Fromm

irreverent
guide to
Las Vegas

Frommer's®

irreverent guide to Las Vegas

1st Edition

By
Jordan Simon

A BALLIETT & FITZGERALD BOOK
IDG BOOKS WORLDWIDE, INC.

a disclaimer

Prices fluctuate in the course of time, and travel information changes under the impact of the varied and volatile factors that influence the travel industry. Neither the author nor the publisher can be held responsible for the experiences of readers while traveling. Readers are invited to write to the publisher with ideas, comments, and suggestions for future editions.

about the author

Jordan Simon is the author of several guidebooks, as well as co-author of the *Celestial Seasonings Cookbook: Cooking With Tea*. He has written on various topics for *Elle*, *Travel & Leisure*, *Town & Country*, *Los Angeles*, *Diversion*, *Ski*, *Snow County*, *Food Arts*, and *Wine Country International*.

Balliett & Fitzgerald, Inc.

Line editor: Holly Hughes / Production editor: Mike Walters / Associate editors: Kristen Couse, Paul Paddock

IDG Books Worldwide, Inc.

An International Data Group Company
919 E. Hillsdale Blvd., Suite 400
Foster City, CA 94404

ISBN 0-02-863153-6
ISSN 1524-4326

Interior design contributed to by Tsang Seymour Design Studio

special sales

For general information on IDG Books Worldwide's books in the U.S., please call our Consumer Customer Service department at 1-800-762-2974. For reseller information, including discounts, bulk sales, customized editions, and premium sales, please call our Reseller Customer Service department at 1-800-434-3422.

Manufactured in the United States of America

what's so irreverent?

It's up to you.

You can buy a traditional guidebook with its fluff, its promotional hype, its let's-find-something-nice-to-say-about-everything point of view. Or you can buy an Irreverent guide.

What the Irreverents give you is the lowdown, the inside story. They have nothing to sell but the truth, which includes a balance of good and bad. They praise, they trash, they weigh, and leave the final decisions up to you. No tourist board, no chamber of commerce will ever recommend them.

Our writers are insiders, who feel passionate about the cities they live in, and have strong opinions they want to share with you. They take a special pleasure leading you where other guides fear to tread.

How irreverent are they? One of our authors insisted on writing under a pseudonym. "I couldn't show my face in town again if I used my own name," she told me. "My friends would never speak to me." Such is the price of honesty. She, like you, should know she'll always have a friend at Frommer's.

Warm regards,

Michael Spring

Michael Spring
Publisher

contents

introduction

I was driving down the Strip, dazed, amazed, and disoriented. There was the erupting volcano, the Eiffel Tower sprouting from the Paris casino, the roller coaster zooming around the Statue of Liberty and the Chrysler Building, a giant pyramid beaming lasers as if sending a beacon to lost E.T.s. And I recalled Hunter S. Thompson's line in *Fear and Loathing in Las Vegas*: "No, this is not a good town for psychedelic drugs. Reality itself is too twisted." It holds even truer today than it did then.

A little later, I sat jawing with an off-duty dealer, one of the rare born-and-bred locals in this transient town. I trotted out my observation that Las Vegas is a town without a history, continually demolishing and imploding its landmarks (The Sands becomes the Venetian; the Hacienda, Mandalay Bay; the Dunes, Bellagio; the Aladdin... the Aladdin). With no culture of its own, it parasitically appropriates architecture, gourmet chefs, artworks, loot from around the world. Las Vegas continually reinvents itself, I opined. The dealer laughed. "Oh EVERYone says that. But really Las Vegas is just a mirror, reflecting our country's values. It's whatever you think the American Dream ought to be." And she was right on the money. Las Vegas has been uncannily taking America's pulse for the last 70 years and transforming itself into whatever we have wanted it to be.

The supreme irony is that this Sin City was founded by

Mormons in 1855, though they soon decamped for Utah (call it a premonition). By 1931, Nevada was on the verge of becoming a ghost state when, at the depth of the Depression, government officials hit upon the brilliant idea of legalizing gambling and prostitution, while easing marriage and divorce laws. It suited an era when people needed to feel alive, to indulge greedily in immediate gratification. Hoover Dam was built at the same time, boosting the country's morale with proof that America was still technologically superior. Raising hopes for a new future, these two developments provided Las Vegas with the first of many tourist attractions it could hype. The first real casinos—and neon signage—appeared shortly after, with the El Rancho Hotel inaugurating the Strip in 1941. The first theme hotel materialized in 1943: the Last Frontier filled its rooms with antique pioneer furnishings, hired Zuni artisans to create baskets and rugs, and picked guests up from the airport in a horse-drawn stagecoach.

But it was Benjamin "Bugsy" Siegel who jumpstarted the good times with the Flamingo in 1946; alas, the current Flamingo Hilton had the temerity to raze Bugsy Siegel's private section of the hotel in a 1993 expansion. Tall, suave, and handsome, Bugsy solidified the Hollywood connection (George Raft supposedly modeled his screen persona after him). Headliners streamed in: Jimmy Durante, Martin and Lewis, Sammy Davis Jr. And where movie stars went to be licentious, so did the public. It was the ultimate "cool" frontier town: no rules, no limits, no covers, no sales (or income) tax, where anything could happen—and usually did. For a while, mob ties glamorized Las Vegas, culminating in the Rat Pack days when martinis, cigarettes, and sex were the order of the day and night. Bugsy created a Vegas in his image: a little garish and gaudy, but smooth, with evening dress mandatory in the casinos and restaurants. His vision for Las Vegas may have been his downfall; he was gunned to death ostensibly for skimming off the cash flow, but it was really because, like many a movie director, he ran over budget.

By the 1950s, when atomic bomb tests were held in the nearby deserts, Las Vegans were already tourism-savvy enough to put chaise longues on hotel roofs and sell tickets. Atomic cocktails were served at bars, casinos featured Miss Atom Bomb beauty pageants, and atomic hairdos were offered at beauty salons; when shock waves broke glass, these entrepreneurs offered the shardsas free atomic souvenirs. Even today, the Department of Energy conducts free once-monthly tours of non-classified areas of the Nevada Test Site, where you can see the moon-like craters formed by detonations, one of them used as a training spot for the Apollo astronauts' lunar landings. But the thrill soon palled with Cold War fears, and during the Kennedy Camelot era, America became disenchanted with organized crime.

The town's unlikely redeemer was reclusive germ-phobic Howard Hughes, who in the mid-1960s moved into the Desert Inn and started buying up hotels as if the Strip was his own private Monopoly game. Though he didn't build any monuments, Hughes made Vegas safe for big business. By the 1970s, it became so corporate that business interests wanted the government to interfere, and it did, via the newly established Nevada Gaming Commission. Gambling became "gaming." By the mid-1980s, Las Vegas was in the doldrums. Enter Steve Wynn, who changed the face of the Strip forever by erecting the glamorous tropically themed Mirage, with its white tiger habitat and jungle interior and its belching volcano. A string of resorts followed, culminating in Wynn's own opulent recreation of a Lake Como villa, Bellagio. Nowadays on the Las Vegas skyline, minarets give way to turrets, domes, arches, Deco skyscrapers, Italian campaniles, even a hundred-foot-tall Coke bottle (a relic of the defunct World of Coca Cola attraction). It all gives rise, of course, to some unintentionally funny juxtapositions. The Luxor's Nile Deli serves kosher sandwiches; at Excalibur, the WCW's Nitro Grill sits just around the corner from Lance-a-Lotta Pasta and Sir Galahad's; New York New York's Motown Café overlooks the Central Park–themed casino. The NASCAR Café brings a whiff of the grease pits to the Moroccan-themed Sahara hotel; a headless Lenin statue looms outside Red Square in the otherwise tropically themed Mandalay Bay. And developers are already fretting where to turn now that they've exhausted the truly recognizable cityscapes like Venice, Paris, New York, and ancient Rome.

In the early 1990s came the single stupidest marketing ploy in Las Vegas history. The town fathers, aided and abetted by Steve Wynn, determined to clean up Sin City's image by promoting it as a family-friendly destination—again reflecting the middle-American zeitgeist, cashing in on the "family values" debate and the baby boom. When that misfired, Wynn and other big-business-dreamers like Sheldon Adelson (the maestro who recreated Venice as The Venetian) anticipated the next trend, of billion-dollar IPOs and mutual fund tycoons. Las Vegas decided it was time to go upscalewith a vengeance, aiming to appeal to that coveted 18–to–49-year-old demographic of dot.com stockbrokers, bankers, and professionals who Internet-work even on vacation. Enter Bellagio, The Venetian, Paris, and Mandalay Bay. All are sumptuous and dazzling, but then you see the Jumbotron sign flashing "Hermès and Prada" or "Now appearing, Picasso and Van Gogh." It's a bit like someone thrusting a 10-carat diamond ring in your face, then adding, "It's Tiffany, you know." The truth is, any schmoe with dough is still welcome. Remember the scene in *Pretty Woman* where Julia Roberts tramps down Rodeo Drive in her hooker garb and is shunned at every chic boutique? Variations now happen hourly at the chichi shops of Las Vegas. Take the couple in pastel polyester who stagger into the Tiffany outpost in the ultra-exclusive Via Bellagio shopping arcade, schlepping bags from Gucci and Chanel. A frosty blonde saleswoman pauses a haughty moment before asking, "What can I do for you, sir?" The man peels off several $100 bills from a thick wad and replies, "We need some souvenirs for the folks back home." It's consumerism in its purest, most naked form.

So how does the city dumb down to the lowest common denominator that has always been its bread and butter while smartening itself up for the new younger upscale crowd? It's a delicate high-wire act, but somehow Vegas manages to offer something for everyone: high, low, and arched brow. Nowhere else will you see dreadlocked gangsta rappers and long-bearded Hasidicrebbes sit side by side at shows, expense account fat cats next to fanny packers in restaurants, blue-haired grannies passing white-collar CEOs in the casinos. Tour buses circle like buzzards, and hookers, hucksters, bimbos, bingo junkies, and pencil-neck geeks alike stare into the maw of the one-armed bandits.

And for all the the architectural excess, neon still winks like a hooker in the night. The Rio's confetti-bedecked marquee explodes in a neon-rainbow riot; light-and-water cylinders at Bally's spout off regularly every evening, changing from lilac to blue to green; the Stardust has a huge spangled fireworks of stars going supernova. Circus Circus features a 123-foot-tall clown marquee—thankfully, it doesn't move and speak.

As proud as many locals are of the town's spiffy resurgence, they're also dismayed by the increased hordes, the traffic, the condescending jokes from outsiders about Vegas being a good-time gal trying to get class. Some even wax nostalgic about the Mob days, when casinos were more generous with their comps than the corporate bean-counters: "Once, if you gambled $100, you got a big steak dinner; now you're treated like meat." I overheard a grizzled bartender at a seedy downtown casino wistfully reminisce about the days when he served Sinatra at the Sands. "You know what he told me he loved about Las Vegas: 'Loose slots and loose slits'."

Okay, so some things don't change. I saw a working girl in black leather miniskirt, five-inch stilettos, and Gucci bag (holding who knows what) walk into an elevator on a room floor at one of the tony new resorts and casually ask if the elevator was going up. A six-foot-tall transvestite in fishnet stockings, blonde wig, and gray mustache bellies up to a table and no one blinks. Titillating magazines are dispensed on the streets; jiggle and burlesque shows remain among the ABCs of tourism. Outside town, in Nye County, where prostitution is legal, the (in)famous Chicken Ranch has its own airstrip. The Stardust and Riviera are legendary for presenting private XXX revues, especially during Comdex (nicknamed by locals ComSex) and the Consumer Electronics Show. The Riv, in fact, brings in porn actresses; they strip and autograph their panties for panting software designers.

Las Vegas, no matter what, will always be about giving into the decadence, the indulgence, the revelry. Where else can you buy a fur-trimmed Rocky Raccoon slinky for $3,000 or a Cokebottle Stonehenge sculpture for $500? Where else would the entrance to the Warner Brothers store be guarded by a giant Porky Pig and Wile E. Coyote dressed in full Roman regalia? So, what to make of this surreal city? When all is said and done, any town that can pack the Seven Wonders of the ancient and modern worlds into a three-mile main drag is surely capableof being simultaneously crass and sublime, of being all things for all people. Under its neon-lit influence, even culture snobs begin to unbend, to enjoy the camp and the kitsch, to let themselves go and just have a good time. Above all else, Las Vegas feeds into theAmerican Dream of get-rich-quick, hitting the jackpot, beating the odds. After all, Las Vegas itself, in the middle of the damned desert, defied the odds to become the entertainment capital of the world—over and over again.

I recall one of Liberace's last shows. He entered in a blizzard of white sequins and announced, "I've only done a couple of numbers and I'm warm already. Why don't I slip out of this and into something more spectacular?" That could be the Las Vegas motto as it sheds its skin, reborn yet again.

Las Vegas at a Glance

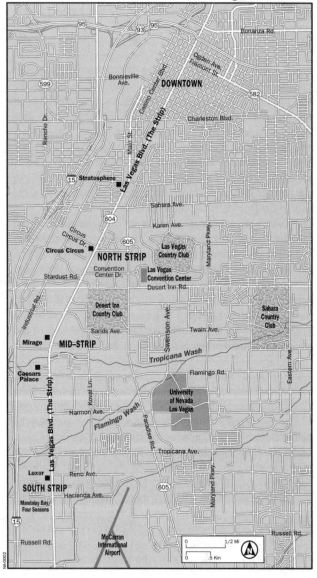

you
probably
didn't know

The Strip is in Las Vegas...right?... Few visitors realize that they're leaving Las Vegas as they drive south on **Las Vegas Boulevard South**, aka **the Strip**, just south of Sahara Avenue. Yes, indeed, the airport, the **MGM Grand**, **Luxor**, **Excalibur**, **Bellagio**, **Mandalay Bay**, **Mirage**, **Caesars Palace**—indeed, most of the famed names, aren't part of incorporated Las Vegas, but rather **Clark County**.

Just how big are those big hotels?... Just listen to these statistics. At the **MGM Grand**, which is the world's second-largest hotel, you'd have to sleep in a different bedroom every night for 13 years and eight months to work your way through its 5,005 guest rooms; there are 18,000 doors (a staffer cracks that it's like Monty Hall's nightmare). The MGM Grand puts roughly 771,700 gambling chips into play annually, which if stacked up would climb 1.5 miles. In 1998, the **Las Vegas Hilton** had 5,290 phones, 603 computers, 224,936 square feet of windows, and 4,552 parking spaces; it used 153,000 decks of cards, 8,357 dice, 101,562 light bulbs, and cleaned 29.8 million pieces of laundry during the year. **Bally's** handled 3,800 pieces of luggage daily, and one million rolls of toilet paper (1,300,000,000 feet; no data available as to single- or double-ply) were flushed in one year. The **Rio**, known for its 15 sumptuous eateries, prepared 1,825,000 pastries, 73,000 cakes, and 91,000 pies utilizing 81,250 pounds of chocolate, 73,000 pounds of sugar, and 730,000 pounds of flour. **Excalibur** goes through 44,100 Cornish game hens, 15,000 pounds of hamburger meat, and 4,200 pounds of prime rib monthly. **Caesars Palace** goes through 2,080,000 maraschino cherries, 114,800 cucumbers, 11,200 ounces of caviar, and 156,000 pounds of coffee, not to mention 2,152,800 ounces of tomato juice and 584,000 ounces of vodka (that's a hell of a lot of Bloody Marys). **Mandalay Bay** has 5,300 palm trees of various species; its wave pool holds 1,640,270 gallons of water and is surrounded by 1,700 tons of sand.

Where can I find a legal hooker?... Nowhere. The world's oldest profession may be legal in some of Nevada, but not in Las Vegas (or Reno) and their counties. The nearest lawful cathouses are 70 miles distant in adjacent **Nye County** (but never fear, many even offer limo service). In town, mind you, hookers are plentiful; a whole strip of little motels caters to the hourly trade. Despite security efforts, there's plenty of play in the big hotels, too. But it is against the law. Furthermore, municipal authorities are trying to change the town's whorier-than-thou reputation (while still upholding the Sin City moniker for horny conventioneers) so the police aggressively pursue solicitation arrests.

Is Vegas still married to the mob?... The old romance of tommy guns, concrete boots, and pinky rings is gone forever—bookmakers have given way to bookkeepers in this increasingly corporate town. Not only the Gaming Control Board but also hotel company stockholders keep a sharp eye out, and today's pit bosses likely boast degrees from high-toned MBA programs like Wharton's and gaming degrees from Cornell and UNLV. Operations such as RICO (Racketeer-Influenced Corrupt Organizations), the Justice Department's Organized Crime Strike Force, and the FBI's ongoing Thincrust Investigation into reputed mobsters have taken the bite out of organized crime's gambling proceeds. Of course, the action has simply moved from racketeering to other rackets, and ancillary businesses are often mob-controlled. The sex industry, for one. The high-toned strip joint **Club Paradise** once was owned by Sam Cecola, reputed to have long-standing ties to the Chicago mob (after he was convicted for income tax fraud, he put the club in his wife's spotless name).

How can I hit the ground running?... The **MGM Grand** and the five Park Place properties (**Caesars Palace, Las Vegas Hilton, Flamingo Hilton, Bally's,** and **Paris**) have set up express registration desks at **McCarran International Airport,** where guests can check in and even purchase show tickets or make dinner reservations—a great way to make an end run around the often-interminable registration lines at the hotels.

Where can I stash the car?... Despite frequent waits for drop-off and pickup, locals know it's much easier to valet than to find a parking spot and walk through acres of asphalt terraces. (Valet parking maybe the only sane way to negotiate **Caesars Palace** and **Bally's**, especially since the latter surrendered its front parking lot to create its bizarre neon walkway and its back parking lot for the **Paris** casino—the remaining lot is a long schlep away, on Paradise Road.) All major hotels offer free valet service but, during holidays and big conventions, many hotels limit their valet service to their hotel guests. Bypass long waits by using valet services at the entrances of hotel shopping promenades (notably the one at **Bellagio**) or side entrances (like **Mandalay Bay**'s west side, inside the parking terrace, which is close to the casino's hippest bars and restaurants including **rumjungle, Aureole,** and **Red Square**). Valet tickets are purposely not identified with the names of hotels and casinos, so hang on to your valet ticket and *remember where you parked.* Without a ticket, no amount of pleading (or moolah; acceptable minimal tips begin at $2 per car and gaming chips are okay) will prompt a Vegas valet to hand over the keys to a red Jag. Don't be like the poor soul—too many freebie drinks— who had absolutely no idea where he left his Mercedes and had to hire a private detective to find it. (It was found at a totally nude strip joint, by the way.)

Can I walk the Strip?... Yes, carefully. There are side-walks along 10-lane-wide **Las Vegas Boulevard South,**

and yes, you'll see masses of people walking on them. But it's deceptively far from one casino to the next, pavements are often ripped up for construction, and pickpockets and smut peddlers line the way. The worst aspect, however, is the kamikaze drivers along certain intersections, particularly the dangerous **Tropicana/Strip intersection**, where a walkway was finally built between **MGM Grand** and **New York-New York**. **Rio All-Suite Casino Resort** is linked to the Strip via a pedestrian bridge along **Flamingo Road**, since 70,000 cars use that turn-off daily. Several hotel groups operate private trams between their affiliated properties, but be forewarned: Tram stations are difficult to find, tucked in the far back corners of hotels and casinos. Trams run between **Bally's**, **Paris**, and **MGM Grand**; **Monte Carlo** and **Bellagio** (not even affiliated properties); **Treasure Island** and the **Mirage**; and **Excalibur** is connected by a moving walkway to the **Luxor** and thence by tram to **Mandalay Bay**.

How can I avoid traffic?... You can't, at least not along **Las Vegas Boulevard South**, which residents have nicknamed the "world's longest parking lot." Sitting in their unmoving cars, people get hotter than the desert in summer, with hardhats and soccer moms giving each other the finger. It's so slow, many motorists actually take out their laptops or write letters. Cabbies say that traffic is the number one reason visitors refuse to return. Avoid the following treacherous intersections if at all possible: where **Sahara Avenue** crosses **Rainbow Boulevard, Decatur Boulevard,** or **Rancho Drive**, and where the **Strip** crosses **Flamingo Road**. Consider taking parallel north-south routes such as **Industrial Road, Rancho Drive**, and **Paradise Road**; the **Desert Inn** superarterial makes east-west traversing much easier, as it swoops over I-15 and down under the Strip. If you're traveling the western side of town, bypass **U.S. 95** in favor of **Lake Mead and Charleston boulevards.** The Interchange between **I-95** and **U.S. 95** is nicknamed the **Spaghetti Bowl** for the tangle of ramps connecting the two highways, used by nearly 350,000 vehicles daily. The whole damn area is being redesigned (right now, omnipresent orange cranes are a hazardous distraction in and of themselves) with a series of bridges, flyovers, and underpasses, some of which have already opened, doubling the number of vehicles per hour. But road engineers can't keep up with the sheer influx of both new residents (5,000 monthly) and tourists (200,000 on the worst weekends).

Leaving on a jet plane... The newest trend in Las Vegas service is pre-checking baggage from your hotel. The **Sahara** offers direct baggage check-in up to 12 hours prior to America West and Delta flights; National Airlines does the same for **Rio All-Suite Casino Resort**.

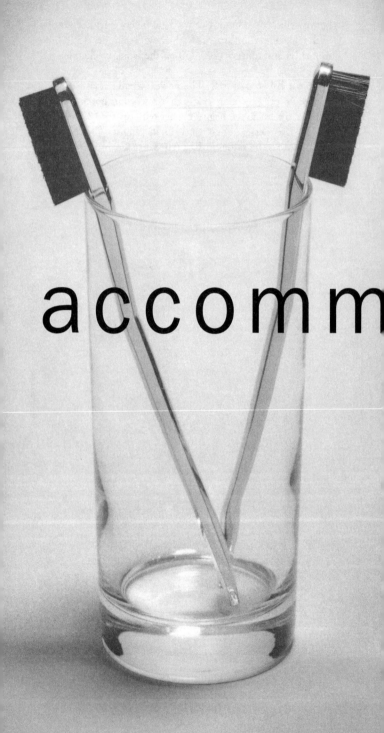

accomm

1

odations

Nowhere else on earth will you find another skyline like that of Las Vegas Boulevard South— otherwise known as the Strip.

A Disney-esque Arthurian castle abuts an Egyptian pyramid and the Statue of Liberty. A Caribbean pirate lair stares down Venice's Saint Mark's Square. Truly, Las Vegas has shouldered aside Hollywood as America's Dream Factory. Novelist Michael Ventura calls Las Vegas "the last great mythic city that Western civilization will ever create"; art critic Robert Hughes calls Las Vegas "a work of art: bad art, but art nonetheless." The extravagant pleasure palaces lining the Strip make a bold, brash architectural statement, with developers increasingly crowing about architectural integrity and authenticity. Replica landmarks are meticulously built to scale, whether half-size (the Eiffel Tower at the Paris hotel), full (the Venetian's Doge's Palace), or oversized (Luxor's Sphinx). To paraphrase Shakespeare's words about another immortal temptress: "Age does not wither nor custom stale her infinite variety."

In Las Vegas, the hotel business is a staggering success story. The city has a total room inventory of 122,000, nearly twice that of New York. The five properties at the intersection of Tropicana and the Strip alone contain more rooms than all of San Francisco. And those rooms aren't standing empty: The Strip has an amazing hotel occupancy level of 90.3 percent. With the city's annual visitor count projected to increase from 30 million to 36 million by 2001, it's a good thing that some 20,000 Strip hotel rooms were added from 1998 to 2000. The latest mega-property is the all-new 3,600-room Aladdin (the original was imploded April 27, 1998), slated to open summer 2000. Needless to say the theme is Arabian Nights. There will be two separate hotels and casinos; nearly 500,000 square feet of retail, entertainment, and dining space; a 20,000 square-foot spa; a 1,000-person-capacity nightclub; a 1,500-seat showroom (with appropriately themed spectacular); and the renovated 7,000-seat Theater of the Performing Arts.

The sheer magnitude of these properties impresses, too. Las Vegas possesses 11 of the world's 12 largest hotels and 14 of the 15 largest in the United States. It even boasts the world's largest Super 8 and Motel 6 properties. A 2,000-room property is considered average size here. No wonder they're cities unto themselves, with everything from ATM machines to fast-food courts, giving guests no reason to leave the hotel—and, more important, the casino, since gaming is still the name of the game (note that main-floor elevator buttons are marked "C" for casino, instead of "L" for lobby).

In that respect, however, things have been changing here.

Non-casino revenues are increasing at nearly quadruple the rate of casino revenues, accounting now for almost half the income. Promoters these days talk of Las Vegas as a true resort, not merely a gambling destination. Every new hotel that's built includes a massive spa, glorified pool area, and fitness facilities—not to mention gourmet eateries, name-brand shops, in-house attractions, and razzle-dazzle shows. Guest rooms themselves have been improving; they're no longer dark, dingy, and cramped chambers calculated to make guests flee to the casino. The typical directory of services looks like a small town's phone book—and it's printed in at least five languages (English, French, Spanish, Japanese, and German).

Developers up the ante in a high-stakes gamble for the tourist dollar. Older hotels constantly receive face lifts (befitting a city renowned for its plastic surgeons). In the newly upscale Vegas, kitschier properties like Circus Circus and Excalibur have "classed up" their cheap motel fantasy suite decor. In a tornado of remodeling, MGM Grand slew the 80-foot roaring lion at its main entrance (which had spooked Asian gamblers to no end), as well as demolished the tacky Emerald City just inside (including the animatronic Dorothys, Totos, and Munchkins). Unfortunately, in the rush to play "Can you top this?" many hotels are constructed little better than mud huts in New Guinea (you may be able to hear your neighbors shower, celebrate their winnings, or consummate their quickie marriages). Typically, Strip resorts settle about two to eight inches just after construction because they're built on rock-like caliche; some sections of Mandalay Bay settled as much as 16 inches, requiring 500 steel pipes to be bored into its foundation to stabilize the tower. Even the Venetian, in its quest to replicate Venice, hasn't sunk to that level.

The new yupscale models, however, will never be the true pampering resorts they claim to be as long as hotels cling to the old casino-centric Vegas standards of guest treatment. Service can be soulless and impersonal, including lengthy check-in periods and waits for your bags or car, even at the ultra-ritzy Bellagio. Conventioneers often arrive early and grab the available rooms; though check-in is normally 3pm, you may have to cool your jets before your room is clean. Hardly luxury coddling. You'd be amazed how difficult staffers find it to switch you from a double/double to the king you'd requested, even with 3,000-plus rooms to choose from. If necessary, make a fuss (politely); blather about being late for meetings. If you wait forever at restaurants or for room service, complain to the MOD (manager on duty) about your hypoglycemia. It might net a few coupons, or a free meal. And be prepared to flash your room key/card as often as a teenager with fake ID at a bar—security is stringent, with the elevator banks staked out by the kind of goons one usually associates with nightclubs.

Winning the Reservations Game

Given the 90 percent average room occupancy rate, you may not be able to book on your preferred dates, so reserve way ahead or be willing to be flexible. Also be aware that there is no rhyme or reason to pricing—any given week, certain hotels will be in greater demand than others (presumably if they host a convention or special event), and rates oscillate wildly. Major holidays, needless to say, are near-impossible. Even more important, avoid the big conventions and special events (see Hotlines & Other Basics), like Comdex, the NAB (National Association of Broadcasters), or National Finals Rodeo week. During these events, rooms are booked a year in advance; people may have to stay as far as 90 miles away in Mesquite. Even something as simple as the latest Mike Tyson fight or Priscilla Presley's Elvis memorabilia auction on Columbus Day weekend 1999 can triple room rates—and not just in the host hotel. There are some rules of thumb. Most properties roughly double their prices over the weekend—except in the dog days of summer. Keep checking the Internet or your travel agent for special deals: They come and go like airline promotions. Consider hooking onto something like a drag-racing promotion so you get the room at 25 percent off (and a free sun visor, too!). You can inquire whether or not a hotel offers casino deals, such as playing three hours straight at the $5 table to gain a free night's stay, but remember that there is a risk here—you might end up losing quadruple the room price. If you win big, on the other hand, most casinos and hotels will "comp" you with breakfast, lunch, and dinner, treat you to a suite, or upgrade you to high-roller digs, all in the interest of keeping you in the casino. High-roller suites are usually obtained via a guaranteed line of credit and a minimum amount (of both time and money) spent gambling, which varies according to property. On rare occasions, usually during slow periods, hotels release higher-end suites (expect to pay anywhere from $1,000 to $25,000 per night). Among the most luxe, with haute bachelor pad decor, are those at Caesars Palace, Las Vegas Hilton, MGM Grand, and Mirage. You can always resort to calling the **Las Vegas Convention and Visitors Authority** reservations line (tel 800/332-5333), which can also inform you about convention schedules, or the discounter **Reservations Plus** (tel 800/805-9528). Both services are free. Among the websites you can try are *www. lasvegashotel.com*, *www.lasvegasreservations.com*, *www.las vegasrooms.com*, and *www.lvholidays.com*. Each offers numerous properties at varying rates; just remember you won't get your choice of room (a higher floor for maximum views, for example).

Is There a Right Address?

Naturally, most people want to stay on the **Strip**. Since this fabled stretch is a mere 3.5 miles long (technically walkable) and the iconic properties are lined up along it—from Circus Circus at one end to the MGM Grand, Luxor, Excalibur, and Mandalay Bay at the other—there is no preferred Strip address. It all depends on the ambience, theme, and facilities you seek. The old Vegas wisdom that a room is just a room no longer applies; posher digs are now available at the likes of Bellagio, Four Seasons, and the Venetian, as well as old stand-bys like Caesars Palace and the Desert Inn. Of course, you pay more for the premium toiletries, turn-down service, and spacious rooms. Prices have risen across the board with the "upscaling" of Las Vegas, but they're still rock-bottom compared to most cities.

While there are still bargains on the Strip itself, many people on a budget prefer to stay **Downtown**, where you can hit 15 casinos in a four-block radius. (Strip hotels are further apart, though there are clusters at the southern and lower-central sections.) Another increasingly popular way to go is to choose one of the moderately priced **Paradise Road** and **Boulder Highway** properties. Three "locals' casino" chains generally offer superior value, whatever the individual hotel's location: Boyd Gaming (California, Stardust, Sam's Town), the Station lineup (Palace, Boulder, Texas, and Sunset Station Hotels), and the Coast chain (Gold Coast, Orleans, Barbary Coast). Though various properties in a chain may have different themes, they offer comparable facilities. Another benefit is that they offer free shuttles between their properties. In fact, most off-Strip properties, such as the Hard Rock, offer complimentary transport to the "action." Wherever you stay, especially if you bring the kids or don't gamble, make sure there are plenty of activities and facilities. All the properties listed below, unless stated otherwise, will include at least a pool, a restaurant, a bar, and a casino.

The Lowdown

New-style glitz... In the late '90s, Las Vegas hoteliers were suddenly struck with a desire for "class," like a retired madam who madly redecorates in an effort to win over her former clients' wives. The prime class-monger is Mirage Resorts' Steve Wynn, whose $1.6 billion Lake Como palazzo, **Bellagio**, is exquisite in every way, even refined (at least by Las Vegas standards). It strives to offer the best of the best, or at least the best that money can buy: world-renowned chefs/restaurateurs, haute couture shops, a spa offering no less than eight facials, the latest Cirque du Soleil extravaganza, *O* (see Entertainment), the Bellagio Gallery of Fine Art, and the Bellagio Conservatory (see Diversions for both). Caviar bars, afternoon teas, graceful fountains, exemplary lounge entertainment—the array begins to feel strained and ostentatious. Its hipster equivalent is the **Hard Rock Hotel & Casino**, where Fendi meets Fender guitars. Its witty rock music theme includes song lyrics posted in the elevators and the usual compliment of gold records, guitars (REM's Michael Stipe, Axel Rose, and The Boss), and memorabilia (Elvis's gold lamé jacket, Ginger Spice's Union Jack bathing suit, Beach Boys' surfboards, '60s and '70s dolls of the Captian and Tamille, Sonny and Cher, and Donny and Marie, even Andy Gibb and Bobby Sherman lunch boxes and Spice Girls and Boy George make-up kits). The decor, with leather, gold, and black accents, is kitten with a whip. There are even four all-music TV channels. The 1999 $100 million expansion and renovation—another 350 rooms and a whole new pool area—only added to the glam factor without sacrificing intimacy (this may change if owner Peter Morton adds another anticipated 340 rooms), and the restaurant menu was upgraded to celeb status with the addition of Nobu (see Dining). These newer properties exerted pressure on Strip institutions like **Caesars Palace**, which responded by building its Palace Tower, with enormous rooms (550 to 750 square feet) that manage to be models of restraint and good taste. Decorated in gold and bronze-tan tones with cherry wood two-poster beds, sponge-painted walls, and subdued classical prints, the rooms' only concessions to razzmatazz are huge gilt mirrors. Bathrooms feature marble vanities, double showers, and whirlpool baths. Add a clutch of truly superb restaurants, high-end shops, and world-class high-roller areas; Caesar's Palace attracts clients so posh, they carelessly leave unopened champagne bottles on their finished breakfast trays. Wynn's older property, the **Mirage**, also remains at the forefront of Las Vegas properties, despite having most of its Picassos spirited away to Bellagio. The lobby lagoon is spectacular (moreso than the pool) and the business center and spa, while not the town's finest, are superior and luxe, with lots of antique chinoiserie and polished hardwood. The restaurants (including Onda and Renoir, by celeb chefs Todd English and Alex Siratta) are superlative, the shops upscale, the look simply ravishing. Wynn's first Vegas property, the downtown **Golden Nugget**, still shows off his famed "touch of class" in an understated way. Public areas display miles of obsessively swept marble floors, etched-glass windows, potted plants, gleaming brass, red carpets, and stained-glass ceilings in the elevators. The cultivated room decor features burnished golden fabrics, gilt mirrors, and a vaguely turn-of-the-century (that last one) feel. The only sign of potential vulgarity is the display of the world's two largest gold nuggets (the 61 pound, 11 ounce "Hand of Faith" and the chunk it eclipsed, "Robin's Nugget"). Excellent restaurants include Lillie Langtry (Chinese, but resembling Marie Antoinette's drawing room) and Stefano's (trellises and lovely murals of the Tuscan countryside). The human-scale casino has a certain Bond-like savoir faire; even the cabaret is intimate and tasteful. With these amenities, it would cost at least twice as much were it not located in budget-conscious Downtown.

Older money... Thanks to its relatively small size, the **Desert Inn** can provide the kind of personalized pampering that the vaunted Bellagio and Venetian promise in vain. It's the one true class act in town; the glorious golf course right outside your door and swellegant public spaces give it a country-club ambience, smarter than ever thanks to a 1998 $200 million renovation. The expanded spa is filled with tasteful (really) Greco-Roman marble statuary and columns and even offers a Champagne Selection facial utilizing "champagne yeast imported from France to nourish and stimulate the skin's metabolism." What more could the discriminating client ask? Discerning moneyed guests quickly discovered the newcomer **Regent Las Vegas**, with its complex of gardens and pools, quietly elegant casino (almost an afterthought), and mind-blowing Aquae Sulis spa. The Regent's Spanish Revival-style architecture blends harmoniously with the surrounding mountains, and the two components—Regent Grand Spa and Regent Grand Palms—both have stylish room decor: golden hues, striped imported fabrics, and plush armchairs; and marble, wrought-iron, and hardwood furnishings, including large desks for working. The Regent is even more golf-frenzied than the D.I., controlling half the tee times at the nationally ranked TPC at the Canyons course and preferred tee times at 10 other premier courses. Though it's the largest property in its chain, **Four Seasons Las Vegas** is an oasis of serenity, perched on the 35th through 39th floors of Mandalay Bay. To enhance its guests' privacy, it has its own express elevators, its own restaurants (two) and lounges, 26,000 square feet of meeting space, an 8,000-square-foot pool area, business center, and spa/fitness club. Many areas are inaccessible to Mandalay Bay guests, though Four Seasons' guests have access to the larger resort's facilities. Rooms are enormous, mostly junior suites with separate parlor, furnished in the usual Four Seasons style—refined, if spare, with hardwood furnishings (including armoires and canopy beds), down comforters, and botanical prints on the walls.

Don't know much about history... A handful of Strip hotels plumb the past for theme concepts, with mixed success. The grandeur of ancient Egypt is actually captured in some parts of **Luxor**, erected in the shape of a Rayban-dark-glass pyramid (the inclined 39-degree elevators are an engineering feat in themselves). Cracked ruins, the Cleopatra's Needle obelisk, and a mysterious 10-story-high Sphinx greet you at the entrance (its eyes shoot lasers at night). The lobby recreates an archeological dig, with exact replicas of Egyptian artifacts and statues, including a 35-foot Ramses; hieroglyphics are stenciled on the walls. Scarabs, cobras, and sacred cats stare you almost menacingly in the eye in the casino. Even the gourmet restaurants include vases, pharaoh images, hieroglyphics—thankfully without being cheesy. Over-the-top as it is, the Roman Empire theme of **Caesars Palace** works (after all, the ancient Romans themselves were given to vulgar excess). The public areas feature a miniature recreation of Imperial Rome at its height, enhanced by holograms and fiber optics; the Garden of the Gods pools, inlaid with Carrara marble, were inspired by the Pompeii Baths; and the Circus Maximus show-room seats guests in booths designed to resemble Roman chariot seats (shades of *Ben Hur*). The north edge of the property features the Quadriga statue: four gold-leaf horses and a charioteer that point the way through five triumphal arches into the Olympic casino. Everywhere you look are neoclassical statues, including reproductions of Michelangelo's *David* (whose marble supposedly came from the same Carrara quarry used by The Maestro), the *Winged Victory of Samothrace*, *Venus de Milo*, and *Rape of the Sabines*. *Veni, vidi, vici.* Less successful is medieval-themed **Excalibur**, where no one acts particularly chivalrous—people shove for a look at the animatronic dragon and cut ahead in the buffet lines. Many of the heraldic banners and halberds, even the actors' costumes, are faintly authentic, but the decor is cartoonish, like a Dr. Seuss rewrite of *La Morte d'Arthur*.

Overrated... In an ill-advised ploy to attract families, **Treasure Island** was conceived as the Mirage's kid sister—they're even connected by a tram. Though the rooms are pleasant enough, with old globe maps and prints of sailing ships, you can hear the plumbing next door, and the kitschy property offers nothing memorable save for the Pirate Battle. It's certainly not worth paying the comparative pirate's ransom to stay here. In its no-mans-land north of the Strip, the high-rise **Stratosphere** sits as if in solitary confinement. The Strat has raised its standards for the new century: Rooms are now stylish, with Deco-style abstract paintings, cherry wood furnishings with black lacquer accents, and dramatically patterned fabrics. But its unsavory surroundings (creatively termed the "Stratosphere District") attract a high percentage of petty theft—

if you stay or play there, drive or cab it. Beautiful—if nouveau riche—as it is, the fantasy Italian villa **Bellagio** can't keep the gawkers out, which diminishes its otherwise haute ambience. Same story at the **Venetian**, which should only get worse as it doubles in size as planned by 2004. Can they maintain its high standards and authentic feel?

Globe-trotting themes... If you can peel your eyes from the half-scale Eiffel Tower at **Paris**, you'll note replicas of other famed landmarks: the Opéra, the Louvre, and the Arc de Triomphe. The 34-story hotel itself is modeled on the 800-year-old Hôtel de Ville, the Paris City Hall. Cobblestone paths wind everywhere and, true to both Las Vegas hotels and the Latin Quarter, they wind tortuously. The shopping areas (wine, cheese, lingerie, mini-Eiffel Towers stamped Paris Las Vegas!) and lounges recreate Parisian street scenes circa the 1920s, striving for that *The Sun Also Rises* feel. There are nine Gallic-themed eateries, and on every hand you'll see Parisian street performers (mimes, musicians, magicians, sword-swallowers), or at least American imitators. Cramped but elegantly appointed guest rooms feature crown molding, rich French fabrics in cool blues and mauves, and custom-designed furnishings (including armoires for closets)—so why no bidets? Unlike the other Vegas "cities," the **Venetian** presents full-size replicas of its landmarks: the Doge's Palace, the 315-foot Campanile Tower, the Rialto Bridge, the Bridge of Sighs, and the Ca d'Oro Villa. Interiors were meticulously duplicated from actual paintings, frescoes, and statues. The Gallery area features copies of artworks by Titian, Bellini, and Canaletto. Okay, so the Grand Canal is only a quarter-mile long and three feet deep, not to mention oddly clean, with motorized gondolas; okay, so the cobblestoned "neighborhoods" lining the canal are full of glass-blowers, jugglers, and other entertainers. Still, white doves take flight in formation five times a day from Saint Mark's Plaza (they may be replaced by animatronic pigeons—cheaper, and no threat of pooping). **New York–New York**'s charm starts with the scaled-down version of the skyline: Statue of Liberty in a miniature New York Harbor (complete with a tugboat to hose her down), Brooklyn Bridge, Chrysler and Empire State Buildings, storefronts, even gargoyles. Inside, on the walkway into Little Italy, manholes emit steam and mail-boxes are covered with graffiti. Cobblestone street scenes are re-created down to the parking meters, fire escapes, hydrants, balconies, street lamps, signs for palm readers, barber shops, and even front stoops. Stroll through a Central Park highlighted with tall, spreading, lifelike trees surrounding a pond and foot bridge—and banks of slot machines (well, it IS a gamble walking through the park at night). Just like its namesake, **Monte Carlo** is opulent indeed—its exterior features three grand arches, the center topped by a Renaissance-style marble grouping of angels, not to mention cascading fountains; the lobby has crystal chandeliers, marble columns, artfully aged paintings, and Aubusson-style rugs. There's a *fin de siècle* feel to the guest rooms, with their cherry wood furnishings, gilt frames, and striped tan wallpaper with fleur-de-lys friezes. It manages to seem refined without going for Ba-roque. **The Orleans** sports the requisite French Quarter look—trompe l'oeil green shutters and wrought-iron balconies outside, French doors and intricate lattice-work, and a festive mauve/key lime/coral color scheme inside. Rooms are enormous but plain. Just don't expect proper mint juleps or Sazeracs (and surprisingly little Dixieland) in the lounges. In a town that generally neglects its Wild-West roots, **Sam's Town** sticks to its six-guns, setting the tone with its enormous bronze "Spirit of Rodeo" sculpture, with three proud cowpokes on horseback carrying banners. A "log cabin" facade surrounds Mystic Falls (see Diversions), a glassed-in recreation of a Rocky Mountain aerie (request a room with this interior view). Dance halls and saloons (see Nightlife) attract genuine boot-scooters. Bona fide antique barn doors, covered wagons, and saddles are strewn throughout; tables are fashioned from old farm implements; rooms have rustic pine furnishings, Native American rugs, and rough-hewn ceramic lamps with cowhide shades. The restaurants lean toward Western theming as well.

Globetrotting themes gone haywire... **Mandalay Bay** wants to offer the "colonial" experience suggested by Kipling, or at least the steamy tropical ambience of a Somerset Maugham novel. (Just for the record, however, the city of Mandalay in Burma sits on a river, not a bay.) Thematically, it really spans the entire Asian continent, with a dash of South Pacific for good measure. And the theme is happily junked to accommodate Brazilian, Russian, Italian, Cajun, and nouvelle American restaurants that lure trendoids. Still, there are exotic notes aplenty. Weathered stone idols stand sentry throughout. Bamboo gates open onto the "beach" pool area, replete with faux stone temple. Lily ponds, fountains, faux grottoes, waterfalls, hibiscus prints, and porcelain chinoiserie dot the public areas. Buddhas and Confucius bless various dining spots. Tropical plants, birds, and fish are seemingly everywhere. **Bellagio** is an overgrown Lake Como villa (with even the lake), with a *porte cochère* modeled after Milan's Galleria and trees imported from Piedmont and Tuscany—but any specifically Italian influence ends there. The upmarket Via Bellagio shopping/dining area, for all its marble and gold-plated fountains, is more Rodeo Drive; the casino area is almost gaudy with orange and red accents. Winking signs advertise Picasso and Monet alongside Armani and Tiffany from the soigné "lakeside" restaurants and lounges—hardly Old-World class. The oversized guest rooms are surprisingly undistinguished, if handsomely appointed with marble floors and surfaces, imported striped and plaid fabrics, and the expected top amenities. Downtown's **Main Street Station** sports a wildly divergent collection of antiques, artifacts, and collectibles, including Buffalo Bill's private rail car, a fireplace from Scotland's Preswick castle, 18th-century Brussels street lamps, a piece of the Berlin Wall for guys to pee on in the brew pub, and woodwork, crystal chandeliers, and stained glass pilfered from various American mansions. The **Stratosphere** features a clutter of unenthusiastic, seemingly unfinished themes winding up through the property's shopping/food court levels: Paris (with *fin de siècle* street lamps, mini-Eiffel Tower, and replicas of Art Deco Metro entrances), Chinatown (with pagodas and dragons—and a Victoria's Secret outlet), and New York City (old Coney Island photos adorning the Nathan's).

Campiest themes... Aside from a surprisingly elegant lobby and spa, the public spaces of **Treasure Island** are as Yo Ho Hokey as can be. The exterior supposedly represents a Caribbean shanty town (complete with lagoon for the Pirate Battle—see Diversions), though it's a weird conflation of Mediterranean (barrel tile roofs, gas lamps, arcades), Pacific (tiki thatching), Caribbean (Creamsicle colors, fretwork balconies, creeping vines), and Hollywood (mermaid figureheads) elements—crowned by a huge skull and crossbones. As you cross the hemp-and-wood "bridge" into the hotel, goats bleat and roosters crow on the sound system. Inside, buccaneers with cutlasses, parrots, and treasure chests jut from the walls. Restaurants have cutesy names like Buccaneer Bay Club and The Plank, shops are called Damsels in Distress, blunderbusses and scimitars hang in the deli. Luckily, the guest rooms don't overdo the theme. **Excalibur** evokes *Monty Python and the Holy Grail:* A purplish dragon languishes in a moat that resembles a mildewed bathtub with clogged drain (well, that might be historically accurate), wildly colored turrets and towers bristle from the roof, and hand-applied stars spangle mock stone wallpaper, with incongruous elements like the WCW's Nitro ("where the big boys eat") theme restaurant. The hell with Camelot, it's as if Mad King Ludwig had dropped acid before designing Neuschwanstein. Fake concrete arabesques, hideous keyhole arches, half-hearted minarets, onion domes—the **Sahara**'s remodeled decor actually makes you long for the tacky old neon and camel. The onion-domed *porte cochère* is attractive, but the entrance with psychedelic stained glass looks like it was designed by a sultan on peyote, and the casinos are headaches waiting to happen, (with gold-painted ceilings and molded columns laced with faux multi-hued vines).

When your chips are down... There are plenty of motels, where "shag" and "rug burn" are double entendres, on the south side of the Strip, with deceptively quaint names like the Pollyanna and the Laughing Jackalope. I wouldn't recommend most of these *Leaving Las Vegas* spots, dubbed by locals "tramp-oline hotels." But there are several relatively safe, clean, even appealing budget properties around town, especially downtown. The **Gold Spike**'s $22 standard room ($33 suite) rate is valid 365 days a year. Rooms are surprisingly clean, though linens and curtains have the grayish tinge of too much laundering (could be worse). Suites are large if spare, with wood-canopied beds and black naugahyde furnishings. For every night you stay, you get a free breakfast or two-fer meal offer in the 24-hour restaurant (which serves $2.50 complete roast beef and ham dinners); the lounges serve 50-cent well drinks. The older rooms at the vintage **El Cortez Hotel & Casino** are dead plain, but rates start at $18 and some still sport the original wooden floors and tiled baths. The mini-suites in the newer tower are also cheap and quite spacious, many with separate sitting and dressing areas. It resembles a retirement home for Runyonesque gamblers—look for them pulling on those slot handles in the casino. El Cortez is a couple of blocks removed from the safety of the Fremont Street Experience and lacks a pool. With the largest convention space Downtown (dodge those low-rent tour groupies and conventioneers staggering through the lobby), **Jackie Gaughan's Plaza** is a good budget bet for those who want the feel and services of a large anonymous hotel. Rooms are serviceable, if strangely shaped, with standard blue carpet and floral spreads. The lobby is incredibly garish, with strobing lights bouncing off brass railings and Carnival motifs everywhere. The casino specializes in $1 tables and nickel slots. Other facilities include a theater (usually with artfully nude X-travaganzas) and a year-round sun deck with a quarter-mile jogging track, pool, and tennis court. Moving on to the Strip, the **Glass Pool Inn** achieved renown for its elevated pool with portholes, where photographers shot spreads for *Playboy* back in the '60s. The motel rooms probably haven't changed since. Fluorescent lighting, fake pine paneling, madras spreads, and—if you're lucky—an honest-to-God avocado-hued bathtub and toilet make this one a collector's item of sorts. No casino, but the adjacent bar, with its dated hula-skirt decor, serves burgers and has live bands on weekends.

Gen-X... The dot.com crowd flocks to **Mandalay Bay**, on the Strip, a testament to the purchasing power of cyber-yuppies who make their fortunes in Internet IPOs. M-Bay's post-millennial look—a futuristic fusion of pan-Asian, Russian, and European elements, is *Blade Runner* meets the Forbidden City. Music folks like Mandalay Bay for its on-site House of Blues, but actual rockers more often head over to the **Hard Rock** to join an effortlessly sexy and cool clientele ranging from Barbie-enhanced gals to WASPy trendoids with a few piercings. There's a remarkable collection of rock-music memorabilia, even in the rooms—about the only thing you have to provide are your own groupies. Though **Bellagio** is often thought of as a "mature" resort, stroll around the pool and you'll see not an ounce of cellulite in sight—the younger men all look fashionably pec-toned and gay, the women as if they're awaiting their second callback for a Victoria's Secret ad. Old and young comfortably intermingle at Bellagio, almost as if it were a high-powered corporate mixer at the CEO's country estate on Lake Como. At **Rio All-Suite Casino Resort**, younger hotshot honchos love the goggle or gourmet restaurants; the fantastic flights of wine in the Wine Cellar; high-stakes gambling; and the party-hearty ambience. These are really junior suites, albeit vast at 600 square feet. But they're smart-looking and full of amenities; all have modified canopy beds, tables of smoked glass and cast iron, deep-hued velour furnishings, marble and brass accents, and floor-to-ceiling windows running the length of the room.

Family-friendly on the Strip... Admittedly, the great experiment to make Las Vegas a family destination failed abysmally, but it still serves the market surprisingly well, if only because Vegas manages to bring out the big kid in every visitor anyway. Always be sure to ask if the hotel is offering a special deal, or if kids under 12, 15, or even 18 can stay free with their parents (yeah, just what that restless hormonal teen craves). Boy, do they pour it on at **Circus Circus**: Clown costumes dangle from ceilings and antique Barnum & Bailey and Ringling Brothers posters adorn public dining areas. Ringmasters walk about in bright purple jackets, clowns offer free face painting; the Midway (see Diversions) features great old-style arcade games, free three-ring acts, even popcorn in huge dispensers; the Adventuredome (see Diversions) is the world's largest indoor theme park. Even adults walk around the casino clutching the stuffed animals they won. Older kids will appreciate **Luxor**'s 18,000-square-foot Sega VirtuaLand, a kids' Arcade-ia where Sega test-markets its latest interactive video games, simulations (the Daytona 500 is a winner), and shoot-outs. The hotel's occasional animatronic camels, Indy Jonesian motion-simulator rides, and IMAX theater will also enchant kids. Baby-sitting services allow parents to wallow in the luxu-

ACCOMMODATIONS | THE LOWDOWN

rious spa, dine at the romantic gourmet eateries, or play in the lively casino. Like a parody of Disney World on an episode of "The Simpsons," **Excalibur** features 265-foot-tall bell towers, turrets, machicolated battlements, and drawbridges in colors Crayola hasn't yet invented. Inside you'll find moats, Arthurian knights and fair damsels, suits of armor, wandering minstrels, jesters, jousters, even free puppet and magic shows; kids happily spend their parents' farthings on the Fantasy Faire level's motion-simulator rides and arcade games. Alas, the formerly blood-red guest rooms with faux stone wallpaper have been stripped of nearly all medieval embellishments save for ye olde carved headboards, cast-iron lamps, and valances shaped like heraldic banners. **Treasure Island** is always jammed with families who enjoy the nutty nautical decor. It's marginally cheaper than its sibling, the **Mirage**, yet only a tram ride away from the Mirage's kid-appealing attractions like the Secret Garden, Dolphin Habitat, and White Tiger Habitat (see Diversions). The roaring lion entrance and animatronic *Wizard of Oz* characters are gone from the **MGM Grand**, and what the property's lost in kitsch value, it's made up for with an excellent Youth Activities Center for 3- to 12-year-olds. Disney movies are pushed, bathrooms are "Munchkin-sized," and cartoon characters make occasional appearances, but tweeners can play air hockey, foosball, Nintendo, and pool, there's a video arcade including virtual reality games right across the hall, and there are special days in the MGM Grand Adventures Theme Park (see Diversions). Warning: Covering 112 acres, this hotel seems simply endless (bring running shoes), even though it's clearly laid out in five wings. The hallways do have stars, sort of a combo of "Follow the Yellow Brick Road" and the Hollywood Walk of Stars. Dauntingly elegant as it may seem, the **Four Seasons** is surprisingly attuned to children's needs. The Kids' Club will note kids' names and ages when you make reservations, then present them with personalized T-shirts, a stuffed animal, and milk and cookies upon arrival. All furnishings are child-proofed; kids receive their own menu along with coloring book and crayons at the Verandah Café.

Family-friendly off the Strip... North of the Strip, the **Stratosphere** never fails to impress kids with its sheer height and the thrill rides at the top; parents appreciate room rates made even more attractive by numerous promotions. It also attracts a fair share of Spring Break types, many affecting that disaffected indie grunge look with baggy pants and bad buzz cuts. Among the many entertainment offerings at **The Orleans**, which is also off-Strip, kids enjoy the 70-lane bowling alley, 12-screen multiplex, enormous Time Out arcade with simulated active video games, and the Kids Tyme child center with a gigantic 3-D Jungle Jim and fun activities like puppet shows, finger painting, even day trips. The festive New Orleans decor includes Mardi Gras costumes, masks, and plaques from various crewes hanging and dangling everywhere, and the good-sized rooms give families space to spread out. Social centers for locals, the Station hotels are very family-oriented, especially **Sunset Station**—aside from the 13-screen cineplex, it boasts a SEGA station (Tuesdays from 5 to 11pm you can play all the video games you want for a mere $10). All the Station properties offer a Kids Quest day-care center, with karaoke shows, video games, a play gym, high-tech Jungle Gym, and vivid playful colors like turquoise and mauve. This is the nicest, with public spaces duplicating a quarter in Old Seville, some eateries with Spanish knickknacks and dishes, and handsome if cookie-cutter rooms with cast-iron lamps, cherrywood furnishings—and hideous Andalucien paintings. As if its Wild-West theme wasn't already a kid-pleaser, **Sam's Town**, out on the Boulder Highway, is bidding for even more family business by adding a video arcade, kids club, and 18-screen cineplex by the end of 2000.

Family-unfriendly... Have a child under 18? Forget traipsing through Euro-elegant **Bellagio**, unless you're a hotel guest and can show your room key. Security guards are posted at all entrances to turn non-registered children and their parents away. Steve Wynn, president of Mirage Resorts, is rumored to have mandated the no-kids rule after he tripped over a baby stroller at another Mirage property. In fact, strollers are banned at all Mirage Reorts properties (Mirage, Treasure Island, Golden Nugget). **Riviera** aggressively markets itself as adults-only in another respect—witness the salacious posters for its NC-17 topless shows like *Crazy Girls* and *Splash* (see Entertainment). Most guest rooms are smallish, resembling a prairie town motel with ugly plum carpets and taupe, dusky rose, or floral fabrics.

Quick getaways... **Best Western Mardi Gras Inn** is just one block from the Strip and the Convention Center. The casino is rudimentary—just slots, video poker, and keno—and there's no restaurant, just a 24-hour lounge. Rooms are sleek, with arches, torchère lamps, and a muted gray-and-green color scheme, as well as wet bar, fridge, and coffee maker (several have full kitchenettes). The tariff is low, and they rarely light the "No Vacancy" neon. **Hotel San Remo** has an unbeatable location a block from the Strip's Tropicana intersection. It offers all the expected facilities—casino, cabaret, restaurants (Italian, Japanese, steakhouse)—at bargain prices, right down to a $4.95 prime rib special in the 24-hour coffee shop and a great slot club. The standard rooms are cramped, with turquoise upholstery and carpets clashing with fussy French Provincial furnishings; suites, however, are more subdued, even monochromatic, with two-poster beds. **La Concha Motel** has a marvelous Strip location, but neither a casino nor restaurant. It's done in standard motor-court style, but set back enough from the Strip to keep noise levels down, and you've gotta love the funky office, a 1961 design by L.A. architect Paul Williams, looking like a pale pink conch shell backed by sharks' fins (or billowing sails). The rooms are good-sized, decorated in frilly floral fabrics with coral the predominant color scheme.

Taking care of business... The **Las Vegas Hilton** enjoys location location location: right next to the Convention Center. Savvy management provides something for the older business traveler (golf course, elegant restaurants) and the new whiz kids, like the Star Trek environment (see Diversions), and a hot dance club (see Nightlife). Standard rooms are plain, though the marbleized desks are long enough to be real working desks. Suites are classier in decor, individually decorated (including four fantasy-theme versions) with hand-carved four-poster beds, modern artworks, crystal chandeliers, and tall wrought-iron lamps. In addition to its own extensive meeting facilities (500,000 square feet, which in phase two will nearly double), the **Venetian** is connected to the Sands Convention Center, making it a whopping 1,700,000-square-foot corporate playground. The 85,000-square-foot main ballroom is the world's largest without columns. In keeping with the rest of the resort, the meeting space has fastidiously duplicated frescoes, murals, and statues, as well as Venetian glass chandeliers and textured wallpaper. Head honchos love the sumptuous if overly ornate 700-square-foot rooms (largest in Vegas) with sunken living room, crown mouldings, iron railings, gilt-trimmed armchairs—and 130-square foot bathrooms with Italian marble. **Paris** offers 140,000 square feet of pillarless function space, including the largest ballroom in Las Vegas, prosaically named the Paris. The convention area is patterned after the Hall of Mirrors at the Palace in Versailles: It's lined with towering mirrored arches, while crystal chandeliers hang from recessed ceilings with gold-leaf cornice moldings, ideal for the CEO who fancies himself Louis XIV. Moreover, Paris is connected via "Le Boulevard" to its sister property, **Bally's**, which offers another 175,000 square feet. Meeting planners can one-stop-shop at the combined sales office for their functions. **Riviera**'s lively "adult" rep (right down to the vulgar gold tassels on guest room furniture in the newer towers) already appeals to certain conventioneers; an added inducement is its 158,000-square-foot convention center expansion, which is already booked into 2002. **Caesars Palace** expanded its meeting space to 170,000 square feet in 1999 and offers rooms fit for any corporate emperor in its Palace Tower: marble pediments atop etched bronze elevators, replicas of Roman frescoes and murals, and barrel-vaulted ceilings in meeting rooms. Fruitwood-paneled board rooms offer plush leather executive chairs, and private mini-offices with phones are available. The business center even has a notary on staff. **MGM Grand**'s separate 300,000-square-foot Conference Center is perhaps the most sophisticated part of this sprawling, amenity-packed hotel. The smart postmodern decor features striking abstract wood "torches," fake palms, and stained-glass panels; board rooms, many with outdoor views, feature plush leather armchairs, marble tables, curved glass pendant lamps, and decorative porcelain in cabinets.

Service with a smile... The **Four Seasons** boasts 10 staff concierges, including six out of the 10 Nevada members of Les Clefs d'Or, the profession's highest award. Their "I Need It Now" program redresses packing lapses: the Concierge Kit includes everything from batteries to birthday candles, cuff links, sleeping masks, thermometers, and reading lights—all delivered within 15 minutes. Guests who go for a run are handed bottled water and a cold towel upon their return, while poolside loungers are offered complimentary Evian spritzing, fresh fruit, even cucumber slices for their eyes. Complimentary overnight shoeshine service, hand-delivered phone messages—so many staffers ask if they can be of service, you feel like you have your own personal butler, giving the Four Seasons more of the "Raj" ambience than its downstairs sibling, Mandalay Bay. **Bally's** has long been lauded for its smooth, friendly service, including some of the most helpful dealers in town and most gorgeous pool attendants. Despite its size, Downtown's **Golden Nugget** has remarkably attentive service: Doormen promptly open doors and the front desk staff or concierge apologize sincerely if they keep you waiting more than 30 seconds—virtually unheard-of elsewhere. The staff is unfailingly discreet at the **Desert Inn**, an oasis of tranquility amid the bustle of the Strip, where good old boys play golf—or CEOs (of either sex) might take their "secretaries" for, uh, dictation, especially in the suites and $10,000-per-night casas.

Old Vegas... The Rat Pack landmarks are gone, but a few hotels, while keeping up with the latest trends, still retain that '60s time-warp feel. **Stardust** has been featured in numerous flicks, including *Showgirls, Mars Attacks!,* and *Casino,* with its vintage cigarette girls, cartoonish neon, multi-hued carpets, mirrored columns, and crystal disco balls in the casino/reception area. Built well after the Rat Pack heyday, **Bally's** has since been surpassed in many ways, but this dinosaur has upheld old-style professionalism—the restaurants are uniformly excellent, the unthemed casino elegant without pretension, the rooms fairly large (450 square feet) with tasteful madras fabrics and dark wood furnishings. Its quiet style appeals to a loyal, discriminating clientele that doesn't want glitz. And dig the reception desk's great mural of Las Vegas characters in action. Downtown, **El Cortez** may be ugly, but it's genuinely historic (it was Bugsy Siegel's first Vegas property, with the oldest casino, built in 1941), just like the many old-time penny-ante gamblers in its casino. Several "updatings" have mercifully left the **Tropicana**'s fun, funky ambience unspoiled. It's a hoot, with Easter Island—style steles in front, lushly landscaped grounds (several plants stemming back 40 years); pyrotechnically hued macaws and parrots in ornate cages in the casino and lobby; elevators painted with jungle wildlife; and faux bamboo trim running around the halls. Tiger skin rugs and jungle murals decorate the gourmet Savannah restaurant, the pool area is just as exotic, and there's even a wildlife habitat with snakes and sloths (just like in the casino) in the walkway between towers. The original (Island) tower carries out the theme with rattan furnishings, pastels, and even the occasional mirror above the bed for those wild nights, though guests can opt for more subdued room decor in the Paradise Tower, which has French Provincial style with gold high-back chairs and armoires.

Best-value casinos on the Strip... Despite a raft of nostalgically honky-tonk attractions, **Circus Circus** displays surprising restraint in other areas. The redecorated rooms are now actually quite nice and subdued, if smallish (just overlook the mauve spread with gold accents); the sizable junior suites have muted tones of gold, silver, gray, and cream, with armoires and wet bars. The busy "back to the future" casino decor of the **Stardust** thankfully isn't carried through into the rooms. In fact, lodgings are mostly in soft dun and gray tones, with distinctly Deco-ish touches—modernist curved cabinets and black torchère lamps. Rooms in the new tower are downright attractive, with black and blood-red upholstery, wicker furnishings, and glass or marble tables. **Sahara** isn't quite the Moroccan fantasia it wants to be after a 1998, $100 million overhaul softened the sultan-on-a-budget decor (save for public spaces). Still, it delivers good value, with such attractions as the NASCAR Cafe and Speedworld (see Diversions) and a showroom featuring the terrific magician Steve Wyrick (see Entertainment). Ignore the neon-splashed prison-like exterior of the **Barbary Coast**—inside are opulent public rooms gleaming with oak wainscoting, brass accents, crystal chandeliers, and stained glass. Guest rooms follow suit with hardwood trim, etched mirrors, original paintings, and textured wallpaper; only the suites go for a glaring '70s-era contemporary look. Pyramid-shaped **Luxor** has plenty of campy attractions in its public spaces, yet its new rooms and lobby are surprisingly restrained, and the spa and gourmet restaurants are ultra-luxurious—good amenities for this price. Avoid the drab tombs in the original pyramid—apart from the camels and pharaoh wallpaper, it's like a cinder-block Sheraton. The novelty of the sloped windows wears off quickly, and many of the Strip views are now obscured by the second tower. How could anyone resist the wonderfully Deco-ish rooms at **New York–New York** or the chance to amble through Central Park at night, even sit on a Greenwich Village stoop? It's the New York of Rudy Giuliani and Disney: no pushers, no hookers, no homeless people, no XXX-shops. But you stay here for less than you'd pay at a seedy Times Square transient hotel.

Where to escape the madness... The **Four Seasons** is like a Bali "High" overseeing the South Seas nuttiness below in Mandalay Bay; you can descend from your aerie and enjoy the mega-resort's facilities, but M-Bay guests can't impinge upon your tranquil experience (though the food-and-beverage outlets are, naturally, open to the public). The M-Bay's exotic motif is echoed upstairs with antique porcelain or cloisonné statues from China, Bali, and India scattered throughout marble hallways, but the rooms are decorated in typical Four Seasons restrained style. You feel as if you've left the Strip's madness as soon as you enter the **Desert Inn**'s soaring, sparkling white atrium lobby with sunbursts on the ceilings, picture windows overlooking the gardens, and handsome WPA-style murals. A lushly landscaped lagoon-style pool overlooks the manicured on-site golf course (see Diversions)—and most of the lovely rooms gaze out at the pool. Villas and suites offer even more seclusion for those who want it. **Alexis Park** is just minutes from the Strip, yet light years away in look and ambience. Its tastefully decorated suites sport soft desert hues, and lush landscaping cocoons it from the Vegas frenzy; most telling of all, it doesn't even have a casino. It's a fave of celebrities who want to keep a low profile, from Whitney Houston to Robert DeNiro.

Regent Las Vegas is set miles from the action in the soigné 'burb Summerlin. Though it offers a "European" casino (read: no theme elements), its emphasis is on restful golf and spa packages. The setting is glorious, taking full advantage of the views of Red Rock Canyon's spires and Toiyabe National Forest.

Where to tie the knot... Nearly every major hotel offers at least one chapel and full wedding-planning services, often including in-house florists, photographers, videographers, and bands (for non-hotel chapels and marriage info, see Diversions). Most also provide themed nuptials of varying levels of campy tastelessness. Neptune's Villa at **Caesars Palace** doesn't just flirt with excess, it marries it, for better or worse. A two-story, double-balustrade staircase encircles a stunning koi fish pond as it rises to a wood-paneled foyer framed by a salt-water aquarium; the chapel practically floats away on white chiffon, hand-painted murals, vine-entwined columns, frosted etched glass panels, and soothing painted ceilings of blue skies. An appearance by Caesar and Cleopatra, accompanied by centurions and handmaidens can be arranged (toga party optional). **Excalibur**'s Canterbury Chapels, gussied up with barrel-vault ceilings, stained-glass windows, and chandeliers with dangling crowns, offer a fairy-tale affair where you're actually dubbed "faire maiden and noble knight." As one couple, married in full medieval garb as King Arthur and Guinevere, exited the chapel, the groom grinned, "Get ready for a lotta lancing, babe." **MGM Grand** offers spectacularly theatrical weddings on its *EFX* set (see Entertainment), with nymphs conjuring Merlin in a haze of fog to perform the ceremony; the bride and groom can even literally take the plunge on the SkyScreamer (see Diversions). Its cinema-themed Forever Wedding Chapels are decorated with sepia-toned celebrity wedding stills (from real and reel life). The dressing rooms are to die for, with marble vanities, frosted-glass lamps, and BIODROGA products from the spa. True to its exotic jungle theme, **Tropicana** offers an Island Wedding Chapel set on an actual island with palm trees, waterfalls, fountain, and swans. The chapel is a thatched hut with a bamboo altar. The classic **Desert Inn** has the Fabergé exclusive: complete Fabergé place settings, Imperial caviar with Russian vodka, and a three-

ACCOMMODATIONS | THE LOWDOWN

tiered wedding cake crowned by a Fabergé wedding egg with 24-carat gold-plated bridal couple. No themed spectacles at **Bally's** tasteful Celebration Wedding Chapel, but it's notable for its renewal-of-vows ceremony and gay-friendly attitude (drag queens often serve as maids of honor).

Cool pools... Lagoons with waterfall and faux grotto are a dime a dozen around here, but **Mandalay Bay** doesn't have a pool—it has an 11-acre aquatic environment with a replica beach that has sand, undertow, the whole bit. There's also a jogging track, lazy river ride, and four pools, including one where you can actually hang ten, surfing six-foot waves. There were a few technical glitches—the waves periodically went typhoon, drenching guests and reputedly washing away the beach and pool bar—but these have been ironed out. **Hard Rock's** new pool is so hedonistic you could imagine you're at Hef's Playboy mansion. Exhibition is rampant: "Full moons" are common from the rooms overlooking the pool, and the hotel website features a live pool cam. It's lushly landscaped with palms, a lagoon, grotto, mini-beaches, hidden Jacuzzis, and connecting lazy rivers. Wild purple lounge chairs give it pizzazz, there's swim-up gaming, and the likes of Dennis Rodman and Arab sheiks retire with willowy models to private cabanas. Caligula would have approved of the 4.5-acre Palace Pool Complex and Garden of the Gods at **Caesars Palace**, its fountains playing around three column-lined pools inlaid with marble and granite surrounded by fragrant Mediterranean gardens. The main Temple Pool is crowned by a giant rotunda shading a central island cooled by mist from giant fountains. Statuaries include centurions in full gallop and mythical griffins (half-eagle, half-lion); even the lifeguard stands are decked out like thrones. Amid the **Tropicana's** vintage Vegas tropical setting—palm trees, several waterfalls, swim-up cocktail bar and blackjack, guests in tacky Hawaiian print shirts and muumuus—you'll find an Olympic-sized pool (one of three) and three hot tubs scattered throughout five acres of lush foliage. The **Flamingo Hilton** also provides acres of greenery, a series of linked pools, waterfalls, water slides (popular with the kiddies), and—you got it—pink flamingoes, both live (in wading ponds) and immortalized in plaster or bronze. **Bellagio** places its six swimming pools in a formal, five-acre garden setting complete with imported Italian cypress trees, arbors, urns, and pattering fountains. Almost 300 pine trees sway in the desert breeze nearby, remnants of the old Dunes golf course. The most classic "traditional" pool on the Strip is at the **Glass Pool Inn**, which got its name from the portholes in the tiny above-ground pool with mermaids painted on its sides. Back in the '50s, the Glass Pool became famous for cheesecake poses from starlets and model wannabes. Sundays at 4pm the tradition continues, with photo shoots accompanied by live music at the pool. While you're waiting to see what sleazebag shutterbugs and would-be *Sports Illustrated* swimsuit-issue centerfolds show up, you can hoist a longneck in the adjacent (what else?) Bikini Cafe.

For the body beautiful... Be prepared to pay exorbitant fees to use the splendiferous fitness centers at several of the major casino-hotels. The most serious may be the **Regent Las Vegas**'s Aquae Sulis (Latin for "waters of the sun"), which offers a United Nations of healing treatments: Asian shiatsu and reflexology, Swedish massage, South Indian Abhyanga massage, Austrian Moor Mud Vichy showers, and Native American hot stone therapy. Among the unique offerings are Microdermabrasion (under renowned plastic surgeon Dr. Zimmerman), Siddha Vaidya (an ancient Hindu medicinal system rserved for royalty, supervised by Dr. Rajkumar Regnuthan, a descendant of the Indian Royal Physicians), and Color Therapy™, in which your aura is photographed and analyzed and a corrective course of therapy designed to balance the seven chakras. If all you want to do is work out, there's top-notch cardiovascular and weight training equipment, as well as personal trainers and stress management consultations. **Bally's** spa/fitness center provides state-of-the-art equipment, saunas, steam rooms, hot tubs, et cetera, but those in the know swear by the Belavi facelift massage—you're slathered with various creams and oils, then toned with herbal mists, finished with a honey-lift masque while you enjoy reflexology treatments. It's said to be more rejuvenating than eye tucks and monkey glands. There are even gender-specific treatments. The **Hard Rock**'s RockSpa skews more toward the vain than the varicose-vein crowd with a state-of-the-art fitness center that includes a cross-training climbing wall, stair machines, treadmills, stationary bikes, and Cybex weight training. The spa's Kerstin Florian skin-care products are utilized in thermal mineral water therapy, aromatherapy, and herbal therapy. Besides massages, facials, and body wraps, guests can get chamomile scrubs, Hungarian Moor mud baths, mineral crystal baths, cellular repair facials, acupressure lifting massages, or Vitamin C antioxidant treatments. The Garden of the Gods at **Caesars Palace** has a fitness center offering all the usual treatments, as well as a rock-climbing wall, virtual reality stationary bikes (you're in the Tour de France!), and Zen meditation chamber. Don't miss the 110-minute Passage to India, a package that includes a dry-brush massage, warm-oil full-body massage, and scalp massage that drips warm oil lightly onto the "third eye." The **Venetian** features the ultra-chic Canyon Ranch SpaClub, where you pay for the privilege of being pummeled and pinched to determine your body fat. Its 125 services include every conceivable massage, therapeutic bodywork, body treatments, and facials. And after your mud bath, it "rains" from the ceiling to rinse you off. The 30,000-square-foot Spa at **Mandalay Bay** has 12 treatment rooms, steam rooms, saunas, and whirlpools; treatments include massages, reflexology, aromatherapy, facials, and body wraps, and personal trainers are available for hire. This is a prime place to see people huffing into cell phones, watching the stock ticker on *Moneyline* as they pedal stationary bikes and stride on treadmills.

Heavy lobbying... Step into the **Mirage** and you've entered a rain forest with real orchids, elephant ears, and banana trees, not to mention a lagoon with waterfalls and rushing rapids, a couple of somnolent white tigers, and a coral reef (actually a 20,000-gallon aquarium stocked with more than 1,000 brilliant-hued fish, as well as several menacing sharks and gliding rays). It even smells tropical, with a faint perfume of vanilla and ginger. The lobby of **Mandalay Bay** seems tame by comparison, featuring only a 14-foot shark-filled pagoda/aquarium along with towering bamboo cages filled with parrots and cockatoos (desk clerks sometimes have to scream to make themselves heard above the birds' screeching). Gals dressed in Dorothy Lamour sarongs with parakeets perched on their shoulders occasionally pass by and flash a dazzling smile at folks in the long registration lines. The **Caesars Palace** entrance is a riot of gilt bas relief, carved and mirrored ceilings, friezes, and reclining marble nudes alongside black marble floors and crystal chandeliers. After more than 30 years, it's still Vegas glitz at its best. But for sheer camp, nothing exceeds the excess of **Excalibur** with its mock medieval stained-glass ceiling, glowing dragons, brightly colored heraldic flags, suits of armor on wooden horses, and amazing turreted chandeliers.

When you enter **Bellagio**, you don't even notice the arcaded interior courtyard effect—sage shutters, marble floors, plush couches, and towering floral arrangements—your eye is so drawn toward the ceiling by "Fiori di Como," the $10 million glass installation designed by the renowned Dale Chihuly (by far his largest project ever). Featuring 2,000 separate pieces of shimmering rainbow-hued glass, the work resembles a profusion of glass jellyfish, a floral explosion, or a '60s LSD nightmare. Impressive, yes, but also overwhelming. The majestic 70-foot rotunda dome in the **Venetian**'s lobby is another jaw-dropper, though much more traditional, glinting with 24K gold leaf and a montage of 21 Renaissance paintings. The tile floors are the real thing, scavenged from condemned palazzi. Marble and Murano glass gleam everywhere, and a photo of Venice canals provides a trompe l'oeil effect behind the reception desk. Less awesome but handsome all the same is **New York-New York**'s registration area, with its Art Deco bronze touches, '40s Times Square photos, and a marvelous mural of the New York skyline at dawn.

Handsomest guest room decor... Hard Rock's rooms are wonderful contrasts of hip and classic. The decor is mostly gold (as in record, babe) tones: French windows, leather headboards, parchment-and-iron lamps, cushy contoured olive velour chairs, and stainless-steel sinks in the marble bathrooms. The music theme is smartly carried out with subtle instrument motifs in curtain fabrics, and walls hung with B&W photos of legends like Jimi Hendrix, Janis Joplin, and James Brown. Despite the tropical rain forest theme downstairs, the **Mirage**'s large rooms favor more subdued shimmering taupes, beiges, and bronzes with black accents, crown moldings, hard-wood and rattan furnishings, magnolia prints, marble entryways, and separate vanities. Rise above the Egyptian kitsch of **Luxor**: Its new wing's guest rooms are quite stylish, with blond wood furnishings, sponge-painted golden walls, and subtle stencils of sunbursts and ancient jewelry. Door handles replicate the Ra sign of life or Isis snake amulet. Well, okay, the faux columns are a mite much. Some of **New York–New York**'s rooms are cramped (just like Manhattan apartments, come to think of it), but they're deliciously Deco-ish: vivid colors, cubistic paint-ings, curved headboards, inlaid burled wood furnishings, with ziggurat and chevron patterns subtly incorporated throughout. Each wing has its own color scheme: golds and yellows in Empire, reds in the Century tower, purples in the New Yorker, greens in the Chrysler. The surpris-ingly inexpensive suites at **New York–New York** sport that high infidelity look: They let loose, with zebra-, tiger-, or leopard-print lounges and antimacassars, streamlined torchère lamps, chessboard-patterned furniture, mar-ble vanities, black tubs and sinks. After a 1998 renova-tion, the perennially fine **Desert Inn** is looking good, with tropical spreads, burnished walnut furnishings, and fun elements like violet chairs—think Martha Stewart on mescaline. Every room has a fridge, and the bathrooms are truly magnificent in black and gray gran-ite, with double sinks, separate shower, whirlpool tub, marble vanity, robes, and Gilchrist & Soames toiletries. Rooms in the Palms section are largest; both the Palms and St. Andrews wings have balconies. There are also two-bedroom villas and individually decorated 9,800-square-foot "casas" with private butlers and 24K gold fixtures. The huge rooms at **Mandalay Bay** strike a nice balance between ultra-modern comfort and an exotic motif, with glazed porcelain plates, hardwood armoires, pineapple-carved beds, leopard skin armchairs, prints of plants and butterflies, and abstract tropical fabrics.

Obsessively detailed... The signature landmark at **Paris** is its 50-story Eiffel Tower replica. To ensure authenticity, designers obtained Gustave Eiffel's original drawings. Although Las Vegas's Eiffel Tower is a half-scale replica, elevators can't be half-scale, so it's made of stronger welded steel, but rivets duplicate the original's wrought-iron appearance. The **Venetian** design team not only took thousands of photos on-site, they hired an architectural consultant from Venezia to ensure accuracy right down to the last detail. Every color exactly matches those in the landmarks; every pediment, capital, frieze, and other embellishment is precise; in an air-conditioned on-site sweatshop, laborers hand-chiseled elaborate replicas of columns, right down to the cherubs' toenails. Marble in the floors comes from the same quarry that yielded the stone for the original Doge's Palace. **Luxor** features an painstaking replica of King Tut's Tomb, with "artifacts" fashioned according to ancient Egyptian methods (see Diversions). Tasteful **Bellagio** didn't strain for authenticity as much as its glitzy rivals, but its designers did import hundreds of genuine Italian cypress trees at a cost of several million dollars.

When the conventions book the biggies... Your best bet may be **The Orleans**, a tasteful little slice of the French Quarter that offers spacious accommodations with separate sitting rooms and large closets and bathrooms; a vast array of restaurants and entertainment/activity options; incredible prices; room availability nearly 365 days a year; and a great location a mere mile from the Strip (east-facing rooms have darn fine views). Southeast of the Strip, Spanish-themed **Sunset Station** and Wild-West **Sam's Town** are further off the beaten path, which is precisely why they usually have availability—and don't gouge prices. As the old song advises, "forget all your troubles, forget all your cares, and go Downtown," especially to the second-largest hotel Downtown, the anonymous-feeling **Jackie Gaughan's Plaza** next to the bus terminal.

Suite deals... A note of quiet elegance is struck immediately in **Alexis Park**'s lobby, with its beige terra-cotta floors, overstuffed chairs, and brass chandeliers. It lacks a casino, but offers the requisite lounge with crooner and high-end restaurant, as well as three pools and a hot tub scattered around the property. The landscaping is lovely, with greenery and rock fountains transporting you from the desert. Suites come in 10 different layouts and decor that varies from French Provincial to Southwest Modern, but the look is generally upmarket Sun Belt condo—light colors, cast-iron chairs, marble fixtures—and even the standard suites feature a fridge and mini-bar, while more than half the units boast a fireplace (fake logs, natch) and hot tub. Great for seduction of clients or dates. The anonymous but clean chain member **AmeriSuites** just across the road from the Hard Rock has no casino or restaurant but offers plenty of gratis extras, such as a Strip shuttle, tiny fitness room, heated outdoor pool, full buffet breakfast, laundry facilities, full business center, and even popcorn and *USA Today*. The smallish units are attractively appointed, with stained-oak furnishings, moss-green carpets, leaf-print fabrics; microwave, fridge, coffeemaker, hair dryer, and iron are standard. Homey **Desert Paradise Resort** was converted from a former apartment complex. There's no casino, bar, or restaurant, but continental breakfast, fitness center, pool with BBQ grills, and strip shuttle are complimentary. Management throws occasional wine-and-cheese parties to introduce everyone. The one- and two-bedroom units—in attractive Mediterranean red barrel tile and faux stucco—are fully equipped with kitchen (including dishwasher and microwave), washer/dryer, irons, patios, and walk-in closets. The decor usually includes lots of handsome cast-iron and glass knickknacks, gold sunburst mirrors, Deco-ish sconces, hardwood furnishings, and vaguely southwestern fabrics.

The Index

$$$$$	over $200
$$$$	$150–$200
$$$	$100–$150
$$	$50–$100
$	under $50

Prices are for a standard double room (averaged between weekday and weekend tariffs), excluding nine percent hotel tax, and do not reflect special promotions, seasonal rates, or peak periods. All properties accept AE, D, DC, MC, V.

Alexis Park Resort and Spa. A 20-acre all-suite getaway just minutes from the Strip. No casino.... *Tel 702/796-3300 or 800/453-8000, fax 702/796-4334. 375 E. Harmon Ave. 496 units. $$$–$$$$$* **(see p. 34, 41)**

AmeriSuites. Comfortable suite property for business travelers and families on a budget.... *Tel 702/369-3366 or 800/833-1516, fax 702/369-0009. 4520 Paradise Rd. 202 suites. $$–$$$* **(see p. 42)**

Bally's Las Vegas. An excellent alternative between the older dowdy properties and the overweening new entries: near the top in every category and blissfully theme-free.... *Tel 702/739-4111 or 800/634-3434, fax 702/739-4405. 3645 Las Vegas Blvd. S. 2,814 rooms (including 265 suites). $$$–$$$$* **(see pp. 31, 32, 36, 37)**

Barbary Coast Hotel. A surprisingly elegant smaller Strip hotel at sensational prices.... *Tel 702/737-7111 or 800/634-6755, fax 702/737-6304. 3595 Las Vegas Blvd. S. 196 rooms. $$* **(see pp. 33)**

Bellagio. Luxe, lavish, and slightly nouveau, this recreation of a villa on Lake Como is made for modern Medicis.... *Tel*

702/693-7444 or 888/987-6667, fax 702/693-8546. 3600 Las Vegas Blvd. S. 2,688 rooms (including 388 suites). $$$$–$$$$$ **(see pp. 18, 22, 24, 27, 29, 37, 39, 41)**

Best Western Mardi Gras Inn. No restaurant and a minimal casino, but a couple of blocks from the Strip, and affordable.... *Tel 702/731-2020 or 800/634-6501, fax 702/733-6994. 3500 Paradise Rd. 314 rooms. $–$$*

(see p. 30)

Caesars Palace. The town's first truly luxe (and themed-to-the-max) property has maintained its standards in the face of stiff competition.... *Tel 702/731-7110 or 800/634-6661, fax 702/731-6636. 3570 Las Vegas Blvd. S. 2,471 rooms and suites. $$$–$$$$$* **(see pp. 18, 21, 31, 35, 36, 38, 39)**

Circus Circus. An exuberant property-as-giant-arcade that appeals to the kid in everyone. Get ready to dodge strollers and wheelchairs alike.... *Tel 702/734-0410 or 800/634-3450, fax 702/734-5897. 2880 Las Vegas Blvd. S. 3,744 rooms (including 130 suites). $–$$*

(see pp. 27, 33)

Desert Inn. The one true class act on the Strip, with impeccable dining, entertainment, superb golf, and an unfailingly courteous staff.... *Tel 702/733-4444 or 800/634-6909, fax 702/733-4676. 3145 Las Vegas Blvd. S. 715 rooms. $$$–$$$$$* **(see pp. 19, 32, 34, 35, 40)**

Desert Paradise Resort. Former cookie-cutter condos transformed into suites—homey accommodations at a decent price.... *Tel 702/257-0010 or 877/257-0010, fax 702/257-0363. 5165 S. Decatur Blvd. 111 units. $$–$$$*

(see p. 42)

El Cortez Hotel & Casino. El cheapo no-frills, but adequate hotel that caters to a senior crowd.... *Tel 702/385-5200 or 800/634-6703, fax 702/382-1554. 600 E. Fremont St. 308 units. $* **(see pp. 26, 33)**

Excalibur. The campiest theme in town—medieval mediocrity.... *Tel 702/597-7777 or 800/937-7777, fax 702/597-7040. 3850 Las Vegas Blvd. S. 4,008 rooms. $$*

(see pp. 21, 25, 28, 35, 39)

ACCOMMODATIONS | THE INDEX

Flamingo Hilton. A pallid replacement for Bugsy ~~original~~, but still a good moderate Strip option, with rooms in warm jewel tones.... *Tel 702/7~~33-XXXX~~, 800/732-2111, fax 702/733-3353. 3555 Las ~~Vegas Blvd.~~ S. $$$*

Four Seasons Las Vegas. Understated luxury, occupying Mandalay's Bay's top five floors, yet with its own entrance, elevators, and facilities.... *Tel 702/632-5000 or 877/632-5200, fax 702/632-5222. 3960 Las Vegas Blvd. S. 424 rooms (including 86 suites). $$$$–$$$$$***(see p. 20, 28, 32, 34)**

Glass Pool Inn. A total throwback motel with peculiarly cheesy allure. No casino.... *Tel 702/739-6636 or 800/527-7118, no fax. 4613 Las Vegas Blvd. S. 100 rooms. $*
(see pp. 26, 37)

Gold Spike. Basic downtown property, but bountiful amenities for the price.... *Tel 702/384-8444 or 800/634-6703, fax 702/384-8768. 400 E. Ogden Ave. 109 rooms. $*
(see p. 25)

Golden Nugget. With a light-handed Victorian theme, this Downtown gem may be the most refined of Steve Wynn's properties.... *Tel 702/385-7111 or 800/634-3454, fax 702/386-8362. 129 E. Fremont St. 1,911 rooms. $$–$$$*
(see pp. 19, 32)

Hard Rock Hotel & Casino. Hedonistic hangout for a hip under-40 crowd, fabulously witty.... *Tel 702/693-5000 or 800/HRD-ROCK, fax 702/693-5010. 4455 Paradise Rd. 670 rooms (including 68 suites). $$$–$$$$*
(see pp. 18, 26, 36, 37, 39)

Hotel San Remo. This comparatively-small property boasts a great location and solid low-end value.... *Tel 702/739-9000 or 800/522-7366, fax 702/736-1120. 115 E. Tropicana Ave. 711 rooms. $$*
(see p. 30)

Jackie Gaughan's Plaza Hotel & Casino. A rather impersonal, shabby, but inexpensive downtown hotel with all the expected facilities. Avoid the garish lobby.... *Tel 702/386-2110 or 800/634-6575, fax 702/382-8281. 1 Main St. 1,037 rooms $–$$*
(see pp. 26, 41)

Concha Motel. Cozy rooms, friendly service, pool and ideal location for the price..... *Tel 702/735-1255, fax 702/369-0862. 2955 Las Vegas Blvd. S. 351 rooms. $–$$*

(see p. 30)

Las Vegas Hilton. Despite its age, the Hilton does everything well, from dining to activities to serving a discerning business clientele.... *Tel 702/732-5111 or 800/732-7117, fax 702/732-5243. 3000 Paradise Rd. 3,174 rooms. $$$*

(see p. 30)

Luxor Hotel & Casino. After a $300 million renovation that eliminated much of the Egyptian kitsch, this may be the best middle-priced entry in town.... *Tel 702/262-4000 or 800/288-1000, fax 702/262-4406. 3900 Las Vegas Blvd. S. 4,467 rooms (including 473 suites). $$–$$$*

(see pp. 20, 27, 34, 40, 41)

Main Street Station. Handsomely outfitted Downtown yuppie hangout.... *Tel 702/387-1896 or 800/465-0711, fax 702/386-4466. 200 N. Main St. 406 rooms. $$*

(see p. 24)

Mandalay Bay Resort & Casino. A hip, corporate frat party with a South Seas theme and cutting-edge fun, from the House of Blues theater to the top-notch eateries.... *Tel 702/632-7777 or 877/632-7000, fax 702/632-7190. 3950 Las Vegas Blvd. S. 3,276 units. $$$$*

(see pp. 23, 26, 36, 38, 40)

MGM Grand Hotel & Casino. The world's second largest hotel, it abandoned its *Wizard of Oz* animatronics in favor of high-end videos at the entrance. The Hollywood theme, though, lingers in a Studio Walk of restaurants and shops, and fun-themed wings (Hollywood, Southern, Marrakesh, and Oz), whose rooms differ only in color scheme and artwork.... *Tel 702/891-1111 or 800/929-1111, fax 702/891-1030. Las Vegas Blvd. S. 5,005 units (including 756 suites). $$$–$$$$*

(see pp. 28, 31, 35)

Mirage. Remarkable jungle lobby, elegant rooms, excellent restaurants, and generally impeccable service.... *Tel 702/791-7111 or 800/627-6667, fax 702/791-7446.*

3400 Las Vegas Blvd. S. 3,044 rooms (including 279 suites). $$–$$$$$ **(see pp. 19, 28, 38, 39)**

Monte Carlo Resort & Casino. This elegant property offers a combination of old-fashioned romance and up-to-date amenities.... Tel 702/730-7777 or 800/3111-8999, fax 702/730-7250. 3770 Las Vegas Blvd. S. 3,002 rooms (including 265 suites). $$–$$$ **(see p. 23)**

New York-New York Hotel & Casino. Merely average restaurants, pool, and spa/fitness club, but otherwise a thoroughly admirable property. Request a room that doesn't look directly onto the Manhattan Express roller coaster—too many screams.... Tel 702/740-6969 or 800/NY-FOR-ME, fax 702/740-6969. 3790 Las Vegas Blvd S. 2,033 units. $$–$$$ **(see pp. 22, 34, 39, 40)**

The Orleans Hotel & Casino. This Big Easy-themed resort doesn't take itself too seriously, and has great diversions for the kids. Attractive and attractively priced to boot.... Tel 702/365-7111 or 800/675-3267, 4500 W. Tropicana Ave. 840 rooms. $–$$ **(see pp. 23, 29, 41)**

Paris. Obsessive replica of the City of Light, with a sense of naughty (G-rated) fun. The replica Eiffel Tower, with legs coming into the casino, is actually quite impressive.... Tel 702/967-4111 or 888/266-5687, fax 702/967-3836. 3655 Las Vegas Blvd. S. 2,916 units. $$$–$$$$ **(see pp. 22, 31, 40)**

Regent Las Vegas. Suburban off-Strip location and luxury style makes this resort feel more like a Phoenix/Scottsdale golf and tennis resort than a Vegas property.... Tel 702/869-7777 or 877/869-7777, fax 702/869-7771. 221 North Rampart Blvd. 540 rooms. $$$$$ **(see pp. 20, 35, 37)**

Rio All-Suite Casino Resort. Exemplary property—huge rooms (most with fab strip views), superlative restaurants, a model beach/grotto pool, fine spa, and extensive gaming, entertainment, and nightlife options.... Tel 702/252-7777 or 800/PLAY-RIO, fax 702/253-0090. 3700 W. Flamingo Rd. 2,563 rooms. $$$ **(see p. 27)**

Riviera Hotel & Casino. This slightly tarnished golden oldie

ACCOMMODATIONS | THE INDEX

markets itself as "The Alternative for Grownups," as evidenced by the NC-17 shows and the gold tassel–heavy decor in the rooms... *Tel 702/734-5110 or 800/634-6753, fax 702/794-9451. 2901 Las Vegas Blvd. S. 2,075 rooms (including 158 suites). $$–$$$* **(see pp. 29, 31)**

Sahara Hotel & Casino. It's questionable whether the recent remodeling job is an improvement or not, but this is still a bargain at the edge of the Strip, popular with families and seniors alike.... *Tel 702/737-2111 or 888/696-2121, fax 702/791-2027. 2535 Las Vegas Blvd. S. 1,709 units. $–$$* **(see pp. 25, 33)**

Sam's Town. A virtual Western theme park, complete with dance halls, saloons, and a recreation of the Rocky Mountains. One of the best buys in town.... *Tel 702/456-7777 or 800/634-6371, fax 702/454-8014. 5111 Boulder Hwy. 650 units. $$* **(see pp. 23, 29, 41)**

Stardust Resort & Casino. Old holdover that remains one of the best values in town, catering to middle-American salesmen and tour groups. Lobby decor runs to mirrored columns and mulicolored carpet, but rooms are thankfully more subdued.... *Tel 702/732-6111 or 800/824-6033, fax 702/732-6296. 3000 Las Vegas Blvd. S. 2,431 units. $$* **(see pp. 32, 33)**

Stratosphere Tower and Thrill Rides. Despite a poor location, the tallest structure in town rises above its surroundings. Good value.... *Tel 702/380-7777 or 800/99-TOWER, fax 702/383-4755. 2000 Las Vegas Blvd. S. 1,500 units. $–$$* **(see pp. 21, 24, 28)**

Sunset Station Hotel & Casino. The newest and arguably best of the Station properties, featuring an attractive Mediterranean theme.... *Tel 702/547-7777 or 800/6-STATIONS, fax 702/547-7606. 1301 W. Sunset Rd., Hendesson. 448 units. $$* **(see pp. 29, 41)**

Treasure Island. Popular but overly themed sibling resort to the Mirage.... *Tel 702/894-7111 or 800/944-7444, fax 702/894-7446. 3300 Las Vegas Blvd. S. 2,891 units. $$–$$$* **(see pp. 21, 24, 28)**

Tropicana Resort & Casino. That rare Strip property that still offers kitsch and glitz with a wink.... *Tel 702/739-2222 or 800/634-4000, fax 702/739-2469. 3801 Las Vegas Blvd. S. 1,874 units. $$–$$$* **(see pp. 33, 35, 36)**

Venetian. For all the excess, an admirable duplication of Venice, inside and out, including ceiling frescoes and a Grand Canal.... *Tel 702/733-5000 or 800/494-3556, fax 702/733-5404. 3355 Las Vegas Blvd. S. 3,036 units. $$$$$* **(see pp. 22, 31, 38, 39, 41)**

North Strip Accommodations

Best Western
  Mardi Gras Inn **10**
Circus Circus **4**
Desert Inn **9**
La Concha Motel **6**
Las Vegas Hilton **7**
Regent Las Vegas **1**
Riviera Hotel & Casino **5**
Sahara Hotel & Casino **3**
Stardust Resort & Casino **8**
Stratosphere Tower
  and Thrill Rides **2**

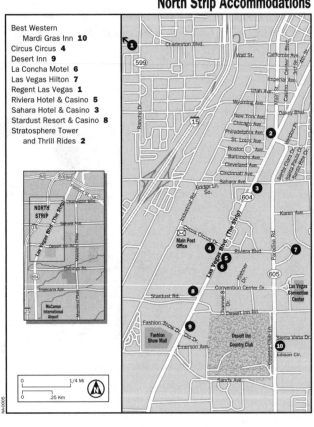

Mid-Strip Accommodations

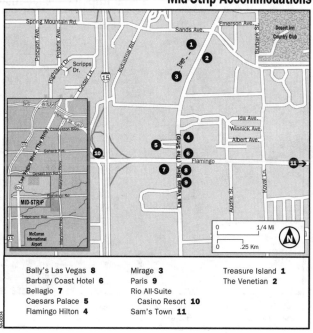

Bally's Las Vegas **8**	Mirage **3**	Treasure Island **1**
Barbary Coast Hotel **6**	Paris **9**	The Venetian **2**
Bellagio **7**	Rio All-Suite	
Caesars Palace **5**	Casino Resort **10**	
Flamingo Hilton **4**	Sam's Town **11**	

NA-0004

South Strip Accommodations

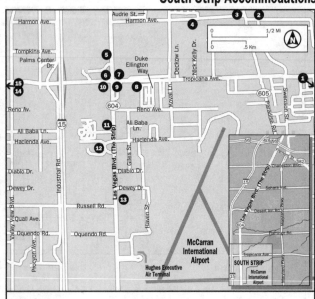

Alexis Park Resort **4**	Hard Rock Hotel & Casino **3**	Monte Carlo
AmeriSuites **2**	Hotel San Remo **8**	Hotel & Casino **5**
Desert Paradise Resort **15**	Luxor Hotel & Casino **11**	New York-New York **6**
Excalibur **10**	Mandalay Bay	Orleans **14**
Four Seasons **12**	Resort & Casino **12**	Sunset Station **1**
Glass Pool Inn **13**	MGM Grand Hotel & Casino **7**	Tropicana **9**

NA-0003

Downtown Accommodations

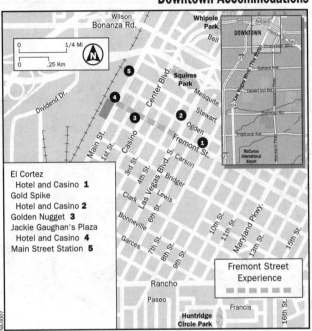

El Cortez
  Hotel and Casino **1**
Gold Spike
  Hotel and Casino **2**
Golden Nugget **3**
Jackie Gaughan's Plaza
  Hotel and Casino **4**
Main Street Station **5**

NA-0007

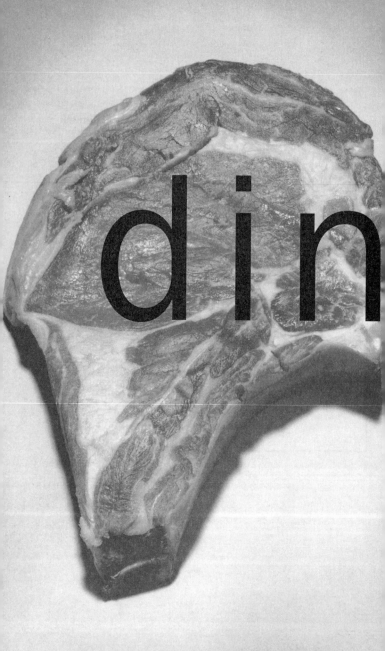

ing

Used to be that Las
Vegas was the city
where the preferred
greens were crisp
laundered C-notes.
You had two dining
choices:

cafeteria-style all-you-can-eat buffets or ornate gourmet rooms with strolling violinists and champagne waterfalls, serving continental cuisine frozen in the Kennedy era (the latter designed for high rollers—90 percent of the meals were comped). Today the baby radicchio/arugula crowd has arrived en masse. Credit it to Wolfgang Puck, who in 1992 opened a branch of his trendy L.A. gourmet pizzeria, **Spago**, in the Forum Shops at Caesars, of all places. It was an instant smash, still his biggest-grossing restaurant with sales in excess of $12 million annually. Once Puck raised the bar, everyone rushed to fill the culinary void, and the dining scene has undergone a change of epic proportions. For every listing in this chapter there are several more in each hotel (Mandalay Bay alone has 15 eateries), all imaginatively themed and boasting different cuisines. The big hotels have made this a prestige competition, courting and coddling renowned chefs (see Where the Chefs Are) like prized acquisitions. The chefs in turn have imported their favorite designers like Adam Tihany and David Rockwell, making these restaurants feasts for the eye as well as the palate. Add to this the incursion of such respected chains as **Il Fornaio**, **Lawry's Prime Rib**, **McCormick & Schmick's Seafood**, and steakhouses like **The Palm**, **Morton's of Chicago**, and **Ruth's Chris Steakhouse**, and you've got a suddenly upscale dining scene. Here's an eye-and cork-popping statistic: Las Vegas even boasts more Master Sommeliers (seven of the world's total 76) than any other city; these "wine directors" often oversee several wine lists, culled from a master list containing thousands of bottles. Bellagio's wine director, Jay James, says 1,000 bottles go every day during peak periods. Unfortunately, these star restaurants seem to be on steroids, conceived on an even grander scale than the originals. Chicago's Charlie Trotter, one of the few high-profile chefs to get away, has been quoted as saying that too much pizzazz was expected of the eateries in every aspect, from look to presentation. But he claims that he enjoyed his stint at MGM Grand and that if the right situation came along, he'd reconsider. Emeril Lagasse, with two restaurants in town, notes a lack of depth. And he's right: Past the top 30 or 40 eateries, there's a significant drop-off in quality. But those 30 or 40 can stand against almost any restaurant in America—in every respect save, perhaps, service. There's such a shallow pool of trained high-end restaurant labor that service here often ends up being maddeningly slow, rushed, or downright incompetent. Just as the new mega-resorts force the older hotels to refurbish, the hot restaurants have had a domino effect. There's so much competition, even for local business, that hotel buffets have done away with the ghoulish goulash, mousy moussaka, and pallid paella. Now live chef's stations are de rigueur, as are fresh ingredients and fresher recipes. There's also a glut of chain theme restaurants (basically T-shirt huts that serve food): **Hard Rock Cafe**, the **All Star Cafe** (at the Showcase Mall), the **Motown Cafe, House of Blues, Harley-Davidson Cafe**, **Planet Hollywood** (in Forum Shops at Caesars), **Dive!** , **Gilley's Western Saloon**, **Rainforest Café**, **WCW Nitro Grill**, and **NASCAR Cafe**. The Venetian even added a Warner Brothers Stage 16 with screening rooms and rotating movie-set decor (start in *Casablanca*, end up in *Batman*; waiters will actually change costumes as the panels shift). It shows that Vegas has merely upgraded from meat-and-potatoes to Porterhouse and pommes frites; some diners appreciate the bill of fare, others the size of the bill. This anecdote overheard at **Le Cirque** tells it all: As one Valentino-clad woman confided to another about her stodgy date, "He's boring and a terrible lay. I would have broken up with him long ago, but all these new restaurants keep opening."

Only in Las Vegas

Las Vegas offers nothing truly original, unless you count the all-you-can-eat buffets that began in the 1940s with El Rancho's Midnight Chuck Wagon: a $1 late-night meal as an inducement to keep customers in the hotel after the second show. By now, that concept has been copied in dozens of touristy towns, not to mention at generic chain restaurants like Red Lobster and Sizzler. What is unique is that in one mega-hotel you can find a themed fast-food court, a 24-hour restaurant, a massive buffet, a deli, and several other eateries, ranging from theme to steakhouse to gourmet—and room service to boot.

Real meal deals

The Golden Gate (tel 702/385-1906, 1 Fremont St.) serves a legendary 99-cent shrimp cocktail 'round the clock: more than 100 shrimp swimming in a big sundae glass. San Remo's Ristorante di Fiori (tel 702/739-9000, 115 E. Tropicana Ave.) has a $4.95 prime rib special (salad, baked potato, veggie, and roll). The Gold Coast (tel 702/367-7111, 4000 W. Flamingo Rd.) serves a heaping platter of ham, eggs, and hash browns for $2.99. The Gambler's Special at Arizona Charlie's Sourdough Café (tel 702/258-5200, 740 S. Decatur Blvd.), available midnight till 7am, rolls a lucky seven: seven different breakfasts, each 77 cents—or, anytime, a top sirloin (or ham) steak plus two eggs, toast, and potatoes for $2.49.

DINING — INTRODUCTION

The basic idea is the same: Keep customers on the property at any cost.

What it Will Cost

The price ranges from a $2.99 steak dinner to a $6,000 bottle of wine and $75 prix fixe menu at the gastronomic temples. Some of the most fabulous deals, advertised all over town, are offered in the wee hours in the casino/hotel 24-hour coffee shops (often far more attractive than the dingy diners and truck stops elsewhere in the country). Coupons in the free rags and the newspapers can help save on meals, and joining a slot club may snag you VIP passes to avoid long buffet lines. Tip the standard 15–20% at restaurants.

When to Eat

Buffet lines at peak hours can entail an hour or more wait (and room service is even worse, especially at 3am after a crappy night at the craps table). Consider going late for breakfast (after 9am); before 11:30 am or after 1:30pm for lunch time; and as early as 4:30 or after 8pm for dinner. Note that surprisingly few hotel dining rooms (save for locals' casinos) are open for lunch; buffets and the malls may be your only noontime choices. Upscale spots rarely serve dinner past midnight.

How to Dress

Usually anything goes, except at the pampering palaces of dining, where shorts, T-shirts, sneakers, and those designer jeans are greeted with a sneer and a fringe table, even at lunch. Las Vegas is cultivating that swankier image, remember. So jacket (and sometimes tie) for guys and appropriate evening garb for dolls are required at the **gourmet rooms** in **Bellagio**, **Las Vegas Hilton**, the **Venetian**, **Desert Inn**, **Caesars Palace**, and the **Rio**, as well as a smattering of other top restaurants around town. Dress codes, if any, are noted in the Index below.

Getting the Right Table

Even in the dead of winter or summer, the trendy eateries require reservations up to two months ahead. Scope out the territory in advance: If you want a window or patio seat, request it—or else your romantic anniversary dinner will be accompanied by a symphony of clashing plates or a serenade of shouts from the kitchen. As in any other gastronomic capital, the only way to ensure prompt service and a prime table is by being a regular or a celebrity. The time-honored practice of tipping the maître d' at see-and-be-scenes is now regarded as gauche. If you notice empty tables, request a better one; most maître d's will accommodate you. If all else fails, walk out—there are probably five or ten other restaurants in the hotel, and many more within a few minutes' walk.

Where the Chefs Are

Nearly all of America's hottest chefs or restaurateurs are in Las Vegas, albeit in absentia much of the time— they're too busy checking on their other outposts, promoting their cookbooks, or taping their TV shows. The kitchens are usually run by hand-picked acolytes, but quality can still be uneven. Bellagio alone holds seven James Beard Award–winning chefs. Über-chef **Jean-Georges Vongerichten** (Manhattan's Jean-Georges, Vong, JoJo, and Mercer Kitchen) has staked out his first steakhouse, **Prime**, at Bellagio, where you'll also find two San Francisco transplants—Michael Mina (**Aqua**, for savory seafood) and Julian Serrano, formerly of Masa's, with **Picasso**. Sirio Maccione's three sons supervise operations at two Bellagio restaurants, **Circo** and **Le Cirque**, whose executive chef Marc Poidevin apprenticed under Daniel Boulud and Sottha Khunn in New York. Charles Palmer has reinvented his New York classic **Aureole** at Mandalay Bay, and was so pleased he also recently opened **Charlie Palmer's Steakhouse** at the Four Seasons. New Orleans' Emeril Lagasse has two places: **Emeril's New Orleans Fish House** at the MGM Grand and **Delmonico Steakhouse** at the Venetian. Joachim Splichal has cloned his L.A. hot spot **Pinot Brasserie** at the Venetian, where L.A. chef Piero Selvaggio brought his top-rated Italian **Valentino** (along with a good chunk of his amazing wine cellar), NYC's Eberhard Müller presides over a new **Lutèce**, and Dallas' Stephan and Alena Pyles opened an offshoot of their **Star Canyon**. Other sizzling Southwestern chefs include Santa Fe's Mark Miller (**Coyote Café** in MGM Grand) and L.A.'s "Too Hot Tamales," Susan Feiniger and Mary Sue Milliken, at Mandalay Bay's **Border Grill**. Boston's Todd English brings his sun-drenched Mediterranean cooking to two restaurants—**Olive's** (Bellagio) and **Onda** (Mirage). The Phoenician's Alex Stratta brought his artistry to Mirage's **Renoir**. Peripatetic Nobu Matsuhisa endows the Hard Rock with sashimi chic at his latest **Nobu**. Jean-Louis Palladin (formerly of Washington D.C.'s sublime Jean-Louis) brings post-nouvelle cuisine to the Rio's **Napa**. Jean Joho (of Chicago's top-rated Everest restaurant) oversees Paris' **Eiffel Tower**. Wolfgang Puck may be over-exposed with five restaurants (the latest is **Postrio** in the Venetian), but they're still drawing crowds.

The Lowdown

Where to go when you hit the jackpot... Perversely located on a balcony overlooking the frenzied Rio casino, **Napa** makes you forget the revel below with shimmering abstract artworks and a centerpiece bronze sculpture of leaves whirling up to a huge oval skylight. From the banquettes, diners can watch the open kitchen turn out well-nigh perfect food. Celebrity chef Jean-Louis Palladin's elaborate concoctions use fresh, often unusual American ingredients (Hudson Valley foie gras, Yukon gold potatoes, and Delaware smoked eel), not to mention caviar and truffles, with wild abandon. Hearty game like antelope loin and partridge is featured, usually in intense wine reductions with wild mushrooms and spicy sausage. At Caesars, the swooningly beautiful **Palace Court** is still a winner—real trees, crystal chandeliers, voluminous drapes, a two-story glass wall, and a 45-by-20-foot mural of the French countryside are crowned by a magnificent stained-glass skylight dome. A haute $125 seven-course feast served on Limoges porcelain includes matching wines in Baccarat crystal. The opulent look of **Gatsby's**, in the MGM Grand, is Wasp-ishly restrained—blown-glass pendant lamps, simple Biedermeyer-style chairs, towering floral arrangements, and large mirrors—much like its older, conservative crowd dressed in elegant monochromes. Terence Fong's cooking adds tropical flair to most presentations. Sumptuous as it is, the **Monte Carlo's** cupid-heavy neoclassical look (at the Desert Inn) is almost more Liberace than Louis XIV. Almost. Still, you can't quarrel with the Fabergé-designed place settings, precision service, and faultlessly classic French/Continental food. Bellagio has a trio of high-ticket restaurants that really stand out. Bucking the bigger, bolder trend, **Le Cirque** is intimate (80 seats) by Vegas standards, with only three seatings, making you feel like a member of a private club. The French gourmet fare is deceptively simple, in brilliant counterpoint to the whimsical circus theme. Despite its "power" look, clientele, and feel, the innovative steakhouse **Prime** is surprisingly unstuffy. Jackets aren't required (though New York black always works); there are even ponytails, earrings, and tattoos in evidence. Then there's **Picasso**, which spotlights an approximately-$30 million collection of the namesake artist's originals, plus carpet and furniture designed by Picasso's son, Claude (all that's missing are Paloma's scarves and perfumes on sale). The Mediterranean-style vaulted dining room sets off chef Julian Serrano's masterworks, inspired by Pablo Picasso's stomping grounds in the South of France and Spain.

Most beautiful clientele... At Emeril Lagasse's **Delmonico Steakhouse**, at the Venetian, Robin Leach wanted a dessert that wasn't on the menu: He laid a model out nude on his table and slathered her with whipped cream and chocolate sauce (merely a whipped cream fight, according to Leach). The equally well-connected Lagasse has since banned Leach, though that hasn't stopped "Lifestyles of the Rich and Famous" types from stampeding this upscale meat-ery. Chi-chi Chinese **P.F. Chang's China Bistro** is a sea of MTV types with earrings and goatees, fresh-faced collegiate jocks, manicured JAPs with nails out to here, and distinguished politicos with slicked-back gray hair (there's a special dining area in the kitchen for power dinners). The Hard Rock's **Mr. Lucky's** is packed with sultry trendoids, leggy models, and members of the band who didn't score at the bar or nightclub. The adjacent restaurant is as exotically decorated, with high star sightings and nouvelle California food (frankly, the more calories, the better the dish). The Mandalay Bay's tropical-themed **rumjungle** attracts the kind of curvaceous gals who aspire to play "Who Wants to Marry a Millionaire?" and the attorneys, surgeons, and bankers who want to avoid major entanglements with them. Vegas doesn't get any dressier than Bellagio's **Le Cirque**, which is jammed with a mature, moneyed set that appreciates finely wrought food. Owned by former dancers Kirk Offerle and Connie Chambers, tiny but sophisticated **Jazzed Café and Vinoteca** is an after-the-show gathering spot for lissome toned dancers of both sexes—open late, off the Strip, with superb Italian food, wines, and espresso.

Overrated... **Michael's** serves sublime Continental food in a

DINING | THE LOWDOWN

prototypically "classy" wood-paneled setting. But after all these years, why is it still such a high-ticket hot ticket? The celeb clientele may be loyal, but they don't get the brusque brush off lesser-knowns endure here. At **Emeril's New Orleans Fish House**, everything seems harried and hurried during peak hours, and the normally superlative fish can be overcooked. At these prices, that's unforgivable. And really, Emeril, a big "BAM! WHOP! SMACK!" for the crass advertising of your merchandise on the menu. The **Rosewood Grill** is bustling and impersonal; though the kitchen still excels, it's clearly been coasting complacently on its rep—and the bill's bigger than the much-vaunted lobsters. With **Spago's** signature items now in supermarket frozen-food sections, the menu at this once-upon-a-time trend-setter almost parodies itself. The current chef David Robins is helping reinvigorate the old Wolfgang Puck warhorse with dishes like spicy chicken pizza with roasted bell peppers, sweet corn, and cilantro; or yellowfin tuna sashimi with daikon/sweet onion salsa, ginger ponzu, and sesame seeds, but it seems tired—or maybe you're just drained by the assault on the senses in the surrounding Forum Shops. At Paris's **Eiffel Tower**, waiters trot out their flat-toned halting French a la Peter Sellers as Inspector Clouseau, or eagerly explain French cuisine and preparations in such detail that your eyes glaze over more than the classic entrecôte demi-glace. Pass the Grey Poupon, please.

Most creative menus... At **Napa**, the groupie waiters idolize star chef Jean-Louis Palladin, breathlessly describing his byzantine preparations: crisp roast suckling pig in rosemary *jus* paired with marshmallows and sweet potato mousseline, or a duck consommé embellished with black truffles and cubes of foie gras, topped with foie gras-infused whipped cream. The endlessly inventive Julian Serrano at Bellagio's **Picasso** roasts scallops in a veal reduction with black truffles or sautés them in a gossamer saffron-infused beurre blanc; slightly smoky medallions of fallow deer are counterpointed by caramelized green apples and Zinfandel sauce. Tasting menus are the only way to go. Perhaps the single most brilliant, gutsy dish in Vegas is at Mark Lo Russo's **Aqua**: seared ahi tuna crowned with sautéed foie gras, with spinach and a crispy potato cake enveloped in a rich port wine reduction and meaty portabellos. An even more audacious variation substitutes sea scallops, caramelized rhubarb-lime compote, and endive. The MGM Grand also has two very creative kitchens: Hawaiian Terry Fong marries classic French preparations to island ingredients and flavors at **Gatsby's** (Kobe steak in ginger soy sauce accompanied by luscious pan-roasted garlic; macadamia nut–crusted escolar served with ginger-cilantro pesto and teriyaki sauce) and **Neyla** (hand-rolled crab cigars stuffed with shiitakes with tomato-coriander relish and tamarind molasses; tilapia encrusted with pistachio and pumpkin seeds with a roasted beet, mango, and vanilla vinaigrette). At **Raffles Café**, Mandalay Bay's knockout version of a 24-hour coffee shop, the kitchen is more inventive than many a gourmet room: Taste firecracker shrimp rolls accented with mint in Thai dipping sauce; blue crab cakes with jicama and watercress salad, lime aioli, and frizzled leeks; and smoked duck confit on rosemary focaccia with red onion–pepper jam and pecan mayonnaise.

Where the Rat Pack might hang out... The Downtown basement location, with exposed brick-and-hardwood walls and vaulted brick ceiling, gives **Hugo's Cellar** a speakeasy air, reinforced by a bar where the city's finest classic martinis are served in decanters buried in ice baths. The retro menu includes tableside salad service from giant carts, the occasional flambé, and decently executed standards like *escargots en croûte*, herb-crusted rack of lamb, and swordfish *en papillote* with julienne vegetables. A '50s-style marquee glows "Cocktails" above tufted oxblood leather doors leading to **A.J.'s**, the Hard Rock's faithful recreation of the Rat Pack era's macho glam look—dark woods, sheer curtains, curved leather booths, and a serpentine elevated bar whose pugilist paintings of martinis are as mouthwatering as the slabs of meat on display. With its oak paneling, stained-glass dome, and pressed copper ceiling, the vintage **Binion's Horseshoe Coffee Shop** has character and characters galore. Everyone's sucking on Marlboros and filling in Keno sheets—at *breakfast*. The retro-swank Italian **Manhattan of Las Vegas** on Flamingo Road is more smart-ass than smart, but Frankie and Dino would slip right into the plush booths like old shoes. And no place in Vegas has more limos waiting outside.

Close encounters of the romantic kind... For all its Egyptian excess, Luxor's **Isis** is an eye-catching room serving smartly conceived gourmet fare. Snuggle into one of the huge scalloped black banquettes and you may feel like you're drifting up the Nile on Cleo's barge. The three tiny timbered rooms at downtown's **André's French Resturant** have that rustic look—stuccoed walls embedded with straw and hung with country crockery, arches crawling with vines—and plenty of nooks and crannies for amorous tête-à-têtes over unfussy French food. The longtime French standard **Pamplemousse** has a rosy glow—maroon and mirrored walls, pink and plum napery, wood beams, and the kindest lighting in town, in pink bulbs, for the gracefully aging clientele. Piaf, Mouskouri, Aznavour, and Brel warble on the sound system. Downtown at the Lady Luck, the **Burgundy Room**'s Deco style, with hardwood and brass accents and artworks by Dali and La Poucette, suggests something out of *Gigi*. Dim lighting and well-spaced tables complete the romantic ambience. **Neyla** at the MGM Grand has a sensuous souk-like ambience: stained-glass chandeliers, arches, Berber rugs, billowing canopies, and a working hookah at the room's center, with a selection of pungent Turkish and Iranian tobaccos that provides instant aromatherapy. The Middle Eastern fusion food awakens the senses, too, with unusual combinations of exotic ingredients. The Desert Inn's **Monte Carlo** out-Versailles Versailles with its cupids, classical murals, and floral patterns, but the French/Continental food and service are sublime. Sit by a Palladian window overlooking the lagoon pool, and the rose tapestry banquettes, pink table lamps, and lambent peach accents will cast their warm glow. Finish off with crème anglaise or a light-as-air Grand Marnier soufflé and the night is yours.

Where to impress clients... The ultra-contemporary, hyperactive **Aqua** has the requisite "hot/cool" quotient for wheeling and dealing; everyone talks rapidly into cell phones as their eyes follow who's entered. Who cares if you have to shout to make yourself heard? Designer seafood is served from specialized carts (including one devoted to caviars) by remarkably deft waiters with the unruffled poise of dealers as they toss toast points or riffle slices of apple. As you might expect at Bellagio, it's hung with fine artwork: specially commissioned Rauschenbergs. Its neighbor **Prime** features an Aubusson wool tapestry by Lichtenstein, paintings by Robert DeNiro, Sr., and a five-paneled water-themed canvas by Joseph Raffael. Designer Michael DeSantis gave this sizzling steakhouse a grand manor-house library look: heavy drapes, marble accents, crystal chandeliers, well-spaced tables, and picture windows overlooking the dancing fountains. The bar at **Bistro Le Montrachet** is hopping with power brokers and conventioneers finagling deals (this is the Las Vegas Hilton, after all). The kitchen's creative tweaks to classic French dishes are impressive, or you can find exemplary renditions of power-eating classics: New York steak in a green peppercorn and cognac sauce or roast breast of Muscovy duck with crème de cassis and black currants. The dining room looks dressed for success—a domed ceiling, mahogany paneling, semi-circular banquettes in floral fabrics, beveled mirrors, and a massive floral centerpiece. The Mandalay Bay's gourmet American **Aureole** manages to be both a relaxing dining experience and a frenetic power room. Though the high-tech space seats 400, designer Adam Tihany has cleverly broken it up with half-walls and water curtains. Earth tones, paper lamps, brass-and-wood sconces, and towering floral arrangements impart the feel of a plush boardroom; for serious deal-hammering, head for the Swan Court area, just nine tables and four booths surrounded by picture windows overlooking a waterfall, pool, and gardens. Only the prix fixe tasting menus can be ordered back here, but all the better to sample the stellar regional American cuisine, which uses fresh seasonal ingredients, layered into skyscrapers of carefully juxtaposed flavors and textures (roasted cod with Parma ham and sage on a bed of cabbage, caramelized pheasant atop truffled potato purée accompanied by Oregon chanterelles and sweet Italian cipollini onions). Tihany also designed the same hotel's Italian charmer, **Trattoria del Lupo**, which strikes a nice medium between the neighboring youthful party restaurants and expense-accounter Aureole. The look is secluded Milanese piazza: wrought-iron gates, wooden ceiling beams, huge earthenware pots, elegantly tiled floors inlaid with wood, and an appetizing sage color scheme. **McCormick and Schmick's** has the look of a Northwest lumber baron's fishing lodge: white tablecloths, cherry-wood paneling, parquet floors, tiled fireplaces, green velvet drapes, dark wood booths, and a mahogany bar. To underscore the fact that seafood's the thing here, stained-glass lamps gleam with fish motifs, and marine life illustrations hang on the walls beside mounted trophy fish.

Frozen in the '50s... A clutch of old-time "high roller" rooms are in a gastronomic time warp. With plush red velvet flocking and mahogany wainscoting, stodgy **Michael's** at the Barbary Coast does a fine job with fine-dining standards like rack of lamb, chateaubriand, stone crabs in season, lobster, veal chops, and cherries Jubilee. The vintage Italian restaurant **Bootlegger Ristorante** has a great retro fireside cocktail lounge with faux stone walls, flickering table lamps, large planters, and red red red napery. The pianist plays everything ever recorded by Bennett, Martin, and Sinatra. Co-owner Lorraine Hunt, the former singer/current Lieutenant Governor, occasionally belts a tune. **Rosewood Grill** is a real "dad" type of restaurant, where you expect a stern lecture on life in between courses. You know the look—booths, dark wood paneling, red carpets, crisp white napery. The invariably excellent lobster, stone crabs, lamb and pork chops, crab cakes, scampi, and wine list are overpriced—just the way dads usually like it. Off the Strip, **Lawry's The Prime Rib** replicates the L.A. original's Art Deco inlaid woods and brass; Benny Goodman and Glenn Miller waft through the background and the extraordinary prime rib is served tableside from elephantine silver carts; even the waitresses "English nanny" uniforms haven't changed since the 1930s. Waiters at the well-aged **Burgundy Room** downtown murmur "excellent choice" no matter which of the fine-dining clichés you opt for—flaming tableside preparations, beef Wellington, steak au poivre, veal Oscar, or fettuccine Alfredo.

Buffet all the way... Sequined ribbons loop everywhere at the Rio's **Carnival World Buffet**, with its booths upholstered in Crayola-bright colors and servers dressed in skimpy carioca outfits. Twelve distinct global dining experiences—Brazilian, Cantonese, Italian, Mexican, BBQ, Japanese sushi, Japanese teppanyaki, et cetera—showcase live-action preparations. No wonder the conga lines are among the longest in town. In gorgeous Tuscan villa surroundings, **Bellagio Buffet** offers the most upscale items: an exceptional gathering of marine delights, such as crab legs, oysters on the half shell, sushi, and the occasional lobster tail. Each station at Paris' **Le Village Buffet** refers to a different French province, with food to match—duck braised with Riesling wine from Alsace, rock crab salad from Brittany, sautéed sea bass with artichoke crust from Provence, coq au vin from Burgundy, and fricassee of scallops with roasted forest mushrooms from Normandy. You can eat "outside" in the town square or in a casual dining room by a fireplace. The **Mirage Buffet** is known for its verdant fountain setting, superb food (very good salads) and scrumptious desserts (sinfully rich bourbon-drenched bread pudding). The **Golden Nugget Buffet** is the most elegant in town, with frosted glass, mirrored ceilings, marble-topped serving tables, and swagged curtains. The food is excellent but limited, though the salad bar entices with almost 50 items. Sunday brunch is best, bringing out owner Steve Wynn's mother's recipes for bread pudding, blintzes, and matzoh ball soup. Bally's **Big Kitchen Buffet** is a splendiferous spread in swank surroundings (crystal chandeliers, plush carpeting, upholstered armchairs) for mid-range prices ($10 lunch, $14 dinner). Its creative entrees include Cajun rubbed pork chops, steak in peppercorn sauce, seafood casserole in creamy dill sauce, king crab legs, and crispy duck.

Bargain buffets... The best bang for your buck (yen/lira/peso) is the global smorgasbord at Fiesta's **Festival Buffet**. The nightly lineup includes Italian, Mexican, and Chinese stations; a Mongolian grill; and a fire-pit barbecue turning out some of the tenderest ribs in town, not to mention shish kebab and smoked sausage. Specialty nights might add sashimi, Hawaiian poi, or fresh shellfish and clams. At Main Street Station, the pretty brick-walled **Garden Court Buffet** offers rotisserie, wood-fired brick-oven gourmet pizzas, Chinese stir-fries, BBQ, carving, Hawaiian, Mexican (delectable salsas and guacamole), even Southern cooking, at very decent prices ($9.99 for dinner most nights). Luxor's **Pharaoh's Pheast** duplicates an archeological dig with papyrus, pottery shards, hieroglyphics, sarcophagi, and khaki-suited servers. The Mexican, Chinese, and Italian stations are the best; desserts are bland. The **Circus Circus Buffet** looks marvelous: abstract circus paintings, barrel vault ceilings, black and white torchère lamps, even paintings of disturbingly posed clowns and turn-of-the-century acrobats.

Alas, they forgot to upgrade the food (hey, dinner's a mere $6.99); and the stainless steel counters and menu ranging from pancakes to prime rib shouts cafeteria. Still, come here for a taste of Vegas at its most surreal: Baptist church groups, bewildered Japanese tourists.

The brunch bunch... Many buffets ladle on the eggs Benedict/Florentine/whatever like there's no tomorrow, but beware of champagne brunches, which usually serve inferior sparkling wine, and only a glass or two at that. Not so **Bally's Steakhouse**, where Sunday's $49.95 Sterling Brunch entitles you to an endless stream of Mumm's Cordon Rouge. Ice sculptures are laden with piles of shrimp, sushi, lobster, and oysters on the half shell; floral arrangements frame sumptuous entrees like roast duckling with black currant and blueberry sauce, steak Diane, or chicken roulade with porcinis and pistachios. With local and national touring acts stirring the soul, the **House of Blues** Sunday Gospel Brunch is as much revival meeting (up to 300 people shouting "Amen!") as brunch. There are two seatings (10am and 1pm), both all-you-can-eat with unlimited champagne (a decent domestic label) and a finger-lickin'-good menu of fried chicken, jambalaya, maple-smoked ham, shrimp remoulade salad, smoked chicken and andouille hash, and fabulous banana bread pudding and peach cobbler. At **Garduno's Cantina**, $10.99 will bag you some turbo-charged chili-packed selections, festive mariachi music, and free-flowing margaritas.

Incredible edible deals... Cheap as the Strip buffets can be, there are even better bargains around if you look for them. **Huntridge Drugstore Restaurant** serves up a mean chow mein at an honest-to-God downtown drugstore lunch counter for under $5—cheaper and more filling than a TV dinner. In a strip mall just off the Strip, **Sam Woo BBQ** has even less atmosphere, but the crispy crackling barbecued flesh, not to mention glistening noodles, are almost as cheap. The 10-ounce New York strip steak at **Binion's Horseshoe Coffee Shop** will set you back (get this) $2.99, baked potato and salad included. Okay, so you have to show up between 10pm and 5:45am, but hey, it's a great time to listen to cabbies and old-timers gossip. Show up between 5pm and 11:45pm and you'll still get a 16-ounce T-bone for $6.75.

We never close... Every major casino (except Bellagio) has a 24-hour cafe, but if you want something more stylish, try these. Mandalay Bay's **Raffles Café** serves a United Nations menu with real flair: A small sampling includes Buffalo wings, brie and avocado bruschetta, chicken piccata, meat loaf, halibut and chips, filet mignon, quesadillas (some gussied up), and more than 10 egg selections, not including quiches or omelets to order. The real winners are the gourmet items like chilled lobster gazpacho or Chilean sea bass with chanterelles. The colonial-tropical look includes Indonesian pottery, elaborate carved chests, folding shutters opening onto a delightful patio, and a large tile fountain. **Mr. Lucky's** is like walking into a Calvin Klein shoot, where buff males and waifish females strike poses on a Route 66 set with battered highway signs, brushed-aluminum tables, leather booths, rock 'n' roll memorabilia, and rescued neon signs from demolished hotels. As you'd expect at the Hard Rock, the food is not your usual coffee shop fare—herb-roasted chicken with garlic mashed potatoes, anyone? At Circus Circus's **Pink Pony Café** everything is cotton-candy pink with Valentine-red trimmings: pink ponies in the carpet, pink pony paintings, even a bubble-gum-hued carousel. Somehow it manages to be playful rather than nauseating, and the food is straightforward burgers and grills, with Chinese after 5pm. Most people are bullish on beef at **Binion's Horseshoe Coffee Shop**; the legendary steaks supposedly come from cattle raised on the family's ranch, though family feuds may have put an end to that. Binion's, long the site of the World Series of Poker, is one of the best places to see authentic, professional, hardened, chain-smoking gamblers at all hours—in a surprisingly handsome oak-paneled room.

Delish deli... **Stage Deli** at Caesars' Forum Shops tries hard to duplicate its New York namesake with "graffitied" walls and Broadway show posters; the service, too, is as brusque as the original. "Skyscraper" five-inch sandwiches (good for two meals) are named for Vegas entertainers: Buddy Hackett, Wayne Newton, Don Rickles, Tom Jones, David Copperfield, George Foreman, Jay Leno (he's the triple-decker turkey, pastrami, roast beef, Swiss, cole slaw, and Russian dressing). Knishes, pierogis, and blintzes—they even whip up a fair egg cream. On Maryland Parkway, **Celebrity Deli** serves the same without the theme and fanfare. In addition to perfectly lean corned beef, pastrami, and brisket, there's decent stuffed cabbage, potato pancakes, borscht, and matzoh ball soup. It's a glorified coffee shop with the usual star portraits (Wayne Newton, Tom Jones, Frank Sinatra, Bill Cosby) and gum-cracking professional waitresses. Also off the Strip, **Freddie G's** is a retro-fitted "Deco" diner, with sleek chrome and black leatherette booths, plentiful old photos of the Rat Pack and their entourage, and a beef brisket so tender it dissolves in your mouth. The great triple-decker sandwiches are cleverly named after demolished hotels like the Hacienda (grilled salami and bologna, Swiss, sauerkraut, and tomatoes).

Chow, bella... Bellagio's **Circo**, Le Cirque's Tuscan cousin (Maccioni matriarch Egidiana designed the menu), dishes up all the standards, from melon and prosciutto to tiramisù. The flavors sing lustily, whether it's a mascarpone and prosciutto pizza, ricotta-and-spinach ravioli in sage-accented brown butter, or simply grilled jumbo shrimp (with heads) artfully arranged atop plump cannellini beans, diced tomato, and basil sprigs. The Barnum & Bailey decor is a bit too bright, but the festive atmosphere is infectious. At Mandalay Bay's **Trattoria del Lupo** former Spago chef Mark Ferguson has adapted more unfamiliar "peasant" dishes to American tastes with smashing success in a handsome contemporary Milanesque arcaded setting. A pizza might marry eggplant, portabellos, and aged balsamic vinegar; fennel ravioli is matched with peas and fava beans; rotisserie chicken has a robust orange and truffle sauce; grilled swordfish brims with raisins and pine nuts. Adventuresome Marco Porceddu of **Francesco's** runs the gamut from veggie ravioli with porcini mushrooms and Sardinian pecorino to a porterhouse with arugula over baked tomatoes and garlic bruschetta. The cozy room is a tranquil oasis in Treasure Island, with wood chandeliers and columns, floral fabrics, and artworks by celebrities such as Tony Bennett and Phyllis Diller. From a seat at the bar at the off-Strip **Jazzed Café and Vinoteca**, you can watch owner Kirk Offerle in the kitchen cooking the velvety risotto (try al prosecco, made with sparkling wine) or eggplant Parmigiana. In Summerlin, **Portobella**'s deceptively simple dishes burst with flavor—potato-wrapped sea bass with tomato-caper butter sauce, lobster ravioli in tomato sauce with pesto cream, or a duo of romano-crusted lamb chop and Barolo-braised lamb shank with natural glaze and zucchini tart.

Mambo Italiano... When it comes to old-fashioned Chianti-and-cannelloni joints, Las Vegas is well-stocked. Well away from the Strip, **Bootlegger Ristorante** was founded in 1949 and seems not to have changed since. Old family photos hang everywhere, the main dining room features dark leatherette booths and a canopied bar, and the lounge is a riot of red. Chef Maria Perri's family recipes include toasted ravioli, fried mozzarella and calamari, lasagna, pizzas, and 10 milk-fed veal dishes, from piccata to pizzaiola. You want red sauce? You want a shrine to Francis Albert? You want straw Chianti flasks? Just a block from the Strip, **Battista's Hole in the Wall** serves inexpensive prix fixe meals that include unlimited red and white wine that didn't come from a carton. The veal's Gotti-tough, but sauces are pleasingly robust. There's a strolling accordion player, and Battista himself might sing arias to your date on bended knee. On the east side of town, local fave **Anna Bella** defines warm, homey neighborhood Italian, with generous portions at paisano prices. Even the hodgepodge decor—trellises, Christmas lights, plaster cherubs—can't spoil the pleasures of well-turned-out veal Marsala, salmon in cream sauce with shallots and mushrooms, penne alla vodka, or orange roughy stuffed with spinach and basil in lemon butter caper sauce. Pinky rings, big hair, and plunging décolletage are still in fashion at **Piero's**, just off the Strip. Waiters confide specials like consiglieres, and shadowy booths and alcoves foster deal-making and discreet groping. The food is inconsistent, but the osso buco melts, the cioppino is hearty, and the linguine alla vongole is about as good as it gets. The luxe **Manhattan of Las Vegas** on Flamingo Road is the kind of place Tony from "The Sopranos" would find romantic, with soft lighting and enormous private booths. The veal is invariably excellent, as are the genuine Caesar salad and decadent tiramisù. Scenes of Venice cover the walls, inside and out, at the **Venetian**, where top choices include grilled veal chop, chilled roasted eggplant, and marinated pork neck bones with pepperoncini. Good place to spot Rich Little,

Marisa Tomei, and cheesecake (no, not ricotta: showgirls and strippers often stop here for a bite way after hours).

Service that sparkles... At tony tiny **Le Cirque**, the seamless service is orchestrated with balletic precision. In the Manhattan original, Sirio Maccione dictates who sits where, like a White House dinner; here things are much more relaxed, and the wait staff attend to even the most outrageous requests (even the maître d' and sommelier will serve dishes when necessary). The front door staff is remarkably adept at placating monied bullies and over-dressed trophy wives. The staff at grande dame **Palace Court** is knowledgeable and discreet; also at Caesars, the **Empress Court** black-clad wait staff glides silently as spies attending to your every whim, like minions of the last emperor in the Forbidden City. At the Desert Inn, **Monte Carlo**'s white-jacketed wait staff seem to divine your every need; they raise the silver cloches with the precision of synchronized swimmers. They're kept very busy, too, by all the tableside presentation, flambéed items ranging from spinach salad to bananas Foster, and lemon sorbet "intermezzos" whisked in front of you to refresh the palate. It isn't just the long-stemmed rose presented to every female customer—every aspect of service downtown at **Hugo's Cellar** has an attentive, Old World manner. Salads are prepared with a flourish and a smile, and the alert waiters are friendly without being overly familiar.

Decor to the max... The Mirage's **Samba Grill** has a witty look that's more skewered than the meats sizzling on the open spits. Eggplant-colored ceilings and mango walls accentuate the free-flowing architectural lines; the plates are as colorful as Fiesta Ware, salt and pepper shakers are shaped like balloons, and a red-and-green contraption signals the wait staff (green means "bring it on," red means "wheel me out"). At yupster-haven **Portobella**, the painted interior courtyard is full of illusions—murals of cypress trees, trompe l'oeil shutters, painted Pellegrino ads, a mix of real and faux brick—while exposed ceiling ducts and tangerine-sponged walls add a note of grooviness. The designer Italian food includes wild mushroom pizza and an interesting four-cheese lasagna. **Parian**, the upscale global cuisine restaurant at the Regent Las Vegas in Summerlin, displays on its wall the chef's amazing collection of cooking artifacts from around the world. The serving pieces in daily use are inventive, to say the least: fanciful miniature silver chairs for dessert plates; footless champagne flutes dangling in special holders; cast-iron urns filled with flatware bouquets; silver water pitchers shaped like giraffes or silly wabbits. Adam Tihany designed **Le Cirque** at Bellagio as a subtler, more intimate version of its New York sister, with vividly-colored Italian silks draping sensuously and lit, tent-like, from within. Yes, there's a circus theme, with big-top murals on cherry-wood walls and jugglers and clowns etched on Lalique frosted glass panels. David Rockwell gave the Hard Rock's chic Mexican **Pink Taco** an updated, tequila-soaked *On the Road* look with corrugated metal, distressed wood, swinging bare-bulb fixtures, even an enormous hubcap chandelier. Leather, canvas, burlap, and denim are incorporated into upholstery and wall hangings; the tin-topped Tequila Bar features a ponyskin drink ledge, while the open-air taqueria has one wall festooned with chili peppers and another with vintage radios. At the Forum Shops, Spago's Chinese cousin **Chinois Las Vegas** is fusion-designed, like the food—on the one hand, bamboo, Asian statues, and porcelain vases, on the other hand a riot of curved and textured surfaces and intense colors worthy of a Miro painting. Mandalay Bay's **House of Blues** has the world's largest folk art collection, including a life-size Elvis outside and funky seating areas formed by hammered license plates, bottle caps, and olive oil and coffee cans. The road-house food is soul-satisfying, too—besides gumbo and grits, you can also find Memphis-style ribs with Jack Daniels sauce, cedar plank salmon with watercress-jicama salad, and Voodoo Shrimp served with rosemary cornbread.

Winning wine lists... Vegas sommeliers are rightly proud of their cellars, which nowadays rank among the best in the world. Of course, the premium labels are often reserved for connoisseurs or high rollers. At Mandalay Bay, **Aureole** features the best range and some of the fairest prices in town, with a particularly superb selection of Burgundies, Bordeaux, and (hot trend) Austrian whites to complement the finely wrought American food. You can't miss the four-story wine tower of stainless steel and glass, with cool chicks clad in *Avengers*-style cat suits and crash helmets rapelling up and down to fetch bottles for customers. Yet the tower only holds a quarter of the restaurant's 40,000 bottles (the rest are conventionally stored). Two -thousand wines are available, ranging from $25 to $45,000, though only a few are available by the glass. At the Rio, **Napa** showcases Barrie Larvin's collection of 65,000 bottles, including 25 vintages of Château Lafite-Rothschild; not all are available, but the menu lists more than 600 bottles, with more than 100 by the glass. The downtown French restaurant **André's French Resturant** has a wine list that includes impressive verticals of all the first-growth Bordeaux (15 vintages of Lafite) and some California prizes; a long brass bar at the entrance features plentiful wines by the glass. The MGM Grand's **Gatsby's** has an extensive, impressive wine list, with absurd markups on higher-end bottles but notable values in the $30 to $50 range. Caesars' exquisite **Palace Court** has a lengthy list covering all the basics, the biggies, and esoterica, with Master Sommelier Barbara Werley (one of only eight women to earn the designation) for informed consultations.

Kidz are us... At the MGM Grand, **Rainforest Café** offers a wonderland (on acid) of animatronic animals and other faux natural touches—tropical rainstorms sweep the room every quarter hour; at night, shooting stars cross the ceiling. The food's surprisingly edible, with a kids' menu including Amazon burgers and Planet Earth Pasta. Steer your family clear of the zoo-like gift shop at the entrance. Captain Nemo meets Captain Kirk at **Dive!**, co-owned by Steven Spielberg (remember *Jaws*?) and docked at the Fashion Show Mall. Designed like a submarine, it has loads of interactive aquatic gimmicks— you enter through a hatch, peep through portholes and periscopes, a shark swims overhead. There's a lengthy kids' menu, but even the regular fare is kid-friendly: pizzas (called "portholes"), "sub-stantial" salads (the four Cs: Cobb, Caesar, chicken, and chicken Caesar), "nautical" nachos (not a trace of seafood anywhere), and gourmet subs by the boatload (blackened ribeye, portabello, BBQ pork, Italian meatball). Excalibur's **Sir Galahad** is one mature restaurant where the kids may not squirm— they'll be too busy goggling at the suits of armor and heraldic banners and watching waiters in Robin Hood green tights carve up enormous prime ribs.

Designer Asians... The futuristic **China Grill** at Mandalay Bay mixes East and West with aplomb— broccoli rabe dumplings with roasted tomatoes and star anise; tempura sashimi in hot mustard champagne sauce; and pan-seared foie gras with caramelized mango, palm sugar, and cashews. The BBQ lamb ribs fall off the bone. The look is very high-tech, with bronze mesh on the domed ceiling, and changing-color mood lighting. At the adjacent China Grill Café and Zen Sum, conveyer belts pass dim sum on colorful plates, and video monitors serve up financial news, fashion, live coverage of world events, and even vignettes of Zen philosophy. At the Hard Rock, **Nobu** showcases chef Nobu Matsuhisa's "new-style sushi and sashimi," with stunning dishes like raw fluke with ponzu and heated olive oil. The striking space, designed by David Rockwell, features live trees, bamboo screens, and walls hung with laminated seaweed; the sushi bar glows ethereally within a curved plane of floor-to-ceiling river rock. Despite a few Chinese warrior sculptures and pagoda murals, the atmosphere at **P.F. Chang's China Bistro** is totally American, with halogen lights and a postmodern warehouse-y look. Northern-style short ribs, vegetarian dumplings, and crispy honey shrimp are old reliables. The muted monochrome elegance, all track-lit angles and curves, of **Chin's** has a similar high-tech tone without P.F. Chang's hipster buzz. Skip the Westernized variations (strawberry chicken instead of lemon, shrimp puffs enhanced with curried cream cheese) and go for standards like sweet-and-sour wonton and Hunan beef. Wolfgang Puck does for Asian food at **Chinois Las Vegas** what he did for pizza at Spago: He tarts it up with unlikely yet savory ingredients. Grilled crab claws with mild shishito green chilis and plum-infused mayonnaise: Shinto Southwestern? Szechuan pancakes with Hudson Valley foie gras, shiitake mushrooms and plum sauce: Nouvelle Chinese-American? Sweet-and-sour sesame chicken with yams and snap peas: Yangtze Delta food? **Second Street Grill** is an unexpected delight in a seedy Downtown hotel: a subdued Deco-ish room serving Hawaiian-accented food minus the Trader Vic's flambéed flamboyance. Lemon chicken potstickers are wonderful, as is the whole fresh fish (which could be mahi mahi, ahi tuna, or opaka paka) steamed in tea leaves with coconut, cumin, and coriander notes.

DINING | THE LOWDOWN

Authentic Asians... Sam Woo BBQ is a storefront in Chinatown Plaza (yes, Vegas has a Chinatown, virtually all in one strip mall), serving amazing BBQ and noodle dishes into the wee hours. Downtown, the 1960s vintage **Huntridge Drugstore Restaurant** could be where the Beave and his family ate Chinese, with classic chow mein and chop suey on the menu—chef/owner Bill Fong actually hails from China. **Empress Court** at Caesars may look futuristic, with star-spangled ceilings, rough stone floors, heavy metal curtains, and green-lit fiberglass columns (gotta fit into Caesars' ancient Rome look somehow), but the food is classic authentic Cantonese and Szechuan cooking: cashew chicken, prime sirloin with onions and green peppers, lobster in a sauce of hot and sweet peppers, braised shark's fin in sea urchin sauce. At the Rio, **Fortune's** looks like it cost a fortune, with walnut wainscoting, serene murals, and more than $100,000 worth of Chinese porcelain and other artifacts. The food is just as artful: beef tenderloin with asparagus in black pepper sauce, shrimp in silky mayonnaise with honey walnuts and sesame seeds, and healthful "nouvelle" Chinese items such as the delectable dried scallops and egg-white fried rice. Across the street, **Thai Spice** is an Americanized but stylish Thai pad that does well by pad Thai, mee krob, curries, pepper garlic pork, and especially labb (steamed minced chicken or beef mixed with a sizzling lemon, onion, and cilantro sauce). The big hotels have numerous tasteful Japanese restaurants to accommodate the Asian gambler clientele, but **Mizuno's** at the Tropicana is a standout: antique shoji screens, marble floors, a glass "stream" lit with twinkling lights, cut-glass dividers etched with irises and cherry blossoms, and chefs slicing and dicing with ginzu knives at marble teppanyaki grill tables (they could do without the flashing lights accompanying this routine, though). Near the Strip, **Hamada of Japan** goes touristy with stone temples, fans, kimono-clad staff, even an antique suit of samurai armor, and the teppan room does the usual ginzu tricks with meats and veggies. Still, real Japanese folks come here for the sushi: marvelous eel and toro (fatty tuna), not to mention the fried clam Vegas Roll. Just stay clear of karaoke nights.

Fishing around... The Tillerman is the old-fashioned "serious" seafood spot, and the seafood (usually at least 10 fresh specials daily) is truly special: planked salmon, sautéed scallops, Dungeness crab cakes, shrimp in garlic cream, herb-crusted tuna steak—nothing fancy, but invariably perfectly cooked. The setting has a big-deal flourish, with a skylight cathedral ceiling, a thicket of ficus trees and carved pillars, and an enormous circular stained-glass window. At the spare but striking **Emeril's New Orleans Fish House**, the fish is so fresh it glistens on the plate; Emeril Lagasse uses his star power to fly in just-caught Okeechobee frogs' legs, Alabama free-range chicken, and Lake Superior pike. Look for Louisianan and Portuguese influences on the menu: Creole salmon with wild mushrooms and andouille sausage étouffée; roasted lobster stuffed with "Reverend Al's" oyster dressing with fried spinach leaves, lobster butter sauce, and tasso hollandaise; BBQ shrimp with rosemary biscuits. The wine list is extraordinarily strong on classic California wines. Á la carte entrees at Bellagio's sleek **Aqua** include ahi tuna tartare in sesame oil infused with scotch bonnet peppers, porcini-crusted wild turbot, seared Dayboat scallops with potato shallot cake and osetra caviar in lemon beurre blanc, and Maine lobster pot pie. Upscale **McCormick and Schmick's** serves 32 fresh fish selections, changed twice daily (for lunch and dinner), geographically pinpointed (as in chunky Oregon dungeness crab cakes with red pepper aioli, Idaho rainbow trout stuffed with bay shrimp and spinach risotto, wonton-crusted Florida red snapper with black bean asparagus sauce). You can never go wrong with the chowders, steamers, and calamari. At the Venetian, **Pinot Brasserie** serves the freshest, most succulent shellfish anywhere; waiters shuck shells at the oyster bar in rubber boots just as they would in Montparnasse. Lobster is king at the Strip's handsome-but-uppity **Rosewood Grill**, which needs three huge tanks to house its leviathan crustaceans, many weighing in at over 10 pounds. At **Francesco's**, the seafood really shines: strozzapreti with crab, shrimp, and zucchini in a light saffron sauce; prosciutto-wrapped scallops over seafood couscous in mint oil and a balsamic reduction; and grilled bass with baked apple in red wine sauce. In addition to the inspired sushi and sashimi, the Hard Rock's **Nobu** offers simple cooked seafood that is saturated with flavor, such as miso-inflected cod and creamy, spicy cracked crab. The Mirage's **Kokomo's** has an exotic lagoon setting; no, they don't haul fish out of the faux grotto and waterfalls, but the seafood is fresh and consistently fine. Try the delectable coconut shrimp with sweet Mai onion and jalapeño chutney or delicate, practically falling-apart escolar with truffles and pasta. Off the Strip, **La Barca Seafood Resturant** offers scintillating Mexican seafood, including fish tacos, a 45-ounce shrimp cocktail, escabeche, and a chopped clam tostada that will have you dreaming of mermaids.

Prime beef... Vegas may have more great steakhouses than even Kansas City. **The Steakhouse** at Circus Circus remains the ringmaster of meateries. It's classic men's-club territory, with oil portraits, parquet floors, tapestries, gas lamps, and stuffed peacocks and deer mounted on the walls. Peek in the glass-enclosed aging room, where slabs hang like abstract sculpture. The dry-aged steaks are cooked over an open-hearth mesquite charcoal broiler, imparting a slight smokiness. Don't overlook the very good Caesar salad, excellent black bean soup, and marvelous oysters. Arnie Morton, founder of the Chicago Morton's, is paid tribute at **A.J.'s** at the Hard Rock, owned by Arnie's son Peter Morton; the ineffable retro masculine look matches the macho cuts of beef that often surpass those at the Vegas Morton's of Chicago. **Bally's Steakhouse** seems straight out of a Polo Ralph Lauren ad: green-and-white-striped fabrics, mahogany wainscoting, enormous banquettes, carved wood railings, and horse prints and bronzes. It's pricey, but you can't beef about the incomparable dry-aged cuts. Bellagio's **Prime** may look like a classic steakhouse, but when chef Jean-Georges Vongerichten adds his Alsatian roots and Asian influences, you get items like short ribs with horseradish spaetzle or five-pepper New York steak with signature chickpea fries. At the Venetian's restrained **Delmonico Steakhouse**, antique tables occupy a stark white glass-enclosed room with barrel-vaulted ceilings and chocolate-brown banquettes, but there's nothing monkish about the richly flavored meats. Wet-aged for two weeks then dry-aged for two more, they're served dripping with herb butter and accompanied by sublime steak fries. Ride on out to the Boulder Highway for **Billy Bob's Steakhouse**'s huge "cowboy" and "cowgirl" cuts that taste staight from someone's ranch, in peppercorn, Béarnaise, and honey Dijon sauces. The BBQ is damn fine, too; to be really macho, order Rocky Mountain oysters (bull's testicles), which are crunchy, greasy, and luscious. At Excalibur's **Sir**

Galahad, enormous silver trays are wheeled out for table-side carving. The meat is served with creamed spinach, Yorkshire pudding (a bit rubbery), soup, salad, and potatoes. **The Range** at Harrah's offers some nice variations on standard steakhouse fare, such as filet mignon in gorgonzola onion croustade; for starters, try the creamy Five Onion soup served in a huge hollowed-out onion. Wraparound picture windows provide a dazzling view of the Strip, especially that Mirage volcano. **The Palm** (Forum Shops at Caesars) retains the caricatures of local celebs and politicos on the walls but has lost the sawdust-strewn tile floors and curmudgeonly waiters of its New York progenitor. The humongous steaks and lobsters are as delectable—and pricey. Standing on its own, **Smith & Wollensky** has replicated the Manhattan original's green-and-white building, right down to the polished wood floors and crisp white napery, albeit with casual grill and three stories. Alongside the steak "classics" (T-bone, porterhouse, filet, New York sirloin) you'll find roasted pork shank with jalapeño applesauce, jumbo crab cakes, and 24-ounce Cajun ribeye. **Lawry's The Prime Rib**: The L.A. original served only prime rib, considered by many the best anywhere. What should you order at this off-Strip offshoot? Prime rib, prime rib, and prime rib, with creamed spinach. You can get one fresh fish (halibut, salmon, or swordfish), and three kinds of lobster tail, but what's the point?

Theme dining: the A list... Out in Summerlin, the Regent's **Parian** sometimes gets cutesy with its menu copy and the whimsical array of tableware and serving pieces. (A dish called Duck, Duck...Goose is a trio of Hudson Valley foie gras, seared with blackberry-apple turnover, made into a country terrine with muscat gelée and seared with petite greens—all shaped like waterfowl and presented on a plate sitting on a webbed-footed iron stand.) But the fresh imported ingredients are expertly paired—witness the pan-roasted halibut with artichoke and goat cheese ravioli in sweet-corn bacon broth, or roast rack of Colorado lamb on tomato-eggplant relish with coriander *jus*. The wondrously silly **Bacchanal** at Caesars Palace, with its skimpily attired handmaidens and centurions offering neckrubs and posing provocatively by the fountains, does suggest Hef does Pompeii, but you'll get a surprisingly haute six-course meal (maybe fennel-dusted sea scallop with braised cannellini and shrimp in lemon-garlic sauce, or rack of lamb in fig syrup with roasted pepper and artichoke ragu and rosemary polenta). You enter Luxor's **Isis** along a colonnade of caryatids and through glass doors embossed in gold with the "Wings of Isis." It's Tut's tomb reconceived as a '70s bachelor pad, with stars sewn into the fabric ceiling, cheetah-skin chairs, Pyramid paintings, metal cobras, pharaoh-motif plates, and three Ramses statues standing sentry. The food's remarkably good: Try baked shrimp stuffed with crab and mushrooms; sesame chicken; or oysters rubbed in coriander and chili with basil vinaigrette. With its beheaded Lenin statue outside (replete with bronze pigeon droppings—the original statue actually aroused an outcry in this capitalist shrine), Mandalay Bay's **Red Square** is a bizarre mix of Tsarist (red velour curtains and banquettes, fringe lamps) and populist (sickles, murals of proletariat rallies) decor. There are 120 varieties of vodka served at a stunning bar made of ice, but when it comes to the menu, American comfort food rules: fried chicken with buttermilk mash and red beans, crab cakes with basil mustard mayonnaise, and a wonderful veal-and-shiitake meat loaf.

Theme dining: the B list... Dive!'s exterior is the nose of a life-sized yellow submarine crashing into a water wall, with periodic depth charges rocking the nearby pool. Underwater sounds are piped into the cylindrical gun-metal interior, decorated with gauges, working periscopes, and exposed pipes hissing steam. Every hour a high-tech video show simulates a submarine dive, and a fighting shark and ocean liner hull circle the room from above. You enter the MGM Grand's **Rainforest Café** underneath a huge aquarium, passing animatronic elephants, leopards, gorillas, and giant pythons hiding behind faux palms, cascading waterfalls, and mock rocks covered with fake flowers. The only living creatures are the fish and a few listless parrots (and the relentlessly perky waiters—or are they robots?). Dishes have cutesy names like Jamaica, Me Crazy (grilled pork chops with jerk seasoning and apple chutney) and The Wallaby's Wok (linguine wok-tossed with organic sun-dried tomatoes, toasted pine nuts, and fresh basil). **Billy Bob's Steakhouse** is a Western fetishist's dream: saddles, lariats, yokes, whips, spurs, ten-gallon hats, steer horns, elk racks, antler and wagon-wheel chandeliers from beamed ceilings, rock and log walls. The live guitarist has the Willie Nelson thing down pat. Like all of Excalibur's "gourmet" dining rooms, the prime-rib joint **Sir Galahad** features suits of armor, royal portraits, coats-of-arms, cast-iron chandeliers and sconces, Tudor-style wood-and-stucco walls, and the usual medieval accoutrements.

For Gen-XYZ... Hard Rock's **Mr. Lucky's** confers instant hipster status the minute you walk in—and you can walk in anytime, 24/7. Artfully weathered furnishings and upscale comfort food give it just the right casual buzz. The decor, wait staff, and clientele are equally sleek and lacquered at **P.F. Chang's China Bistro**. The service, unfortunately, is slacker-than-thou. Mandalay Bay's trendoid troika of sex-on-the-beach **rumjungle**; Asian-inspired **China Grill**; and Commie-kitsch **Red Square**, all scream, "This isn't where your parents eat," with unorthodox menus and hopping bar scenes. The latter two feature "communist" unisex bathrooms, another hip "Ally"-ish touch. Cunningly situated between the Armani and Hermès boutiques at Bellagio, **Olive's** is a "name" restaurant (Todd English) at casual prices. The look is playful, with yellow-and-white striped columns and hand-painted ceramic walls swirled with childlike designs, and chef Victor LaPlaca deftly executes the Mediterranean-inspired dishes (try grilled sea scallops mated with woodsy trumpet mushrooms on a bed of truffle mashed potatoes and spinach, or the white clam pizza with prosciutto and balsamic fig jam). The patio is primo at lunch (cheaper selections). Minuscule **Jazzed Café and Vinoteca** lures the chic bohemian set off the Strip with fab risotto, cappuccino, and wines by the glass. Blue walls display unusual artwork (like a woman's navel above denim cutoffs and a Warhol-esque abstracted JFK portrait with a bullseye in the forehead).

Voulez-vous manger avec moi?... Downtown, the long-established **André's** is a charmingly cluttered cottage without a trace of Gallic hauteur. Stay away from the fusion experiments and stick with brasserie fare—sole meunière, capon breast in broccoli cream sauce, seared foie gras with apple purée, and the finest escargots and onion soup gratin in town. Just off the Strip, **Pamplemousse** defines

DINING | THE LOWDOWN

rustic French bistro, from the complimentary basket of crudités, olives, and hard-boiled eggs offered when you sit to the escargots in Burgundy sauce, roast duck, rack of lamb, and a marvelous "hobo" steak encased in salt. Tuxedoed waiters recite the convoluted menu, testing both their memory and their occasionally mangled French. Chef François Meulien is the French standard-bearer at the D.I.'s gloriously baroque **Monte Carlo**: boneless duck à l'orange, Maine lobster Thermidor, filet mignon in Armagnac Bordelaise sauce, and veal chops in morel sauce are signature dishes, but he's not above inspired flights like shrimp and wild rice crêpes with blue Curaçao and tandoori paste and curry dip. Venetian's **Pinot Brasserie** has imported French artifacts (a wooden door from a 19th-century Lyon hotel, Baroque-style murals of wild game from a Paris *maison*) to match its nonpareil bistro food. The rotisserie and oyster bar are superlative; braised meats explode with flavor; the onion soup is dazzling; and the hangar steak with garlic french fries is the town's best. Paris's **Eiffel Tower** is blessedly kitsch-free (no waiters and waitresses in French peasant garb breaking into song) and its solid brasserie food hits all the Gallic highlights, from coq au vin to coquilles Saint-Jacques. Within the Louvre facade in the shadow of the Eiffel Tower, James Beard Award–winning chef Gabino Sotelino opened a branch of his hot Chicago property, **Mon Ami Gabi**, where the cuisine is *très bonne*—fluffy omelets at breakfast, gooey croque-monsieur sandwiches, robust cassoulet, and an almost definitive steak frites. Don't sit in the back room; it's worth the no-reservation wait to nab a front room or, better yet, sidewalk café table (the only outdoor Strip dining).

High-falutin' French... Calling Bellagio's **Le Cirque** a French restaurant oversimplifies things. Chef Marc Poidevin extracts the purest flavors and intensifies them through canny pairings—filet mignon topped with foie gras and brilliantly undercut by tart shallot marmalade; sea scallops swaddled in black truffles; roasted duck with honey-spice glaze and figs; or my favorite, a classic *cuisine paysanne* blanquette de lapin (rabbit in white-wine cream sauce). A $90 five-course *dégustation* (tasting) features seasonal specialties. At Caesars Palace's stunning **Palace Court**, Olivier Valleau experiments with Asian and

Mediterranean accents—witness sautéed scallops in a coriander soy nage or rack of lamb with smoked flageolets, fresh goat cheese, and baby artichokes in an artichoke/lamb juice emulsion—but he can also keep it admirably simple, as in a flaky halibut with artichoke, asparagus, and potato crisps, a lesson in subtle texturing. Cap it off with almond soufflé or passion-fruit crêpes. The tony **Bistro Le Montrachet** offers haute cuisine, with imaginative additions to keep pace with the well-traveled, well-heeled businesspeople that frequent the Las Vegas Hilton. Thus seared Sonoma duck foie gras is served atop spinach mashed potatoes with pine nuts and mushrooms in Madeira sauce; fried bananas and nut-brown lemon butter give Dover sole an exotic twist.

South of the border... One of the few worthwhile Mexican restuarants in town is the colorful, family-run **Lindo Michoacan**, which admirably avoids gringo-izing its food. Chicken mole is dark and bittersweet, and real Mexican dishes such as beef tongue, menudo (tripe, chilis, and hominy stew—served only on weekends) and barbecued goat with tortillas and fresh lime appear on the menu. Beware: The colorado (red) chili sauce will detonate your palate. Unlike many greasy taquerias, **Viva Mercado** stresses healthful cooking: No animal fats are used, and there are several vegetarian specialties. Dino-sized burritos and create-your-own chimichangas are joined on the menu by lobster and fish tacos. Try the intriguing Mex-Ital Marisco Vallarta (orange roughy, shrimp, and scallops swimming in coconut tomato sauce with capers and olives). Off the Strip, the weekends-only **La Barca** is like entering a fiesta, with a great mariachi band, splashy murals of Mexican history and folklore, and remarkable Mexican seafood. A relic from the 1950s, **El Sombrero** is an unprepossessing downtown dump, with a couple of serapes and sombreros sufficing for decor. But the clientele is a vibrant mix of yuppies and ethnic laborers, all rocking to the tremendous jukebox of Latin American songs. Dirt-cheap enchiladas, tamales, tacos, and flautas are served in asbestos-proof colorado (red) and verde (green) chilis. At the Mirage's **Samba Grill**, skewered rotisserie meats are roasted over coals at the open kitchen (the slowly dripping juices and pungent aromas should make any carnivore salivate), then carved tableside. For appetizers, try duck tamales and coconut prawns; the caipirinhas (sugar-cane liquor and limes) deliver a knockout punch. The unlimited rodizio grill is the best bet at Mandalay Bay's tropi-chic **rumjungle**; it includes chicken with chipotle guava sauce, grilled pork loin in tamarind jerk marinade, flank steak with chimichurri, lamb skewers with green curry coconut glaze, and blackened black angus with creole marinade. At the Hard Rock, **Pink Taco**'s Tacho Kneeland earned his chops with the Too Hot Tamales, Mary Sue Milliken and Susan Feiniger (and often surpasses their Border Café in Mandalay Bay). He reinvents tacos and quesadillas (his pink salsa is marvelous), but also turns out properly spicy achiote-rubbed chicken and chicken-and-cheese enchiladas in tomatillo sauce.

Southwest sizzle... Stephan and Alena Pyles' **Star Canyon** sizzles at the Venetian: a fun Texas-sized room featuring hand-scrolled copper and leather accents, earth-packed ceilings, rawhide chairs, steer's horns, and C & W music hooting and hollering through the space. The chefs stick to the items that practically created new Texas cuisine: tamale tart with creamy garlic flan, dense wood-grilled rib-eye with smoky gravy and mounds of yummy onion rings, and more delicate dishes such as halibut in a fennel-orange sauce. With its pumpkin-colored walls adorned with photos of New Mexican staples like chilés and etched art-glass and copper panels, the MGM Grand's **Coyote Café and Grill Room** has a festive yet elegant Southwestern feel, right down to the waiters' bolo ties and chilé-patterned plates. Try the chipotle-marinated shrimp on blinis with avocado relish or the portabello tamales paired with sun-dried tomato corn salsa and portabello cream sauce. Flavors are brilliantly counterpointed: cumin and pumpkin seed or cranberry and chipotle. The livelier and more informal cafe features an authentic exhibition cazuela (casserole oven) and comal (grill) under a ceramic hood, not to mention more than 60 tequilas by the glass. **Garduno's Cantina** serves nasty margaritas and dumps classic green chilé sauce from New Mexico recipes over the tacos and enchiladas, but the seafood-stuffed jalapeños, posole (hominy), and carne adovada are superb. The tableside guacamole preparation is quite a show.

Arabian nights and Turkish delights... Marrakech has cheap chic Sheik ambience with tiled walls and intricately inlaid wood tables in a billowing tent; you slump on throw pillows at uncomfortable low tables and eat with your hands while belly dancers in pink-and-gold costumes undulate nearby, attracting a surprising number of business lunchers. The prix fixe items might include flambéed lamb skewers, flaky chicken pastilla (with raisins and nuts), or a Cornish hen in a light lemon-olive sauce. The MGM Grand's **Neyla** mates Turkish, Egyptian, and Lebanese cuisine with broader Mediterranean influences—witness the duck breast lacquered with tamarind and jasmine topped with macadamia nuts, or the dry-aged strip steak smothered in seven spices and stuffed with feta cheese. You can easily make a meal of the traditional mezza, tapas-style portions of stuffed grape leaves, kebabs, merguez sausage, falafel, spinach pie, etc. Near UNLV, **Mediterranean Café & Market** serves excellent homemade hummus, particularly fine grilled kebabs, thick Turkish coffee, and to-die-for baklava cheesecake. Ignore the misguided decor—weird murals (cavorting Greeks and animals), plastic vines on the ceiling, and marbleized tables. The UNLV crowds love when the vivacious owner makes like Zorba the Greek.

$$$$	over $50
$$$	$30–$50
$$	$15–$30
$	under $15

Price categories reflect the cost of a three-course meal, not including drinks, taxes, and tip.

A.J.'s. A swaggering retro steakhouse.... *Tel 702/693-5000. Hard Rock, 4455 Paradise Rd. Reservations required. $$$*
(see pp. 63, 78)

André's French Restaurant. The perfect French bistro: country antiques, excellent food and wine, and no attitude.... *Tel 702/385-5016. 401 S. 6th St. D not accepted. Jacket, reservations required. $$$–$$$$* **(see pp. 64, 74, 81)**

Anna Bella. Delicious, affordable Italian food.... *Tel 702/434-2537. 3310 Sandhill Rd. Lunch Tue–Fri. Closed Mon. $$–$$$* **(see p. 71)**

Aqua. Buzzing crowd enjoying sensational seafood.... *Tel 702/693-8199. Bellagio, 3600 Las Vegas Blvd. S. DC not accepted. Reservations required. $$$$* **(see pp. 62, 64, 77)**

Aureole. Charlie Palmer's superb regional American cuisine. The subdued lounge is a wonderful spot for a quick bite and a glass of wine.... *Tel 702/632-7401. Mandalay Bay, 3950 Las Vegas Blvd. S. Reservations required. $$$$* **(see pp. 65, 73, 79)**

Bacchanal. Six-course prix fixe meal with Roman orgy trappings. Four seatings nightly.... *Tel 702/731-7731. Caesars Palace, 3570 Las Vegas Blvd. S. No lunch. Closed Sun, Mon. $$$$* **(see p. 79)**

Bally's Steakhouse. Dark, smoky, clubby steakhouse.... *Tel 702/739-4661. Bally's, 3645 Las Vegas Blvd. S. Jacket required; reservation required for brunch. Closed Tue, Wed. $$$$* **(see pp. 68, 78)**

Battista's Hole in the Wall. Priceless Southern Italian kitsch.... *Tel 702/732-1424. 4041 Audrie St. $$* **(see p. 71)**

Bellagio Buffet. Gussied up like an outdoor marketplace, serving everything from calamari ceviche to crème brulée.... *Tel 702/693-7223. Bellagio, 3600 Las Vegas Blvd. S. DC not accepted. $–$$* **(see p. 66)**

Big Kitchen Buffet. Lavish, classy buffet.... *Tel 702/739-4111. Bally's, 3645 Las Vegas Blvd. S. $* **(see p. 67)**

Billy Bob's Steakhouse. Big local hangout with a near-genuine yippie-ai-oh-kai-ay feel.... *Tel 702/454-8031. 5111 Boulder Hwy. $$$* **(see pp. 78, 80)**

Binion's Horseshoe Coffee Shop. Legendary steak specials and Runyonesque patrons.... *Tel 702/382-1600. Binion's Horseshoe, 128 Fremont St. $*   **(see pp. 63, 68, 69)**

Bistro Le Montrachet. Old-fashioned but still superlative French restaurant.... *Tel 702/732-5755. Las Vegas Hilton, 3000 Paradise Rd. Closed Tue, Wed. Jacket, reservations required. $$$$*   **(see pp. 65, 83)**

Bootlegger Ristorante. A local favorite Italian.... *Tel 702/736-4939. 5025 S. Eastern Ave. Lunch served Tue–Fri. Closed Mon. $$*   **(see pp. 66, 71)**

Burgundy Room. Old-fashioned gourmet dining at throwback prices.... *Tel 702/477-3000. Lady Luck, 206 N. 3rd St. Closed Tue, Wed. Reservations required. $$$*   **(see pp. 64, 66)**

Carnival World Buffet. Colorful surroundings, long lines, and fresh savory food from around the globe.... *Tel 702/247-7923. The Rio, 3700 W. Flamingo Rd. $*   **(see p. 66)**

Celebrity Deli. Reasonably priced New York-style delicatessen.... *Tel 702/733-7827. 4055 S. Maryland Pkwy. Lunch served. No dinner Sun. $–$$*   **(see p. 69)**

China Grill. The best of the Orient filtered through a high-tech capitalist haze.... *Tel 702/632-7404. Mandalay Bay, 3950 Las Vegas Blvd. S. Reservations required. $$$ (cafe $$)*
(see pp. 75, 81)

Chinois Las Vegas. Wolfgang Puck's take on Chinese cuisine.... *Tel 702/737-9700. Forum Shops at Caesars, 3500 Las Vegas Blvd. S. Reservations required. Lunch served. $$–$$$$*   **(see pp. 73, 75)**

Chin's. Slightly Westernized Chinese in a starkly high-tech setting.... *Tel 702/893-4045. Fashion Show Mall, 3200 Las Vegas Blvd. S. Lunch served. D not accepted. $$$*
(see p. 75)

Circo. Le Cirque's younger, more festive sibling.... *Tel 702/693-8150. Bellagio, 3600 Las Vegas Blvd. S. Lunch served. $$$*   **(see p. 70)**

Circus Circus Buffet. Jammed and fun as a school cafeteria—

with food barely a cut above.... *Tel 702/734-0410. Circus Circus, 2880 Las Vegas Blvd. S. $* **(see p. 67)**

Coyote Café and Grill Room. Santa Fe import, a standard-bearer for nouvelle Southwestern.... *Tel 702/891-7349. MGM Grand, 3799 Las Vegas Blvd. S. Café open for lunch. Reservations required for Grill Room (not accepted for Café). $$$ (Café $$)* **(see p. 84)**

Delmonico Steakhouse. Emeril Lagasse's top steakhouse.... *Tel 702/414-3737. The Venetian, 3355 Las Vegas Blvd. S. Jacket, reservations required. $$$$* **(see pp. 61, 78)**

Dive! Co-owner Steven Spielberg sells subs in a submarine.... *Tel 702/369-2270. Fashion Show Mall, 3200 Las Vegas Blvd. S. Lunch served. $–$$* **(see pp. 74, 80)**

Eiffel Tower. Great views, pleasant music, and worthy French classics.... *Tel 702/967-4111. Paris, 3655 Las Vegas Blvd. S. Reservations required. $$$–$$$$* **(see pp. 62, 82)**

El Sombrero. The oldest Mexican in the city.... *Tel 702/382-9234. 807 S. Main St. Lunch served. D, DC not accepted. $* **(see p. 83)**

Emeril's New Orleans Fish House. Superb seafood, but the place can get frenzied.... *Tel 702/891-7374. MGM Grand, 3799 Las Vegas Blvd. S. Reservations required. $$$–$$$$* **(see pp. 62, 77)**

Empress Court. Hong Kong chefs and black tie/china/crystal service.... *Tel 702/731-7731. Caesars Palace, 3570 Las Vegas Blvd. S. Jacket and reservations required. $$$–$$$* **(see pp. 72, 76)**

Festival Buffet. Around the world for 800 cents.... *Tel 702/631-7000. The Fiesta, 2400 N. Rancho Dr. $* **(see p. 67)**

Fortune's. Exquisite Chinese food in a dining room that's practically a museum.... *Tel 702/247-7923. Rio, 3700 W. Flamingo Rd. Reservations required. $$–$$$* **(see p. 76)**

Francesco's. A serene spot for delightful Italian food.... *Tel 702/894-7111. Treasure Island, 3300 Las Vegas Blvd. S. Reservations required. $$$* **(see pp. 70, 77)**

Freddie G's. Self-consciously classic deli.... *Tel 702/892-9955. 325 Hughes Center Dr. Lunch served. $–$$* **(see p. 70)**

Garden Court Buffet. Especially good Asian and Polynesian specialties.... *Tel 702/387-1896. 200 N. Main. St. $*
(see p. 67)

Garduno's Cantina. Feisty crowd and feistier margaritas.... *Tel 702/631-7000. The Fiesta, 2400 N. Rancho Dr., N. Las Vegas. $* **(see pp. 68, 84)**

Gatsby's. Big money destination with superlative food.... *Tel 702/891-7337. MGM Grand, 3799 Las Vegas Blvd. S. Jacket, reservations required. $$$$* **(see pp. 60, 63, 74)**

Golden Nugget Buffet. An ornate room that really doubles as a gourmet restaurant.... *Tel 702/385-7111. Golden Nugget, 129 E. Fremont St. $* **(see p. 67)**

Hamada of Japan. Reliable sushi and teppan grill.... *Tel 702/733-3005. 598 E. Flamingo Rd. $$* **(see p. 76)**

House of Blues. Un-hokey decor and fine Southern fare.... *Tel 702/632-7600. Mandalay Bay, 3950 Las Vegas Blvd. S. Lunch served. $–$$* **(see pp. 68, 73)**

Hugo's Cellar. Throwback restaurant for martinis and stolid Continental food.... *Tel 702/385-4011. Four Queens, 202 Fremont St. $$$* **(see pp. 63, 72)**

Huntridge Drugstore Restaurant. A drugstore counter improbably serving authentic Chinese food.... *Tel 702/384-3737. 1122 E. Charleston Blvd. No credit cards. Lunch served. $* **(see pp. 68, 76)**

Isis. Egyptian theme lends a sultry romantic ambience.... *Tel 702/262-4773. Luxor, 3900 Las Vegas Blvd. S. Jacket, reservations required. $$$–$$$$* **(see pp. 64, 80)**

Jazzed Café and Vinoteca. Arty hangout with yummy Italian food and espresso, good wine selection.... *Tel 702/798-5995. 2055 E. Tropicana Ave. Closed Mon. D, DC not accepted. $$* **(see pp. 61, 70, 81)**

Kokomo's. Worthy lagoon-ish setting for steak and seafood....

Tel 702/791-7223. The Mirage, 3400 Las Vegas Blvd. S. DC not accepted. Lunch served. $$$ **(see p. 77)**

La Barca Seafood Restaurant. Hole-in-the-wall with great Mexican seafood.... *Tel 702/657-9700. 953 E. Sahara Ave. Closed Mon–Thur. No credit cards. $–$$* **(see pp. 78, 83)**

Lawry's The Prime Rib. Primo prime rib for meat connoisseurs.... *Tel 702/893-2223. 4043 E. Howard Hughes Pkwy. Reservations required. $$$* **(see pp. 66, 79)**

Le Cirque. Not as over-the-big-top as its New York sibling, it's soothing and sumptuous.... *Tel 702/693-8150. Bellagio, 3600 Las Vegas Blvd. S. Jacket and tie, reservations required. DC not accepted. $$$$* **(see pp. 60, 61, 72, 73, 82)**

Le Village Buffet. Specialties from various regions of France.... *Tel 702/967-4111. Paris, 3655 Las Vegas Blvd. S. $* **(see p. 67)**

Lindo Michoacan. Bona fide Mexican food from a family proud of its roots.... *Tel 702/735-6828. 2655 E. Desert Inn Rd. $$* **(see p. 83)**

Manhattan of Las Vegas. Swellegant Italian Rat Pack wannabe.... *Tel 702/737-5000. 2600 E. Flamingo Rd. Reservations required. $$$* **(see pp. 63, 71)**

Marrakech. A decent Americanized Moroccan prix fixe.... *Tel 702/737-5611. 3900 Paradise Rd., Suite Y. Lunch served. $$* **(see p. 84)**

McCormick and Schmick's. Mellow power-and-single scene serving fresh seafood.... *Tel 702/836-9000. 335 Hughes Center Dr. Lunch Mon–Fri. $$$* **(see pp. 65, 77)**

Mediterranean Café and Market. Casual spot for fine homemade Middle Eastern cuisine.... *Tel 702/731-6030. 4147 S. Maryland Pkwy. Lunch served. $–$$* **(see pp. 85)**

Michael's. Outrageously expensive, sometimes haughty, but marvelous Continental.... *Tel 702/737-7111. Barbary Coast, 3595 Las Vegas Blvd. S. Reservations required. $$$$* **(see pp. 61, 66)**

Mirage Buffet. Class buffet act with lush garden setting...*Tel 702/791-7111. The Mirage, 3400 Las Vegas Blvd S. $*
(see p. 67)

Mr. Lucky's. Hippest 24-hour joint in town.... *Tel 702/693-5000. Hard Rock, 4455 Paradise Rd. $* **(see pp. 61, 69, 81)**

Mizuno's. Soothing ambience and superior teppan cooking.... *Tel 702/739-2713. Tropicana, 3801 Las Vegas Blvd. S. Reservations required. $$–$$$* **(see pp. 76)**

Mon Ami Gabi. Simple, worthy bistro fare, open late and opening right onto the Strip.... *Tel 702/967-4111. Paris, 3655 Las Vegas Blvd. S. Lunch served. No reservations for front room and patio. $$–$$$* **(see p. 82)**

Monte Carlo. So soigné, it's like dining chez Rainier and Grace in the 1960s.... *Tel 702/733-4444. Desert Inn, 3145 Las Vegas Blvd. S. Closed Tue, Wed. Jacket and tie, reservations required. $$$$* **(see pp. 60, 64, 72, 82)**

Napa. A sublime dining experience.... *Tel 702/247-7923. The Rio, 3700 W. Flamingo Rd. Closed Sun, Mon. Reservations required. $$$$* **(see pp. 60, 62, 74)**

Neyla. Sexy seraglio setting with imaginative Near-Eastern fare.... *Tel 702/736-2100. MGM Grand, 3799 Las Vegas Blvd S. $$$* **(see pp. 63, 64, 85)**

Nobu. Taking sushi to the next dimension.... *Tel 702/693-5090. Hard Rock, 4455 Paradise Rd. Reservations required. $$$–$$$$* **(see pp. 75, 77)**

Olive's. Todd English fuses dishes from his acclaimed Olive's and Figs.... *Tel 702/693-8150. Bellagio, 3600 Las Vegas Blvd. S. Lunch served. No reservations. $$$* **(see p. 81)**

P.F. Chang's China Bistro. California-tinged Asian, notable more for its sexy scene than its food.... *Tel 702/792-2207. 4165 Paradise Rd. $$* **(see pp. 61, 75, 81)**

Palace Court. The loveliest dining room in Vegas, with constantly revitalized gourmet food.... *Tel 702/731-7110. Caesars Palace, 3570 Las Vegas Blvd. S. Reservations required. $$$$* **(see pp. 60, 72, 74, 82)**

DINING | THE INDEX

The Palm. New York steakhouse clone, minus the crotchety waiters.... *Tel 702/732-7256. Forum Shops at Caesars, 3500 Las Vegas Blvd. S. Lunch served. Reservations required. $$$$* **(see p. 79)**

Pamplemousse. Serving French comfort food over the years to star regulars, from Wayne Newton to Robert Goulet to Sinatra himself.... *Tel 702/733-2066. 400 E. Sahara Ave. Closed Mon. Reservations required. $$$***(see pp. 64, 81)**

Parian. Witty, truly worldly dining.... *Tel 702/869-7777. Regent Las Vegas, 221 N. Rampart Blvd., Summerlin. Reservations required. $$$–$$$$* **(see pp. 72, 79)**

Pharaoh's Pheast. Acceptable food at $10 and under, amid excavations, columns, and maps of Egypt.... *Tel 702/262-4000. Luxor, 3900 Las Vegas Blvd. S. $* **(see p. 67)**

Picasso. Mediterranean showcase for art and culinary artistry.... *Tel 702/693-7223. Bellagio, 3600 Las Vegas Blvd. S. Closed Wed. Reservations required. $$$$*
(see pp. 61, 62)

Piero's. Goodfellas-style hangout with inconsistent Italian food.... *Tel 702/369-2305. 355 Convention Center Dr. $$$* **(see p. 71)**

Pink Pony Café. Kitschy but adorable.... *Tel 702/734-0410. Circus Circus, 2880 Las Vegas Blvd. S. $* **(see p. 69)**

Pink Taco. With-it crowd, nouvelle Mexican food.... *Tel 702/693-5000. Hard Rock, 4455 Paradise Rd. $–$$*
(see pp. 73, 84)

Pinot Brasserie. Joachim Splichal's bistro cooking and fresh shellfish.... *Tel 702/414-8888. The Venetian, 3355 Las Vegas Blvd S. Reservations required. $$$–$$$$* **(see pp. 77, 82)**

Portobella. An engaging Italian with appealing decor, crowd, and food.... *Tel 702/228-1338. 8427 W. Lake Mead Blvd. Lunch Mon–Fri. $$–$$$* **(see pp. 70, 72)**

Prime. Porterhouses, T-bones, and rib-eye steaks, with stylish culinary tweaks.... *Tel 702/693-8484. Bellagio, 3600 Las Vegas Blvd. S. Reservations required. $$$$* **(see pp. 61, 65, 78)**

Raffles Café. Striking 'round-the-clock cafe with innovative food.... *Tel 702/632-7777. Mandalay Bay, 3950 Las Vegas Blvd. S. $$* **(see pp. 63, 69)**

Rainforest Café. Kids love this Disney-fied ecological theme park.... *Tel 702/891-8580. MGM Grand, 3799 Las Vegas Blvd. S. $$* **(see pp. 74, 80)**

The Range. Strip views and New York Strips.... *Tel 702/369-5084. Harrah's, 3475 Las Vegas Blvd. S. Reservations required. $$$* **(see p. 79)**

Red Square. A postmodern luxe vision of Russia.... *Tel 702/632-7407. Mandalay Bay, 3950 Las Vegas Blvd. S. Reservations required. $$$* **(see pp. 80, 81)**

Rosewood Grill. Handsomely appointed eatery, great lobsters, obtrusive service.... *Tel 702/792-5965. 3339 Las Vegas Blvd. S. Reservations required. $$$–$$$$*
(see pp. 62, 66, 77)

rumjungle. Carib-Latin overkill, but hip, youthful, and high-energy.... *Tel 702/632-7408. Mandalay Bay, 3950 Las Vegas Blvd. S. No reservations. $$$***(see pp. 61, 81, 84)**

Sam Woo BBQ. Shrine to Chinese barbecue. No English spoken.... *Tel 702/368-7628. 4125 W. Spring Mountain Rd. $–$$* **(see pp. 68, 76)**

Samba Grill. Sexy rodizio grill with wacked-out decor.... *Tel 702/791-7111. The Mirage, 3400 Las Vegas Blvd. S. $$$*
(see pp. 72, 83)

Second Street Grill. Innovative Pacific Rim–tinged California cuisine.... *Tel 702/385-6277. Fremont, 200 E. Fremont St. $$–$$$* **(see p. 75)**

Sir Galahad. Affordable prime rib dinner in medieval surroundings.... *Tel 702/397-7589. Excalibur, 3850 Las Vegas Blvd. S. Reservations required. $–$$* **(see pp. 74, 78, 81)**

Smith & Wollensky. The Manhattan power-broker hangout's very authentic duplicate.... *Tel 702/862-4100. 3767 Las Vegas Blvd. S. $$$–$$$$* **(see p. 79)**

DINING | THE INDEX

Spago's. Designer pizzas by Puck.... *Tel 702/369-6300. Forum Shops at Caesars, 3500 Las Vegas Blvd. S. $$$*
(see p. 62)

Stage Deli. New York ripoff serving pastrami and pickles imported from Manhattan.... *Tel 702/893-4045. Forum Shops at Caesars, 3500 Las Vegas Blvd. S. Lunch served. $$* **(see p. 69)**

Star Canyon. Nouvelle Southwestern cuisine.... *Tel 702/414-3772. The Venetian, 3355 Las Vegas Blvd. S. Reservations required. DC not accepted. $$$* **(see p. 84)**

The Steakhouse. Elegant room, fabulous steaks at unheard-of prices. Sunday champagne brunch at 9:30 and 11:30am, 12:30pm.... *Tel 702/794-3767. Circus Circus, 2880 Las Vegas Blvd. S. Brunch served. Reservations required. $$–$$$* **(see p. 78)**

Thai Spice. Excellent Thai dishes (be sure to tell your server your heat tolerance).... *Tel 702/362-5308. 4433 W. Flamingo Rd. Lunch served. Closed Sun. DC not accepted. $–$$* **(see p. 76)**

The Tillerman. Serious seafood, condescending service.... *Tel 702/731-4036. 2245 E. Flamingo Rd. No reservations. $$$* **(see p. 76)**

Trattoria del Lupo. Wolfgang Puck's true Italian trattoria, with marvelous haute peasant food.... *Tel 702/632-7710. Mandalay Bay, 3950 Las Vegas Blvd. S. $$$*
(see pp. 65, 70)

Venetian. Classic Italian.... *Tel 702/876-4190. 3713 W. Sahara Ave. $$–$$$* **(see p. 71)**

Viva Mercado. Superior, health-conscious Mexican.... *Tel 702/435-6200. 4500 E. Sunset Rd.; Tel 702/871-8826. 6182 W. Flamingo Rd. No reservations. DC not accepted. $$* **(see p. 83)**

Dining Downtown

André's French
　Restaurant **11**
Binion's Horseshoe
　Coffee Shop **7**
Burgundy Room **6**
El Sombrero **13**
Festival Buffet **1**
Garden Court
　Buffet **5**
Garduno's Cantina **2**
Golden Nugget
　Buffet **8**
Hugo's Cellar **10**
Huntridge Drugstore
　Restaurant **12**
Parian **3**
Portobella **4**
Second Street Grill **9**

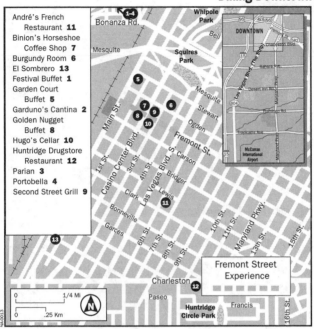

Dining East of the Strip

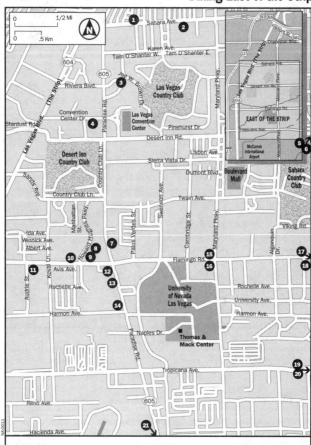

North Strip Dining

Chin's **5**
Circus Circus Buffet **2**
Dive! **4**
Monte Carlo **3**
Pink Pony Café **2**
The Steakhouse **2**
Venetian **1**

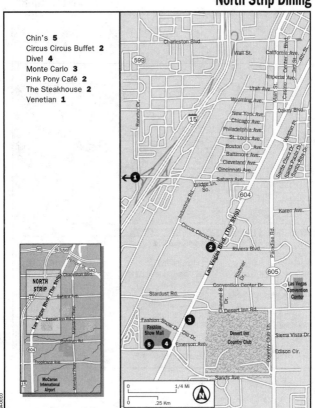

Mid-Strip Dining

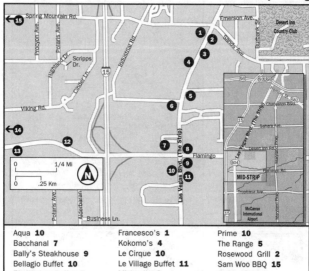

Aqua **10**
Bacchanal **7**
Bally's Steakhouse **9**
Bellagio Buffet **10**
Big Kitchen Buffet **9**
Carnival World Buffet **12**
Chinois Las Vegas **6**
Circo **10**
Delmonico Steakhouse **3**
Eiffel Tower **11**
Empress Court **7**
Fortune's **12**

Francesco's **1**
Kokomo's **4**
Le Cirque **10**
Le Village Buffet **11**
Michael's **8**
Mirage Buffet **4**
Mon Ami Gabi **11**
Napa **12**
Olive's **10**
Palace Court **7**
Picasso **10**
Pinot Brasserie **3**

Prime **10**
The Range **5**
Rosewood Grill **2**
Sam Woo BBQ **15**
Samba Grill **4**
Spago Las Vegas **6**
Stage Deli **6**
Star Canyon **3**
Thai Spice **13**
Viva Mercado **14**

South Strip Dining

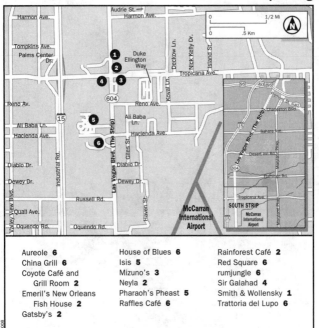

Aureole **6**
China Grill **6**
Coyote Café and
   Grill Room **2**
Emeril's New Orleans
   Fish House **2**
Gatsby's **2**

House of Blues **6**
Isis **5**
Mizuno's **3**
Neyla **2**
Pharaoh's Pheast **5**
Raffles Café **6**

Rainforest Café **2**
Red Square **6**
rumjungle **6**
Sir Galahad **4**
Smith & Wollensky **1**
Trattoria del Lupo **6**

NA-0008

3

sions

Think of Vegas as the
real-life equivalent of
those virtual
reality/IMAX/3D
motion simulators:
non-stop, dizzying
excitement, with

sights and sounds assailing you from every angle. **The Strip** itself is one giant theme park. Hotels install attractions not only to keep guests on the property but to lure outside revenue as well; you can ride gondolas (indoors), zoom up the Eiffel Tower, or hurtle around the Statue of Liberty and Empire State Building on a roller coaster—and if that's too mundane, you can visit Atlantis and Star Trek. Everywhere you wander are serenading minstrels, tumbling acrobats, animatronic statues, resplendent fountains that kick-step like showgirls, buccaneers battling a British naval frigate, and volcanoes spewing lava dozens of feet into the air. Hotel lobbies are virtual zoos or jungles filled with exotic wildlife. Simple shops contain museums of memorabilia. Restaurants have black-clad, harnessed "angels" scaling wine towers or walls of fire encased within water. And those aren't even the official attractions. Though many Las Vegas attractions are designed to be interactive, they also offer the expected shrines to glitz and kitsch (like the **Liberace Museum**) and the gambling industry. Today, there are even prominent art collections as well as cutting-edge galleries. Some of the most glorious offerings are outside town, from the man-made splendor of **Lake Mead** and **Hoover Dam** to the ruddy desert terrain of **Red Rock Canyon**. And within an hour's drive, you can also tour the former atomic Nevada Test Site or a proposed radioactive dump facility, even snoop for military hardware and aliens near top-secret Area 51. But ultimately, is anything more other-worldly than what you find along that glowing strip???

Getting Your Bearings

All roads lead to **the Strip**, the long axle from which most main arteries emanate. The first time doing the Strip can be a profoundly disorienting experience. What other street's skyline includes an Egyptian pyramid, Italianate villa, Arthurian castle, Roman palace, and miniature versions of New York, Paris, and Venice—in many places linked by futuristic monorails? Driving it (with the infamous traffic jams) is daunting; walking can be downright dangerous at major intersections like Flamingo and Tropicana, where pedestrian overpasses were constructed. At least there's a shuttle that crawls along fairly reliably. The 3.5-mile-long Strip (officially **Las Vegas Boulevard South**) can be divided into lower (south) and upper (north) segments. The **southern section** begins near the airport at **Hacienda Avenue**, where you'll encounter such monsters as Mandalay Bay, Luxor, and Excalibur and, across Tropicana Avenue, New

York New York and the MGM Grand. Continuing north, you hit Monte Carlo, Aladdin, and Paris. The lower section ends at **Flamingo Road**, site of the Bellagio, Caesars Palace, Bally's, and Barbary Coast hotels on each corner. Just to the west lie two more mega-properties, Rio and Gold Coast. The **upper section** roughly begins with the Caesars Forum Shops and, across the Strip, the seedy-Chinatown facade of the Imperial Palace. Proceeding north, you hit the Mirage, Treasure Island, Venetian, Stardust, Riviera, and Circus Circus. The uppermost limit is the halfheartedly Moorish Sahara (conveniently at Sahara Avenue). Now you reach an unsavory netherland known as the **Stratosphere district** after the hotel (tallest structure west of the Mississippi) of the same name. From here on, the Strip becomes a dingy, sordid lineup of quickie wedding chapels, bail bondsmen, sex emporia, seedy bars, tattoo shops, and at-your-own-risk motels that often rent by the hour. Turn east on Charleston Avenue, though, and you'll find the blossoming **Gateway district**, the southern fringe of downtown, which is atmospherically skanky, scuzzy, and sleazy in a proto-boho SoHo sorta way. Galleries, thrift-chic shops, and coffeehouses are springing up, where grungeniks etch their bodies with graffiti and discourse knowledgeably on herbal remedies. Continue up Las Vegas Boulevard to reach **Downtown**, aka Glitter Gulch, a few square blocks of tourist area centered around Fremont Street. The Strip is just that—a narrow swath through a sprawling town, though there are several other neighborhoods of interest off the Strip. Near the Convention Center and Las Vegas Hilton, a mini-area has sprouted along **Paradise Road**, which roughly parallels the Strip, anchored by the glittery Hard Rock Hotel. The UNLV campus lies just east, as does the Liberace Museum, about a mile down on Tropicana Avenue. Even further east is the **Boulder Strip,** along the Boulder Highway, home to many of the so-called locals' casinos. Proceed further in any direction and a confusing grid of streets and cul-de-sacs with look-alike residential developments takes over. Like any other Sunbelt city growing too big for its britches, Las Vegas has a score of planned communities: the tony nouveau enclave **Green Valley** to the southeast (where Mike Tyson and Wayne Newton have spreads) and the even ritzier **Summerlin** (replete with a Regent resort) on the other side of town. Summerlin has so many lovely greenspaces, it almost seems as if all the irrigation in the valley was diverted here. **Henderson** (the less exclusive area surrounding Green Valley) boasts several attractions. Drive through here to head toward **Lake Mead** and **Hoover Dam**; continue northwest along the Summerlin route and you'll hit the marvelous **Red Rock Canyon** and **Mount Charleston**, both enormous recreational areas.

The Lowdown

Where the hell am I?... Ah, Las Vegas, City of Themes. At the **Eiffel Tower Experience**, passengers wait to board the elevators on a replica of the Pont Alexandre II that spans Paris's Seine River. At 50 stories, it's a half-size to-scale replica—and it's even the right rusty color. Riders may be too busy losing their Nathan's hot dogs to appreciate New York New York's **Manhattan Express** roller coaster, but they do get a bird's-eye view of the Chrysler Building, the Empire State Building, the Statue of Liberty—in cars duplicating yellow cabs, no less. You board the **Venetian Gondolas** at the end of the Venetian's mall in Piazza San Marco; swept under the Bridge of Sighs, you traverse a "Grand Canal" surrounded by impeccably recreated Venetian neighborhoods (all except the squalor and foul water, that is), where glass blowers, jugglers, and sword swallowers stroll the narrow "alleys." Made by the oldest gondola firm in Venice, these boats are only a foot shorter than Venice's, but they cheat—there's a tiny whirring motor underneath (indistinguishable from the sounds of the slots in the casino below). Pharaohs, Sphinxes, obelisks, hieroglyphs, and other Egyptian symbols greet visitors on their way to **Luxor's King Tut Tomb and Museum**. It's so obsessively "authentic," they even resisted the impulse to include animatronic mummies. Knights in shining armor, troubadours, even an animatronic dragon lurking beneath the drawbridge lure tourists to King Arthur's court in **Excalibur Medieval Village**. The **MGM Grand Adventures Theme Park** includes movie-set street scenes from around the globe: Asian Village (temples, pagodas), Canterbury Junction (Ye Olde Tudor style), Salem Waterfront (shingled clapboard houses), and on to French Street, Gold Rush Junction, New Orleans Street, et al.

Freebie spectacles... Ever wonder why traffic screeches to an abrupt stop on the Strip? It's usually the numerous free spectacles that stop cars in their tracks. In the

Treasure Island Pirate Battle, the British frigate *HMS Britannia* and pirate ship *Hispaniola* skirmish on an elaborate recreation of Robert Louis Stevenson's immortal Buccaneer Bay. Cannon fire, great stunt dives, a sinking ship (the pirates always win), and B-movie dialogue titillate audiences and stop traffic dead. Best views are from the excellent if pricey Buccaneer Bay Club, north end of Battle Bar, or outside on the plank bridge by the frigate-side rope railing (get there 30 to 45 minutes in advance). **Fountains at Bellagio** offers techno-wizardry, as 1,200 choreographed dancing fountains sway and spray under colored lights. Programs vary from a frisky Frank Sinatra rendition of "Luck Be A Lady" to Pavarotti singing "Rondine al Nino" to a tongue-in-cheek "Hey, Big Spender" (which should be the property's theme song). In **Lost City of Atlantis**, at Caesars Forum Shops, an animatronic Neptune (sounding suspiciously like James Earl Jones) shakes his trident at his rebellious, hard-bodied Baywatch-cartoonish offspring Gadrius and Alia. Crowds clamor like they're at the Roman Colosseum, fountains play, statues descend, mists swirl, crystals rise, and lasers shoot. When the **Mirage Volcano** erupts, it spews smoke, steam, flames, and simulated lava 100 feet into the air. A few times, errant sparks have set the nearby palm trees ablaze, which may be the only times this spectacle is really as impressive as it wants to be. Somewhat lamer, the **Excalibur Medieval Village** features decent magicians, jugglers, clowns, and the like on its Court Jester's Stage. Fantasy characters like knights riding unicorns and damsels in distress (usually because their long hair's caught in a suit of armor) add an appropriately absurdist note. The gaudy if somewhat hokey **Fremont Street Experience** is essentially a five-block-long screen presenting neon "moving pictures" (dive-bombing jet fighters, dancing showgirls, and the like). At least it's helped to make Downtown safe, if somewhat sanitized. Out at Sam's Town, **Sunset Stampede**, located in a 25,000-square-foot indoor atrium, is a sound-and-light extravaganza that "takes" the audience across the Great Plains, over the Rockies, through the desert, and into a Gold Rush settlement. An animatronic wolf howls atmospherically as mist shrouds a concrete cliff; animatronic woodpeckers peck and beavers build a dam. Flowers, streams, waterfalls, mountain vegetation, and air conditioning make you feel as if you're on a Rockies plateau.

Best shows for kids... Kids clamor for shoulder perches at the **Treasure Island Pirate Battle**. The bombardment includes more explosions than all three *Die Hard* movies, and while the actors don't buckle the swash as well as Errol Flynn, they do many circus-worthy stunts. At the **Circus Circus Midway**, acrobats somersault, clowns cavort, and an indoor carnival tempts kids with huge popcorn dispensers, face painting, and old-fashioned arcade games (skeeball, Camel Chases, claw machines). And the circus acts, from trapeze artists to trained dog-and-cat acts (using rescued abused or abandoned animals), are top-notch, dazzling even jaded parents. Clown costumes and harlequins dangle from high wires while plastic ice cream cones jut from the walls, giving this "permanent circus" a slightly demented air. Similarly, **Excalibur Medieval Village** offers free stage shows, carnival games, wandering minstrels, Arthurian characters, and two Round Table–themed motion simulator rides (both real yawns, despite the input of George Lucas). But, no surprise, kids prefer the 51-foot-long animatronic dragon belching fire at Merlin (who answers with fire balls), from the slimy green scales of his tail to his glowing yellow eyeballs and blood-red grin. At **M&M's World**, the interactive M&M's Academy "graduates" young children after they follow the story of the good and bad M&M's, complete with a 3-D movie starring "Red" and "Yellow." Who'd have imagined the rigorous demands placed on a chocolate candy? This four-story multi-media "experience" is heavy on the logo merchandise, but has lots of sassy animatronic characters, and the M&M's in 21 colors are da bomb.

Thrill rides... Recently touted by Robbie Knievel as one of the five best thrill rides in the U.S., **Stratosphere**'s Big Shot launches riders 160 feet straight up the outside of the tower in two startling seconds to nearly 1,100 feet above the Strip with four G's of force from the thrust. Then, WHOOSH! Teeth and butt clench, head flattens, and you're trying to remember your chiropractor's number. Just listening to the heartfelt screams of sheer terror is horrifying. At all of 12 seconds, it's a rush job, but a real adrenaline rush. The only thing recommending the Strat's coaster, the High Roller, is its status as the world's highest. Otherwise, it goes at a snail's pace along the mildest of inclines. Vegas being Vegas, even the roller coasters come with themes: The **Adventuredome**'s Canyon Blaster, the world's only indoor double-loop, double-corkscrew roller coaster, packs a lot of punch in an innocuously small area as it loop-the-loops through adobe pueblos and zooms through rock tunnels. New York New York's **Manhattan Express** careens through the New York skyline, threatening to decapitate the Empire State and Chrysler Buildings, ascending to a maximum height of 203 feet. At one point it seems as if you'll kamikaze-dive 144 feet into the valet entrance on the Strip at nearly 70 mph (wusses, be forewarned, it's the second plunge). Next come 540-degree spirals, camelback hills, and high-banked turns before diving back through the casino roof. Wheee! For a literally breathtaking view, check out Las Vegas while you're plunging 70 miles per hour headfirst toward the ground on the SkyScreamer at **MGM Grand Adventures Theme Park**. The world's tallest SkyCoaster thrill ride, it hoists you in a horizontal position to the top of a 220-foot tower, where you pull your ripcord and free fall 100 feet, then swing like a human pendulum. A rocket-shaped elevator ascends to vertiginous heights at **AJ Hackett Bungy**: Even the most valiant have wobbly legs after playing human rubber band, plunging 201 feet. If you feel really daring, do it at night, when it's like swan diving into a vacuum surrounded by psychedelic colors. Just beware of the cost, a jaw-dropping $69. **Flyaway Indoor Skydiving** simulates a 35-foot free fall in a 21-foot-high wind tunnel. An airplane propeller sends blasts of air upward, suspending you for 15 thrilling minutes. (There's also a 20-minute training session). Beware of the ridiculous equipment, including a padded suit that makes you look (and walk) like the Michelin Man. At **Wet 'n' Wild**, Banzai Banzai (a double-slide water coaster where you race side by side) churns up tidal waves in your stomach; Royal Flush (the world's tallest water slide) plunges you down a steep chute at 45 mph before flushing you into a bottomless pool; Bomb Bay is a 76-foot vertical twisting chute whose bottom literally drops out, dunking daredevils into the drink: It's like bungee jumping without the cord (only far safer).

Overrated... If Steve Wynn truly cared about sharing his artistic sensibility with like souls, as he claims, he wouldn't charge $12 admission for the **Bellagio Gallery of Fine Art**. The Louvre and Metropolitan don't charge as much. Don't fall for it: Several fine, if lesser works are displayed for free throughout the hotel's public spaces and restaurants, and the gallery is so small, only 60 paintings can be shown to the jostling crowds. But hey, $12 includes the audio tour by Wynn himself, rambling lectures cooked up with help of several prominent curators that label nearly every piece in his for-sale collection a "masterpiece" or "seminal work." Another faux European experience, the **Venetian Gondolas** glide along a Grand Canal that's a quarter mile long—and only three feet deep. *Gondolieri* in striped shirts and red bandanas say "It's-a real nice, no?" and sing those classic Venetian standards "That's Amore" and "O Sole Mio." ("This is the equivalent of playing a Smurf in a kiddie park," confided one disgruntled boater.) Despite its lofty perch 106 floors above Las Vegas, **Stratosphere**'s High Roller ride is strictly no-thrills, with speeds maxing out at 35mph. Riders are strapped in, with limited views (best after dark to experience any sensation) for a tame ride twice around the top of the tower. The motion-simulator **Race for Atlantis** advertises continuous shows—of course, you have to wait in line for 15 minutes, sometimes half an hour during peak periods. The "chariots" tilt and whirl at six degrees, feeling like a bucking bronco. Not only that, you've got to wear a visor that looks like a cross between fighter pilot goggles and Elton John's eyewear. Bring your Dramamine if you're at all prone to motion sickness, though you're more likely to feel queasy over the price charged for five minutes. Another rip-off is **MGM Grand Adventures Theme Park**. The vague global environments are lame, and most of the rides are tame '50s stuff like a carousel, log flume, and bumper cars. The rides and fine entertainment are "free," but the real attraction, the SkyScreamer, is outrageously priced atop the $10 admission. Downtown, the **Fremont Street Experience** sound-and-light shows are followed by commercials for buffets and shows downtown before the overhead canopy returns to plain old mesh. Plus, you get a neck-ache trying to take everything in above you. Despite the technical wizardry, it's basically a high-wattage attraction for the dim-witted. But worst of all may be the fabled **Mirage Volcano**—its lava sprays look like mere flumes of colored water spitting into the Mirage Lagoon, and the deafening soundtrack recalls a bull elephant in heat.

Au naturel... At the **Bellagio Conservatory**, ponds, bridges, wrought-iron gazebos, arbors, and trellises duplicate an exquisite European garden, albeit one underneath a sculpted green copper ceiling frame. Its vast array of blooms, from perennials to exotics, is impressively color-coordinated. Autumn showcases actual fall foliage, pumpkins, colossal cornucopias; spring features delicate cherry and apple blossoms; holidays bring extras like a 32-foot Christmas tree (decorated by Martha Stewart) and poinsettias and mistletoe everywhere. But nature's not enough for Bellagio founder Steve Wynn; he hired seven-time Tony Award–winner David Hersey to design lighting that would subtly reflect the changing seasons and spotlight each individual flower. Forget the candy factory tour at **Ethel M's Chocolate Factory**; the real sight here is its three-acre Botanical Cactus Garden, where more than three hundred species, from prickly pears to vaulting saguaros, flourish.

Lions and tigers and bears, oh my... Siegfried & Roy's trademark White Himalayan tigers are extinct in the wild, but not at the Mirage lobby's **Tiger Habitat**, which features a rotating cast (the tigers all take their turns between hanging out at Siegfried & Roy's home or performing in their act). Fake concrete palms and a fountain in the pool lend a truly authentic Vegas touch. One tiger reputedly once ate another one; no one said the new Las Vegas still wasn't a jungle out there. While you're here, check out the enormous salt water aquarium behind the hotel's registration desk, complete with menacing sharks and gliding rays. Siggy and Roy's pets are also part of the larger **Secret Garden and Dolphin Habitat**, a twofold outdoor attraction also on the Mirage grounds. Siegfried & Roy's Secret Garden showcases white tigers, the White Lions of Timbavati, Bengal Tigers, and for diversity's sake, one snow leopard, panther, and Asian elephant in an exquisitely landscaped tropical sanctuary, a cool respite dotted with Indian- and Asian-themed pagodas, rock gardens, Buddhas, and Hindu deity statues. The Dolphin Habitat, four connecting pools holding 2.5 million gallons of man-made sea water, is even more fascinating. Underwater and poolside viewing areas let you watch the resident dolphins; incredibly nice staffers will toss beachballs at the Flippers, who'll bat them back to you. Not to be outdone, the **MGM Grand Lion Habitat** plays up its own trademark; three of the big cats here are direct descendants of the MGM mascot, Leo. The

5,345-square-foot habitat is cleverly designed, with several glass walkways that allow the seven lions (of 18 on rotation) to prowl, stalk, and stretch above and below you, so you feel part of their glass-enclosed faux "natural" world. Fortunately, they eat frequently, so you can watch trainers toss slabs of fresh meat. Chiming in with its own mascot, the **Flamingo Hilton Wildlife Habitat** presents flamingos (duh), as well as ducks, swans, cockatoos, and cranes, all cawing, squawking, and whooping like they've just won $100 at the slots. Koi and goldfish swim in the surrounding pools. Wallabies were recently added to provide the requisite "awwww" factor, but the penguins are the real lure, especially at 3pm feeding time. Even the **Las Vegas Museum of Natural History** has live animals ranging from turtles to tarantulas, scorpions (which glow under UV light) to snakes, not to mention the eggs of 35 bird species. But the majority of the exhibits at this temple of taxidermy are fossils, including sabre-toothed cats and ancient crocodiles, and wonderfully posed dioramas of civets, caracals, coyotes, even African water chevrotain in impeccably rendered natural habitats from around the world.

Kids' favorite theme parks... **Adventuredome** is an amazing climate-controlled five-acre park enclosed by a 150-foot-high pink glass dome. Kids of all ages will find something to do: traditional rides like a carousel, Ferris wheel, and bumper cars; SEGA arcade; vicious rides that would make adults lose their hot dogs; animatronic dinos stuck in tar pits; continuous circus acts; mini-golf; hair-braiding; and removable tattoo booths. Older kids will like the Xtreme Zone's climbing wall, "rad bungee" (you do flips on a special trampoline while harnessed), and Lazer Blast for team laser tag (way cool in the black-light room). Beware of the Fun House Express, an IMAX 180-degree wraparound motion simulator ride that goes inside the mind of a very twisted clown. The family that sprays together stays together at **Wet 'n' Wild**, a 15-acre water park right on the Strip: the ideal place to cool off in the Las Vegas summer swelter. There are cannon-shot chutes, a lazy river for the less active, sunbathing areas with cascading waterfalls, video and arcade games, snack bar, swimwear shop, even pockets of green space where families picnic. The Orlando-wannabe **MGM Grand Adventures Theme Park** has some forgettable rides, expensive fast food, souvenir outlets, and halfhearted international-themed sections; concentrate on the Sky-Screamer and the invariably excellent 20 free perfor-mances throughout the day. *Rated X-Treme* showcases BMX riders, boarders, and skaters doing wheelies and twisties on indoor ramps, to the accompaniment of rap, jungle, and hip-hop, but it's creepy watching grown-up dancers in red vinyl bras, hot pants, and black boots cheer them in front of 10-year olds.

Theme parks for grownups... **All-American Sport Park** allows anyone to live out jock fantasies without embarrassment. Major League Slugger Stadium includes a batting cage (slow- and fast-pitch) overlooking a major league-size stadium; the indoor 18-hole putting course is surrounded by a huge photographic mural of spectators, so you can imagine yourself as Tiger Woods. The Rock-reation Sport Climbing Wall offers different obstacles and toeholds, and there's even an in-line skating arena—or, if you don't crave actual exercise, watch games on numerous TVs throughout the Boston Garden Experience cafe, which even has a piece of the parquet floor from the orig-inal Boston Garden. **Star Trek: The Experience** is not just a ride but an entire environment. Its History of the Future Museum includes a nifty Trek timeline (all four shows and eight feature films), costumes, genuine props, and fun factoids. (Didja know Geordi's V.I.S.O.R. was modeled after a 79-cent barrette? That the Klingons drink from goblets used in Cecil B. DeMille's 1956 *The Ten Commandments*?) As for the "ride": You're beamed aboard the starship *Enterprise* and interact with the crew on the bridge; a red alert sounds, you're abducted by Klingons, a Turbolift takes you to the shuttle bay (ignore the worn hotel carpeting here). Klingon blasts rock the bay and you quickly board a 27-seat shuttlecraft on a mission to rescue Captain Picard from the Borg and repair a rift in the time-space continuum. The ride uses a six-axis simulator similar to those used to train NASA astronauts, tilting your perspective so you never get a view of the "real" world.

Honeymoon in Vegas... Las Vegas bills itself not only as the "Entertainment Capital of the World," but the "Marriage Capital of the World" as well, with approxi-mately 120,000 couples getting hitched here annually. You

THE LOWDOWN | DIVERSIONS

can plan a wedding months in advance (hotels specialize in one-stop matrimonial shopping; see Accommodations for top choices) or you can say your vows on the fly in a drive-up chapel or hovering in a helicopter above the Strip ("I do; Roger and out," responded one blushing bride over the propeller noise). You might take the plunge literally, bungee-jumping 175 feet hitched together in a double harness, swooping and whooping "I do's" on **MGM Grand Adventures Theme Park**'s SkyScreamer. Elvis, Captain Kirk, or King Arthur can perform the ceremony. You can even kneel before your future master/mistress in an S&M dungeon, where black leather is accessorized with white lace cat o' nine tails. A civil ceremony costs $25, while elaborate themed weddings run $1,000 and up. No blood test (or marital counseling) is required, and there's no waiting period. A license (one is issued every 6.5 minutes) costs $35; just show up at the **Marriage License Bureau** (tel 702/455-3156, 200 S. 3rd St., 1st floor; open Mon-Thur 8am-midnight, Fri, and Sat 24 hours) with government-sanctioned picture ID. **A Little White Wedding Chapel** (tel 702/382-5943, 1301 Las Vegas Blvd. S.) is one of the more venerable chapels (celebs have included Judy Garland, Bruce Willis and Demi Moore, Sally Jessy Raphael, and Sinatra). It was also the first to offer drive-through service (the $30 Limo Lovers and Liplockers special includes a single red rose). A mere $45 includes limo service from your hotel, non-denominational minister (slip him/her money separately), and free witness. You can get married in the Cherub Chariot underneath a canopy of Cupids, enjoy a dignified wedding under a charming gazebo surrounded by fountains, or soar in a floral hot air balloon accommodating up to 14 guests ($500 to $1,000), called "The Little Chapel in the Sky." The most tranquil is **Little Church of The West** (tel 702/739-7971, 4617 Las Vegas Blvd. S.), open for business since 1942. Elvis Presley and Ann-Margret staged a happy ending here in *Viva Las Vegas*, and movie-mad Japanese have invaded in droves ever since. Real-life celebrity hitchings include Dudley Moore, Judy Garland, Bob Geldof, Zsa Zsa Gabor, Cindy Crawford, and Mickey Rooney (who ought to have been the chapel spokesman, having married all eight of his wives here, starting with Ava Gardner). The faux pine cabin has a certain rustic charm, with an adorable steeple and bell tower, delightful garden, and, inside, cedar-paneled tower, candelabras, and lace curtains. **Graceland Wedding Chapel** (tel 702/474-6655, 619 Las Vegas Blvd. S.) is equally historic, even spanning generations (both 1950s Latin heartthrob Fernando Lamas and C-action-movie king son Lorenzo Lamas); Jon Bon Jovi is the most notable recent guest. Norm "Elvis" Jones performs roughly 40 Elvis weddings a week, finishing with a 15-minute concert. Graceland has a long-running rivalry with **Viva Las Vegas Wedding Chapel** (tel 702/384-0771, 1205 Las Vegas Blvd. S.), where owner Ron DeCar (a singer and Elvis impersonator at the Tropicana for 12 years) conducts approximately 10 to 15 *Blue Hawaii*–inspired weddings weekly, replete with hula girls accompanying the bridesmaids. But Viva Las Vegas offers other movie-themed weddings as well: disco ceremonies with polyester-clad John Travolta minister, *Godfather*-style weddings, and *Beach Blanket Bingo* bashes. The carpet is exchanged for artificial turf for sports fans who want to tackle each other. There's even a gothic package, replete with Grim Reaper pronouncing "Till Death Do You Part" in a darkened candle-lit chapel. Viva Las Vegas is one of many chapels to provide themed weddings for Trekkies (and Trekkers), but only the full-scale attraction **Star Trek: The Experience** can transport beaming couples to the bridge of the *Enterprise*, replete with flickering control panels and Star Fleet officers. They'll even customize; weddings in full Klingon makeup and regalia are particularly popular, staffers confide.

Neon dreams... Neon art may be the great Las Vegas contribution to American culture. The most spectacular example of it is the **Fremont Street Experience**, a five-block pedestrian mall semi-enclosed by a 90-foot vaulted steel-mesh canopy sprinkled with more than two million computer-controlled bulbs (with 35 computers, it's amazingly complex, with fiber optics as sophisticated as spy satellites) and a concert-quality half a million-watt sound system. There are several different "shows." For more of a historical perspective, walk through the open-air **Neon Museum**, which rescued such classics as the horse and cowboy from the Hacienda (1967), the flickering conflagration from the Flame Restaurant (1961), and the lamp from the original Aladdin (1966). Another six are being restored. A couple of blocks down Fremont (off 1st St.), are the legendary downtown glowing icons: Vegas Vic and Vegas Vickie. Vic waves his arm in welcome while puffing a cig, looking like a cross between Howdy Doody and the Marlboro Man. Sultry Vickie looks like she's trying to get his attention across the street, kicking up her heels as if to say, "Wanna good time, stranger?" Old neon signs don't really die: They have a half-life at the **Young Electric Sign Company**, the premier creator of those fantasias. There's no official entry fee, and it's fenced off, but you can peer through. Alas, the neon boneyard has been picked clean by those developer coyotes, but arrows and Stetsons can still be seen, robbed of their glory.

Don't be a dummy... Madame Tussaud's Celebrity Encounter is a $23-million two-story showcase presenting nearly 200 American celebrity figures. You start out at a VIP party with the likes of Oprah Winfrey, Arnold Schwarzenegger, Jerry Springer, Whoopi Goldberg, and Brad Pitt in a swank Art Deco-style room; you then enter a sports arena where Muhammad Ali and Evander Holyfield are supposedly poised to punch in the ring, with jock celebs like John McEnroe, Florence Griffith Joyner, Joe Montana, and Babe Ruth milling about. There's a pop concert where you can sing with Bruce Springsteen and Elton John or dance with Tina Turner and James Brown; another room features Las Vegas legends such as Sinatra, Tom Jones, and Wayne Newton performing in a stunning showroom setting. Paul Newman and Joanne Woodward welcome visitors to a classic Vegas chapel adorned with photos of other celebrities who got hitched here, where you enjoy refreshments such as wedding cake (yes, the frosting does taste a tad waxy). Far less glitzy is the absorbing **Magic and Movie Hall of Fame and Museum**, which has wax figures of famous magicians and a shrine to ventriloquism, with displays on its roots, which can be traced back to ancient Greece as well as the time of King Saul; a video on how it's done, footage of the greats like Edgar Bergen, Shari Lewis, and Paul Winchell; a booth where you can practice with your own dummy; and naturally, dummies galore.

Kidding around... Relics of Las Vegas's attempt to market itself as a family destination are still scattered around town. The best is the outstanding **Lied Children's Museum**, set in an architecturally innovative building full of colors and shapes, where you can become a human battery, stand in a giant bubble, play disc jockey at KKID radio, check out conditions in the Las Vegas Valley at a real weather station, or harness excess kid power (aka hyperactivity) into a lightning spark. Parents will really appreciate the Every Day Living area, where young visitors earn a "paycheck," use the ATM machine in the bank, and shop for groceries. It's not all fossils and stuffed animals at the **Las Vegas Museum of Natural History**: Five robotic dinos include a 35-foot T-Rex and cute Troödons, and the Young Scientist Center offers such interactive displays as "Whose Foot Is It?" (comparing animal tracks) and Dig A Fossil (mini-T-Rex bones). In the Learning Center, kids can dissect owl pellets and cow eyes: gross but fun. Even grosser are exhibits such as the contents of a shark's stomach (in the Marine Life Room), or gruesomely realistic dioramas like the gory scene of caribou fighting off two wolves. Might as well learn it's the law of the jungle out there. Kids who love animals can admire the big cats at **MGM Grand Lion Habitat** (just don't let them talk you into the $20 lion cub photo op) and **Secret Garden and Dolphin Habitat**, which also has elephants, a lovely outdoor setting, and eight show-Flippers. Adults have been known to shove kids out of the way, it's so much fun. **Bonnie Springs Ranch/Old Nevada** is a genuine Wild West theme park (well, it's on a real ranch in a real desert with real pioneer buildings) that enchants kids right from the start, as a mini-choochoo chugs from the parking lot to the entrance. Stagecoach rides on weekends and horseback riding are also available, along with cheesy tourist stuff like a photo shop where you can dress up in period costume and get a tintype. Staged gunfights and saloon melodramas, complete with mustachio-twirling villains, Gary Cooper–esque cowboys and cavalry officers, and beauteous schoolmarms, play up the Wyatt Earp/Billy the Kid shtick for all it's worth. Kids adore the aviary (peacocks for sale) and petting zoo with goat, deer, and pot-belly pigs—but watch out for the greedy llamas.

For high-tech kids... **Gameworks**, developed by Universal Studios, Dreamworks SKG, and Sega Enterprises, has a distinctly macho edge and Nike-esque spirit. Motto: "Life's a game. It's meant to be played." Different "zones" offer more than 300 games of all types (including multi-player and virtual reality), as well as a 75-foot climbing rock and Internet access for playing games with contestants as far afield as England and Japan. You can duke it out with a range of nasty cinematic aliens, battle baddies on a ski lift, or hovercraft your way through the Martian canals. Supervise your kids: Some of the games are graphically violent. You have to be 42 inches tall to compete in **Speedworld**'s simulated Speedway, two 24-seat 3-D theaters with six-seat motion pods resembling NASCAR vehicles (basically a huge video game with near-realistic 3-D visuals projected onto the screen). Skip the nausea and go into the new NASCAR Cafe, with its crash helmet lamps, walls painted with sponsor logos, and servers dressed as grease monkeys. In the IMAX 3-D motion simulator ride **Race for Atlantis**, you're "chosen by the gods" to race a daunting field of competitors in "fighter chariots," all in order to retrieve a magic ring that will determine the fate of the sea-world. The flocks of birds, dragons, dolphins, and weapons are startlingly realistic—3-D spears and shrapnel seem to fly straight at you. Zooming and twisting through canyons, you'll feel like you're in the climactic scene of *Star Wars*. That other sci-fi staple, **Star Trek: The Experience**, transports visitors from the Hilton across Space Bridge into a neon 24th-century universe, where you're encouraged to shop and dine in an exact recreation of the "Deep Space Nine" promenade, or play in the SpaceQuest casino. Cool masks, model starships, and weapons attract kids, not to mention the Trek-inspired names of menu items in the restaurant.

Kitsch collections... Don't miss the **Liberace Museum**, which houses Mr. Showmanship's elaborate bejeweled costumes, bejeweled cars, bejeweled pianos, and bejeweled candelabras. The collection of rare and antique pianos includes a diamond-studded, gold-plated, 7-foot Baldwin covered in rhinestones, but that is counterpointed by the violet 1830 Graffe inlaid with brass and tortoise shell or a Boesendorfer played by Liszt, Schumann, and Brahms—there *was* a quiet, introverted, tasteful pianist somewhere inside the feathers, furs, and rhinestones. Cars range from sublime (one of only seven Rolls Royce Phantom V Landau limos, worth over $1 million) to the ridiculous (the red-white-and-blue Rolls Royce commissioned for his Bicentennial salute, with matching feathered cape and hot pants). Costumes, in every conceivable material from chinchilla to gold lamé, are displayed, along with such trinkets as a 50-pound rhinestone presented to Liberace by a grateful Austrian jeweler. The setting abounds in velvet screens, gilt mirrors, crystal, and marble statues of naked men; the bedroom suite has fur bedspreads; and a family photo room features a "royal portrait" of his mother surrounded by cherubs and Cupids. Not included are his death from AIDS and covert gay lifestyle (including orgies at his home). Ask about his private life and the sweet old ladies, keepers of the flame, blurt "Oh, ohhh no. No, I can't answer that." Sorry, there's only one velvet painting of the King at the **Elvis-a-Rama Museum**, but it's still a must for fans, with gold records; documents (like an American Express application listing his income at $3 million annually); costumes—gold lamé, natch, alongside spangled white jumpsuits; cars (Liberace might have coveted the purple Cadillac); a 1959 full dress Army uniform; and original wardrobe items from *King Creole*, *Clambake*, and *Fun in Acapulco*. And who could resist a free 30-minute concert with an Elvis impersonator in the '50s-style soda shop/cafe? Animatronic Elvii welcome you at **Madame Tussaud's Celebrity Encounter**, where you can interact with the waxwork celebs in various multimedia environments. Many celebrities personally sat for their casts; the modelmakers uncannily captured Michael Jackson in black fetishistic gear, a beatific-looking Shirley MacLaine, the smarmy smile of David Copperfield, and the grin of Eddie Murphy.

Memorable memorabilia... Easily overlooked in a rather seedy Strip hotel, the **Magic and Movie Hall of Fame and Museum** is an unsung pleasure; the fact that it's usually deserted just gives it an appropriately eerie, creepy feeling. The tour begins with waxworks of magicians who revolutionized the entertainment world in their times—Harry Kellar, Thurston, Harry Blackstone Jr., Servais LeRoy, and, of course, Houdini (who must have had a kinky side, judging from the leather straitjackets). The ventriloquist section is spookily cool; other sections are devoted to fake spiritualists and witchcraft; nickelodeons and vintage arcade games, many interactive; and movie posters, autographed photos, and costumes—including Clark Gable's suit coat from *Gone with the Wind*, Errol Flynn's Robin Hood tights, and Elizabeth Taylor's Cleopatra headdresses. In the Houdini Theater, local magicians perform levitations, escapes, and prestidigitation acts that are nearly as

DIVERSIONS | THE LOWDOWN

impressive (and far cheaper) than the famed Siegfried & Roy. The **Casino Legends Hall of Fame** at the Tropicana is more fun than it sounds—artifacts from 738 casinos (550 of which no longer exist), including old menus, showgirl costumes, video clips, vintage movie posters (*Viva Las Vegas*, *Vegas Vacation*), and cancelled checks made out to performers ($406 to Tony Bennett in 1952 from El Rancho, $7,000 to Eartha Kitt in 1954). Car lovers will be astounded by the **Imperial Palace Auto Collection**, one of the largest privately owned collections in world (fittingly located in the Imperial Palace's parking facility). Classics include cars of presidents (Truman, Eisenhower, JFK), dictators (Hitler, Mussolini), and celebrities (Elvis's powder-blue 1976 Cadillac Eldorado, Liberace's 1981 cream Zimmer replete with candelabra, and Sammy Davis, Jr.'s 1972 Stutz). Oddities include Howard Hughes' eccentric 1954 Chrysler (with an air-purification system in the trunk for the germ-phobic titan), Al Capone's 1930 V-16 Cadillac, a 1965 Batmobile (for the TV series), a 1947 Tucker (one of only 51 produced), and even the steel armor-plated Range Rover Popemobile for the Pope's 1982 U.K. trip. Forty-three Model J Dusenbergs, including Jimmy Cagney's, occupy their own room. There are taxis (including a 1908 French model), fire engines, old Harleys, dump trucks, motorized rickshaws, tractors, army vehicles, delivery vans, racing cars, and a 1925 Studebaker paddy wagon. Can you say magnificent obsession?

Show me the cheese: gift shops... The disappointingly tasteful **Elvis-A-Rama Museum** finally gets good and tacky in its gift shop, with Elvis mouse pads and temporary tattoos. The **Liberace Museum** shop comes through in high camp style with red-white-and-blue spangled vests, James Dean ties (huh?), candelabras, and Liberace piggy banks, dolls, and fridge magnets in several resplendent costumes. As expected, **M&M's World** purveys numerous logo items, from ties and T-shirts to teacups, calculators to cuff links to cocktail dresses (gotta have that slinky $2,000 number covered with sequined M&M's, Snickers, and Twixs wrappers). The otherwise scholarly **Titanic Exhibition** reveals its underlying commercial spirit by selling Titanic T-shirts and jigsaw puzzles (rather morbid when you think about it). Shops at **Star Trek: The Experience** pry open the wallets of

Trekkers with the world's largest collection of Trek merchandise and memorabilia. Yes, you too can have Vulcan ears, tribbles, Ferengi masks, a gold-plated communicator, or a $3,000 duplicate of the captain's chair.

Foreign history lessons (why not?)... More often than not in Vegas, the past is no more than a springboard for hotel themes. Witness **Luxor's King Tut's Tomb and Museum**, which recreates the boy pharaoh's tomb with hundreds of items, from the guardian statues and the fabled sarcophagus itself to vases, beds, and basketry, all reproduced using the same gold leaf, linens, pigments, tools, and original 3,300-year-old Egyptian methods. There's even one authentic stone fragment. Overseen by renowned Egyptologist Dr. Omar Mabreuck, the project is so obsessive that artifacts are placed in the precise order in which the originals were first found. Just when you thought it was safe to go back in the water, the **Titanic Exhibition** at the Rio Suites rises as if from the ocean floor, with admirably researched historical photos, multimedia displays on salvaging expeditions, artifacts including personal effects (a shaving brush!), and parts of the ship (the telegraph, a vase etched with the White Star cruise line emblem, and the entire 1,200-pound D deck portal used by first-class passengers to board the ship).

Thumbs up from the galleries... Though locals joke that there's more active culture in the nearest frozen yogurt shop, Las Vegas's arts scene is blooming like a delicate cactus flower in the desert. The prime irrigator is Mirage Resorts' Steve Wynn, who opened the **Bellagio Gallery of Fine Art** with a flurry of press releases pompously comparing Wynn to great art patrons of the past like the Medicis, Henry Clay Frick, or Andrew Mellon. Wynn is indubitably art-savvy (his collection has probably doubled in value from the initial $285 million investment since 1996), with a modern art collection that includes Miro's fanciful *Dialogue of Insects*, Matisse's disturbingly sensual *Odalisque*, Monet's *Water-Lily Pond with Bridge*, Picasso's brooding portrait of then-mistress Dora Marr; and Willem de Kooning's swirling, feverish burst of colors and shapes, *Police Gazette*. Rubens and Rembrandt are even represented. But all these airs mask the fact that the gallery's masterworks are actually for sale—a Roy Lichtenstein painting, for instance, sold

DIVERSIONS | THE LOWDOWN

before the gallery even opened—and that Wynn, who shrewdly leases the collection to his own resort company, managed to finesse a tax break for the Belaggio Gallery as a civic cultural contribution while still charging $12 admission. The aggressively contemporary building design (blazingly white, monumental, with curves and angles like the Frank Lloyd Wrong school of architecture) of the **Sahara West Library and Fine Arts Museum** reflects the solemn agenda of the **Las Vegas Art Museum** within, which presents nationally renowned artists, as well as major international exhibits like a recent comprehensive Chagall retrospective. Despite its noble aspirations, the museum has only 7,000 square feet of exhibition space (smaller than many Strip restaurants). More current works are the stock-in-trade of the **The Arts Factory**, the brainchild of commercial photographer Wes Isbutt, who bought a block-long rundown 1944 warehouse to set up a mini-Soho/artists' commune. There are nearly 20 tenants, with a long waiting list; some are exhibit spaces, some ateliers closed to the public, but you never know who might be smoking outside and let you in. Contemporary Arts Collective (tel 702/382-3886, Room 102) often shows members' work in a variety of media; the Photographic Arts Gallery (tel 702/471-7001, Room 103) hangs ravishing wildlife photos, landscapes, and portraits of local characters; the Nevada Institute of Contemporary Art (tel 702/434-2666, Room 101) is an adventuresome small facility with rotating exhibits, mostly touring shows; the more mainstream Smallworks Gallery (tel 702/388-8857, Room 201) shows leading regional artists such as Robert Beckmann and Barbara Kasten. The George L. Sturman Fine Arts Gallery (tel 702/384-2615, Room 204) is an eccentric, jam-packed grab bag—Disney animation cells, early Christos like wrapped phone books, Calder mobiles, king and queen thrones from Cameroon, Hockneys, Oldenbergs, De Koonings, Rouaults, Dürer etchings, and Milton Avery and Ansel Adams photos. The *pièces de résistance* are shoes collected from various artists, from Chihuly to Rauschenberg.

Rev your motors... **Speedworld** at the Sahara outraces the competition with three-quarter-scale amazingly detailed NASCAR Winston Cup–style cars that sit in service bays replicating pit areas. In a simulated version of the Las Vegas Motor Speedway, you "race" Richard Petty, Jeff Gordon, and Dale Earnhardt, competing in actual time; the thrum and hum is surprisingly realistic. Take turns at speeds approaching 200mph, screech around corners, blow tires, get clipped by fellow racers: it's literally heart-pounding (those with cardiac or respiratory problems are not allowed). **All-American Sport Park** has go-karts, Winston Cup–style cars, and a NASCAR speed park in a less frenzied atmosphere.

For your viewing pleasure... The quickest way to see all the lights on the Strip is via chopper with **Sundance Helicopters**. Its nighttime tours offer eye-level views of the ironwork of the Eiffel Tower at Paris, the roller coaster atop the Stratosphere, hotel penthouses, and fly-bys of the Fountains at Bellagio and the Mirage volcano. Sundance's pilots enjoy angling the aircraft for better views, providing a nice adrenaline rush. If you'd rather keep your feet on solid ground, the 1,149-foot **Stratosphere Tower** is the tallest free-standing observation tower in the U.S. (it was originally supposed to be taller, but the FAA objected) with 360-degree panoramic views. Mind you, you can get the same view with a sunset drink or dinner at the **Top of the Tower** bar and restaurant (see Nightlife). The **Eiffel Tower Experience** may not be the real thing (one leg actually breaks through the Paris's casino ceiling), but 50 stories is still enough to out-Strip most other contenders.

Away from the Strip... If you hanker after greenery, drive to **Mount Charleston**, a cool respite no matter what the time of year. Climb through several distinct ecosystems to the 11,218-foot summit for splendid panoramic views of the valley; the Desert View Trail (seven miles down NV 158) is where locals repaired to watch the mushrooming atomic explosions in the 1950s. A raft of recreational opportunities, from golf to skiing, is available. Ask at one Visitors Center on a hiking trail map. **Red Rock Canyon National Conservation Area** is a brilliant red splash of sandstone, its bacon-like striated exposed rocks revealing more than 600 million years of geological history. The phenomenal terrain features arches, natural bridges, 3,000-foot cliffs, sandstone boulders, and peaks in a striking palette of colors. Ponderosa pines tower, bighorn sheep and desert tortoises wander through, and you may stumble on ancient petroglyphs, arrowheads, and pottery shards of the Anasazi and Paiutes who called the area home centuries ago. There's a 13-mile driving loop (beware of feeding cute but rabid wild burros), but hiking is the best way to appreciate the terrain (be alert for scorpions and snakes). The similar, less trammeled **Valley of Fire State Park** is named for the fiery red sandstone sculpted by wind and rain into spectacular domes, spirals, and beehives (resembling the hairdos of some of the senior citizens back in Vegas). The boulders and pinnacles similarly range in color from deep red to white, with pink, lavender, burnt orange, sienna, and russet highlights. There are also areas of fossilized logs that rival the Petrified Forest.

Head for the lake... If you're feeling parched, head to **Lake Mead/Hoover Dam**, a haven for water sports less than 40 miles away. Drive out State Highway 167, aka North Shore Road, past stunning desert scenery—rugged dark mountains, fiery sandstone outcroppings, gaping canyons, and bluffs reflected in the lake. Turn-offs lead to warmsprings and beaches (those past Callville Bay Marina toward Echo Bay are sandier and less crowded). As a bonus, there are many secluded coves, accessible only by long hikes or boat, for anglers and sunbathers (including some that are unofficially nude or gay). Created by the dam, Lake Mead is the largest manmade lake in the Western hemisphere, with an amazing 550 miles of shoreline; you can sail, jet-ski (tel 702/564-5452 for Las Vegas Adventure Tours), water-ski, river-raft, even scuba dive; fisherman pull in bass (both striped and large-mouth), bluegills, catfish, and crappie. Equipment and so forth can be obtained from **Lake Mead Resort and Marina** (tel 702/293-3484), **Las Vegas Bay** (tel 702/565-9111), and **Callville Bay Marina** (tel 702/565-8958). Ranger-led hikes (from wetlands to vividly hued eroded sandstone formations) and bird-watching expeditions are organized at the **Lake Mead Visitors Center** (tel 702/293-8990 or U.S. 93 at NV 166). **Lake Mead Cruises** (tel 702/293-6180) operates a Mississippi-style paddle wheeler, the *Desert Princess*, a delightful ride through the Black Canyon, past the colorful rock formation nicknamed Arizona's Painted Pots, up to Hoover Dam itself, lit spectacularly at night. If you'd prefer to get your awesome view from the dam itself, take one of the **guided tours of Hoover Dam** (tel

702/293-8367 or 702/294-3522; admission charged); after prowling around the dam's working parts, you'll emerge onto the Overlook Level to gaze at a panorama of Lake Mead, the dam, the Colorado River, and the Black Canyon. Hoover Dam towers an imposing 726 feet (that's 60 stories) above Black Canyon; spanning 1,244 feet, the dam is every bit the engineering marvel it's built up to be. Despite a few Art Deco and Spanish Mission elements, its starkness harmonizes with the desert setting—its honest grandeur puts the pompous palaces of the Strip to shame. Exhibits at the visitors center detail its arduous five-year construction (completed amazingly ahead of schedule), along with Ripley's-like factoids (Lake Mead could cover the state of Pennsylvania in a foot of water, the amount of concrete in the dam could pave an entire cross-continental highway).

Par for the course... The magnificent desert setting, year-round play, and the high percentage of corporate and convention visitors actually make Las Vegas a golfing mecca with dozens of courses. Peak season is from October to May, when top courses schedule tee times up to two months in advance. (If you're fool enough to play at high noon in summer, you'll be pleased to hear that greens fees plunge dramatically.) The **Desert Inn Golf Club** (tel 702/431-4653, 3145 Las Vegas Blvd. S.), the last remaining course that actually sits on the Strip, has hosted the PGA Tour, the Senior PGA Tour, and the LPGA Tour, and is perennially ranked among *Golf Digest*'s top 75 courses. It's a killer, with water in unexpected places, undulating greens, tight fairways, vicious doglegs, sloping greens, and mammoth sand traps. The fabulous pro shop is the highest grossing in the U.S.; the high-tech Pro-link system on the carts digitally notes yardage to pin, time ahead of next quartet, and even calls the clubhouse for lunch reservations. It's pricey (around $225 for non-guest play), but so's a Rolls Royce. The par-72, 7,250-yard **Rio Secco Golf Club** (tel 702/889-2400, 2851 Grand Hills Dr., Henderson) is primarily for guests of the Rio Suites Hotel and Casino; proles can prowl it for $300 and up. Designed by Rees Jones, this is a heartbreaker, with treacherously curvaceous greens; the front six holes snake through a canyon, and the middle six skitter along the plateau, while the back six range along a dry riverbed. Half the tee times at the **Tournament Players Club at the**

Canyons (tel 702/256-2000, 9851 Canyon Run Dr., Summerlin) are controlled by the tony Regent Las Vegas Resort, but non-guest rates (averaging $125) are more than fair. There's a lot of desert to clear before reaching those emerald greens, with arroyos and rocky outcroppings posing as very scenic hazards. The 7,261-yard par-72 **Reflection Bay Golf Club** (tel 702/740-4653, 75 Montelago Blvd.) is the first Jack Nicklaus–designed course in Nevada, primarily for use of guests at the Lake Las Vegas Resort. It features an unusual water hazard for Las Vegas: five holes straddling 1.5 miles of lakefront beach. The aquatic theme is carried through with a four-acre lake on holes one and 10 as well as three major waterfalls, ranging between 25 and 40 feet. The **Angel Park Golf Club** (tel 702/254-4653, 100 South Rampart Blvd.) is the town's most complete facility, with two full courses and a 12-hole par-3 course and 18-hole putting course lit for night play (you can tee off at 6am and play through midnight). Designed by Arnold Palmer, the two 18-hole courses, the 5,438-yard Mountain and 5,751-yard Palm, are both short, placing a premium on shot placement rather than power. Mountain is known for its narrow fairways, tiered greens, and tricky uneven lies, while the Palm incorporates nasty features like natural canyons as bunkers. The Cloud Nine short course has 12 holes modeled after (in)famous holes around the globe (in the Las Vegas spirit of appropriating everything from somewhere else), including the "Double Green" from St. Andrews, the "Postage Stamp" from Royal Troon, and "Island Green" from the Tournament Players Club at Sawgrass. The Cloud Nine fee is just $22 to $35 (compared to $100 and up on the two full courses). The par-72, 7,029-yard **Royal Links Country Club** (tel 888/427-6682, Vegas Valley Rd. at Nellis Blvd.) goes even further with a Perry Dye-designed course simulating the look of famed Scottish, Irish, and British courses (not only Royal Troon's "Postage Stamp" but also St. Andrews' nefarious "Road Hole," where you must clear a section of old wall with blind tee shots). The clubhouse is patterned after a Scottish castle and contains collections of golfing monuments and memorabilia; the single malt selection at the bar is predictably well above par. The oldest course in the city, the **Las Vegas Golf Club** (tel 702/646-3003, 4300 W. Washington Ave.) can be ragged around the edges and brown in spots, but the rates are the lowest around, with a year-round rate (including cart) of $27.75 for tourists. The austerely beautiful, Johnny Miller–designed **Badlands Golf Club** (tel 702/242-4653, 9119 Alta Dr.) has two courses: the original 18 holes, a hellacious drive through natural washes, cantons, and arroyos that favor the straight shooter; and the newer nine-hole Outlaw course, which has fewer desert obstacles to shoot past. Two pluses are a raft of reduced rates ("twilight tees" after 2pm are as low as $39) and golf carts equipped with Skyline, a satellite system that calculates distances and offers tips. Of course, there's also the ultra-exclusive private Shadow Creek Country Club in North Las Vegas, which Mirage Resorts chairman Steve Wynn underwrote to the tune of $40 million so he could play in peace with his buddies (Michael Jordan and former president George Bush are frequent guests). Greens fees are astronomical, so if you have to ask....

Rockin' it... Thousands of climbers from around the globe come to **Red Rock Canyon**, making it one of the top five climbing areas in the United States, with dozens of moderate and tough ascents. The sandstone boulders and 3,000-foot cliffs provide endlessly diverse features, holds, iron nubbins, ledges, and cracks. There are so many side canyons that even on the busiest days, you can claim your own turf. The ultimate macho climb is the 7,068-foot ruddy sandstone peak Mount Wilson. If you want to climb in town, **Gameworks** boasts the world's tallest freestanding rock-climbing structure—75 feet, with more than 900 holds. It attracts lots of exhibitionists who scale the heights in front of passersby on the Strip.

Parking it.... There are more than 60 parks in the greater Las Vegas area, many offering pools, tennis courts, soccer and baseball fields, and paths for biking and in-line skating. Leagues, tournaments, and various cultural events are held throughout the year—call the **Las Vegas Department of Parks and Leisure Activities** (tel 702/229-6297) for activities and schedules. Joggers appreciate **Sunset Park** (2601 E. Sunset Rd.) for the paths snaking through copses of trees and past limpid ponds; it's also a smash with tennis players for its eight courts, all lit for night play—just be prepared to wait (and wait...). Players sometimes hold courts until they drop from heat exhaustion. Fortunately, reservations are accepted, including round-robin play to prevent too much hogging. **Lorenzi Park** (3300 W. Washington Ave.) serves up a completely unpretentious tennis experience; the courts are well-maintained and usually crowd-free. **Floyd Lamb State Park** (9200 Tule Springs Rd.) comes up aces in the natural beauty department, with ponds stocked with trout, peacocks strutting about like showgirls, and an extensive wetlands area filled with mallards, teals, and bullfrogs. For getting away from it all within city limits, you can't do better for picnicking, hiking, and fishing.

The Index

DIVERSIONS | THE INDEX

Adventuredome. America's largest indoor theme park, under an enormous skylit pink dome.... *Tel 702/794-3939. 2880 Las Vegas Blvd. S. Open daily, hours vary (usually 10am–6pm weekdays and off-peak, 10am–midnight otherwise). Admission free; ride tickets $2–5, or buy an unlimited rides pass.* **(see pp. 106, 110)**

AJ Hackett Bungy. Pleasant, efficient instructors do much to alleviate the terror of jumping off a 201-foot tower. And hey, you get a free T-shirt (the video's another $20).... *Tel 702/385-4321. 810 Circus Circus Dr. 11am–9pm daily (till 11pm Fri, Sat). Admission charged.* **(see p. 107)**

All-American Sport Park. This sleek 65-acre complex offers a host of athletic possibilities, both real and simulated.... *Tel 702/798-7777. 121 E. Sunset Rd. 11am–11pm Sun–Thur, 10am–1am Fri, Sat. Fees vary by activity.* **(see pp. 111, 121)**

The Arts Factory. A cutting-edge compound with numerous exhibition spaces, mostly high-quality.... *Tel 702/434-2666* *or 702/383-3133. 101–3 E. Charleston Blvd. Gallery hours vary; most closed Mon.*   **(see p. 120)**

Bellagio Conservatory. A remarkable three-story glass dome botanical garden, where the flowers change seasonally at a cost of $5 million annually (a 90,000-square-foot greenhouse behind the hotel nourishes the various varietals).... *Tel 702/693-7111. Bellagio, 3600 Las Vegas Blvd. S. Open 24 hours daily. Free.*   **(see p. 108)**

Bellagio Gallery of Fine Art. A preeningly self-important Who's Who of Modern Art that undeniably puts Las Vegas (or at least Steve Wynn) on the international art map.... *Tel 702/693-7111. Bellagio, 3600 Las Vegas Blvd. S. 9am–midnight daily. Reservations required. Admission charged.*
(see pp. 107, 119)

Bonnie Springs Ranch/Old Nevada. A combination of cutesy commercialism and delightful Old West ambience in a "ghost town" desert setting.... *Tel 702/875-4191. 1 Gunfighter Lane. 10:30am–6pm daily. Admission charged.*
(see p. 115)

Casino Legends Hall of Fame. Collection traces the development of gambling in Nevada from its 1931 inception to the present.... *Tel 702/739-2222. Tropicana, 3501 Las Vegas Blvd. S. 8am–10pm Sun–Thur, 8am–midnight Fri, Sat. Admission charged.*   **(see p. 118)**

Circus Circus Midway. Dazzling circus acts, decor, and ambience, not to mention free popcorn.... *Tel 702/734-0410. Circus Circus, 2880 S. Las Vegas Blvd S. 11am–midnight daily. Free.*   **(see p. 106)**

Eiffel Tower Experience. A half-sized replica for those who've never experienced the real thing.... *Tel 877/796–2096. Paris, 3655 Las Vegas Blvd. S. 10am–2pm daily (except during high winds). Admission charged.*   **(see pp. 104, 121)**

Elvis-a-Rama Museum. With almost $4 million worth of Presley's personal effects, the largest collection outside Graceland.... *Tel 702/309-7200. 3401 Industrial Rd. 9am–7pm daily. Admission charged; children under 12 free.*
(see pp. 117, 118)

Ethel M's Chocolate Factory. Where Ethel Mars started her cottage industry a century ago. Skip the factory tour for the wonderful cactus gardens. Shuttle buses from M&M's World.... *Tel 702/458-8864. 2 Cactus Dr., Henderson. 8:30am–7pm daily. Free.* **(see p. 109)**

Excalibur Medieval Village. From the animatronic dragon to the fantasy characters, it's cut-rate, but free free free.... *Tel 702/597-7777. Excalibur, 3850 Las Vegas Blvd. S. Stage acts 10am–10pm daily, dragon battle 6pm–1am. Free.* **(see pp. 104, 105, 106)**

Flamingo Hilton Wildlife Habitat. 15-acre Caribbean-themed jungle with all manner of exotic waterfowl.... *Tel 702/733-3111. Flamingo Hilton, 3555 Las Vegas Blvd. S. 24 hours daily. Free.* **(see p. 110)**

Flyaway Indoor Skydiving. A remarkably effective simulation of skydiving.... *Tel 702/731-4768. 200 Convention Center Dr. 10am–7pm daily (till 5pm Sun). Admission charged.* **(see p. 107)**

Fountains at Bellagio. After-dark sight-and-sound show sends geysers of water 240 feet in the air out of Bellagio's eight-acre lake.... *Tel 702/693-7111. Bellagio, 3600 Las Vegas Blvd. S. Every half hour, dusk–midnight. Free.* **(see p. 105)**

Fremont Street Experience. Sound-and-light extravaganzas on the canopy of this five-block-long pedestrian promenade.... *Tel 702/678-5777. 425 Fremont St. Hourly dusk–11pm (till midnight Fri, Sat). Free.* **(see pp. 105, 108, 113)**

Gameworks. This 47,000-square-foot entertainment experience offers hardcore games, a climbing wall, drinks, music, and food.... *Tel 702/432-4263. Showcase Mall, 3785 Las Vegas Blvd. S. 10am–2am daily. Admission free; games vary in price.* **(see pp. 115, 125)**

Imperial Palace Auto Collection. An astonishing collection of motorized vehicles.... *Tel 702/731-3311. Imperial Palace, 3535 Las Vegas Blvd. S. 9:30am–11:30pm daily. Admission charged.* **(see p. 118)**

Lake Mead/Hoover Dam. The big dam and the big lake it created.... *Tel 702/293-8367. 30 miles SE of Las Vegas on US*

Highway 93. From Las Vegas go southeast on I-515, which into US-93. 8am–5:45pm daily. Admission charged.
(see p. 122)

Las Vegas Museum of Natural History. Surprisingly fun stop, with several environments, ranging from old-fashioned dioramas to state-of-the-art interactive displays.... *Tel 702/384-3466. 900 Las Vegas Blvd. N. 9am–4pm daily. Admission charged.* **(see pp. 110, 115**

Liberace Museum. High-camp shrine to Mr. Showmanship.... *Tel 702/798-5595. Liberace Plaza, 1775 E. Tropicana Ave. 10am–5pm Mon-Sat, 1–5pm Sun. Admission charged.*
(see pp. 116, 118)

Lied Children's Museum. Wow! Cool! Geared to the emotional, intellectual, and physical perspective of a child, with more than 100 hands-on displays in its 22,000 square feet.... *Tel 702/382-3445. 833 Las Vegas Blvd. N. 10am–5pm Tue–Sat, noon–5pm Sun, closed Mon. Admission charged.* **(see p. 114)**

Lost City of Atlantis. One of the best animatronic shows, which isn't saying much. Neptune gets pissy with his offspring and sinks Atlantis in retribution.... *Tel 702/893-4800. The Forum Shops at Caesars, 3500 Las Vegas Blvd. S. 10am–11pm Sun–Thur (till midnight Fri, Sat). Alternates on hour and half hour with Caesars Animatronic show. Free.*
(see p. 105)

Luxor's King Tut's Tomb and Museum. Exact reproductions of items found in King Tutankhamun's tomb by the 1922 Howard Carter expedition.... *Tel 702/262-4555. Luxor, 3900 Las Vegas Blvd. S. 9am–11pm daily (till 11:30pm Fri, Sat). Admission charged.* **(see pp. 104, 119)**

M&M's World. Four stories devoted to videos, 3-D movies, commercials, bad M&M murals, tastings, and sassy animatronics.... *Tel 702/736-7611. Showcase Mall, 3785 Las Vegas Blvd. S. 10am–midnight daily (till 1am Fri, Sat). Free.*
(see pp. 106, 118)

Madame Tussaud's Celebrity Encounter. Not just a wax museum, but a multi-media interactive extravaganza done with Vegas pizzazz.... *Tel 702/367-1847. The Venetian,*

3355 Las Vegas Blvd. S. 10am–10pm daily. Admission charged. **(see pp. 114, 117)**

Magic and Movie Hall of Fame and Museum. Lovingly intricate displays of memorabilia, interactive displays, recreations of famous acts, even live magic/comedy performances.... *Tel 702/737-1343, 702/697-2711. O'Shea's, 3555 Las Vegas Blvd. S. 10am–6pm Tue–Sat. Admission charged.*
(see pp. 114, 117)

Manhattan Express. Prepare to lose your spare change on this "twist and shout" coaster through the New York New York skyline. Lines are long, especially on weekends, for the five-minute ride.... *Tel 702/740-6969. New York New York, 3790 Las Vegas Blvd. S. 10:30am–10:30pm daily (till midnight Fri, Sat). Admission charged.* **(see pp. 104, 107)**

MGM Grand Adventures Theme Park. 33 acres of ordinary (with one exception—the SkyScreamer) rides, themed streets, entertainment, restaurants, and shops.... *Tel 702/891-1111 or 702/891-7979. MGM Grand, 3799 Las Vegas Blvd. S. 11am–7pm daily June–Labor Day, Fri–Sun only mid-Apr–early June. Admission charged, SkyScreamer tickets extra.* **(see pp. 104, 107, 108, 110, 112)**

MGM Grand Lion Habitat. Multilevel glass enclosure and "see-through" walkway allows you to view the majestic cats.... *Tel 702/891-1111. MGM Grand, 3799 Las Vegas Blvd. S. 11am–11pm daily. Free.* **(see pp. 109, 115)**

Mirage Volcano. Three-story volcano, flames, fake lava, gaping crowds.... *Tel 702/791-7111. Mirage, 3400 Las Vegas Blvd. S. Every 15 minutes dusk–midnight (cancelled during windy periods). Free.* **(see pp. 105, 108)**

Mount Charleston. Skiing, hiking, horseback riding and golf.... *Tel 702/872-5462. State Highway 156, 36 miles north of Las Vegas. Free.* **(see p. 121)**

Neon Museum. An admirable attempt to resurrect old signs from the neon boneyard.... *Tel 702/299-5366. Fremont St. between 3rd and Main streets. 24 hours daily. Free.*
(see p. 113)

Race for Atlantis. A giant-screen IMAX 3-D motion-simulator

thrill ride, projecting everything from sea dragons to spears on an 82-foot-diameter dome.... *Tel 702/733-9000. Forum Shops at Caesar's, 3500 Las Vegas Blvd. S. 10am–11pm daily (till midnight Fri, Sat). Admission charged.*
(see pp. 108, 116)

Red Rock Canyon National Conservation Area. Just 20 miles from town, a dazzling repository of neon-colored rock formations, rich wildlife, and recreational activities.... *Route 159 (head west from the Strip on W. Charleston Blvd.). Visitors center open 8am–4:30pm daily; loop accessible 7am–dusk. Admission $5 per car.* **(see p. 121)**

Sahara West Library and Fine Arts Museum. Eclectic exhibits by locally, nationally, and internationally renowned artists. Note that several libraries in the system have occasional exhibits; scan local papers for info.... *Tel 702/360-8000. 9600 W. Sahara Ave. 10am–5pm Tue–Sat, 1–5pm Sun. Admission charged.* **(see p. 120)**

Secret Garden and Dolphin Habitat. All about glorious animals and the efforts of Siegfried & Roy (not to mention Steve Wynn) to conserve the environment.... *Tel 702/791-7111. Mirage, 3400 Las Vegas Blvd. S. 11am–5:30pm daily, Secret Garden closed Wed. $10 ($5 Wed Dolphin Habitat only). Children under 10 free.* **(see pp. 109, 115)**

Speedworld. Testosterone test-driving for guys and gals alike in a heavily themed environment.... *Tel 702/737-2111. Sahara, 2535 Las Vegas Blvd. S. 10am–10:30pm daily (till midnight Fri–Sun). Admission charged.* **(see pp. 116, 120)**

Star Trek: The Experience. A genuine effort at recreating a futuristic environment and ambience, plus one of the town's best virtual reality rides.... *Tel 888/GOBOLDLY. Las Vegas Hilton, 3000 Paradise Rd. 11am–11pm daily. Admission charged.* **(see pp. 111, 113, 116, 118)**

Stratosphere Tower and Thrill Rides. An observation tower, the world's highest roller coaster, and a truly scarifying G-force ride. Rides often closed due to high winds or inclement weather.... *Tel 702/380-7777. Stratosphere, 2000 Las Vegas Blvd. S. 10am–1am daily (till 2am Fri, Sat). Admission charged to Tower; rides additional.* **(see pp. 106, 121)**

THE INDEX | DIVERSIONS

Sundance Helicopters. The longest view tours of Vegas. Like all the heli-companies, they also offer weddings and Grand Canyon tours ($299).... *Tel 702/736-0606. Tours take off two blocks east of Mandalay Bay.* **(see p. 121)**

Sunset Stampede. This dancing water and laser journey through the Western frontier acknowledges the town's roots.... *Tel 702/456-7777. Sam's Town, 5111 Boulder Hwy. 2, 6, 8, and 10pm daily. Free.* **(see p. 105)**

Tiger Habitat. Royal Himalayan White Tigers playing, swimming, and usually sleeping right inside the Mirage lobby.... *Tel 702/791-7111. Mirage, 3400 Las Vegas Blvd. S. 24 hours daily. Free.* **(see p. 109)**

Titanic Exhibition. Titanic videos and memorabilia, sans DiCaprio... *Tel 702/252-0315. Rio Suites, 3700 W. Flamingo Rd. 10am–10pm daily. Admission charged* . **(see pp. 118, 119)**

Treasure Island Pirate Battle. Naval battles are staged in this block-long replica of Buccaneer Bay.... *Tel 702/894-7111. 3300 Las Vegas Blvd. S. Every 90 minutes 4pm–11:30pm daily. Free.* **(see pp. 105, 106)**

Valley of Fire State Park. Nevada's first state park is another exceptionally gorgeous expanse of wind-carved red sandstone.... *Tel 702/397-2088. I-15, 60 miles northeast of town. 8:30am–4:30pm daily.* **(see p. 122)**

Venetian Gondolas. 236,000 gallons of water simulate the Grand Canal, which sits above the casino. The fleet of 40 gondolas, like everything else in Vegas, is certified authentic.... *Tel 702/733-5000. Venetian, 3355 Las Vegas Blvd. S. 10:30am–10:30pm daily. Admission charged.* **(see pp. 104, 108)**

Wet 'n' Wild. Water park with thrill rides, beach, river, and pool for more serene pastimes.... *Tel 702/737-3819. 2601 Las Vegas Blvd. S. 10am–6pm daily late Apr–early Oct. Admission charged.* **(see pp. 107, 110)**

Young Electric Sign Company. Top neon sign manufacturers— peer into their yard through the gate.... *Tel 702/876-8080, 5119 Cameron St. off Industrial Blvd. Free.* **(see pp. 114)**

Las Vegas Diversions

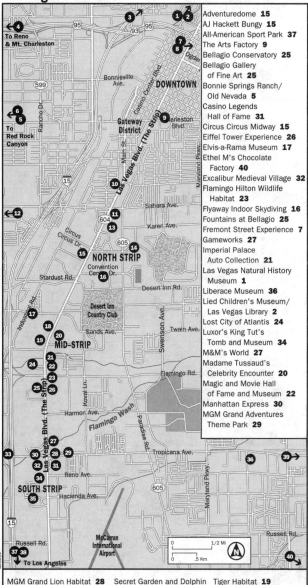

Adventuredome **15**
AJ Hackett Bungy **15**
All-American Sport Park **37**
The Arts Factory **9**
Bellagio Conservatory **25**
Bellagio Gallery
of Fine Art **25**
Bonnie Springs Ranch/
Old Nevada **5**
Casino Legends
Hall of Fame **31**
Circus Circus Midway **15**
Eiffel Tower Experience **26**
Elvis-a-Rama Museum **17**
Ethel M's Chocolate
Factory **40**
Excalibur Medieval Village **32**
Flamingo Hilton Wildlife
Habitat **23**
Flyaway Indoor Skydiving **16**
Fountains at Bellagio **25**
Fremont Street Experience **7**
Gameworks **27**
Imperial Palace
Auto Collection **21**
Las Vegas Natural History
Museum **1**
Liberace Museum **36**
Lied Children's Museum/
Las Vegas Library **2**
Lost City of Atlantis **24**
Luxor's King Tut's
Tomb and Museum **34**
M&M's World **27**
Madame Tussaud's
Celebrity Encounter **20**
Magic and Movie Hall
of Fame and Museum **22**
Manhattan Express **30**
MGM Grand Adventures
Theme Park **29**

MGM Grand Lion Habitat **28**
Mirage Volcano **19**
Mount Charleston **4**
Neon Museum **8**
Race for Atlantis **24**
Red Rock Canyon National
Conservation Area **6**
Sahara West Library and
Fine Arts Museum **12**

Secret Garden and Dolphin
Habitat **19**
Speedworld **11**
Star Trek:
The Experience **14**
Stratosphere Tower
and Thrill Rides **10**
Sundance Helicopters **35**
Sunset Stampede **39**

Tiger Habitat **19**
Titanic Exhibition **33**
Treasure Island
Pirate Battle **18**
Valley of Fire State Park **3**
Venetian Gondolas **20**
Wet 'n' Wild **13**
Young Electric
Sign Company **38**

nos4

Forget the PR blather about Las Vegas becoming an upscale destination—sure, they're importing world-class restaurants, shows, and shops, installing artworks, and fabricating increasingly tasteful surroundings, but local shorthand still refers to all those "resorts" and "hotel/casinos" as casinos, plain and simple. The extracurricular activities may generate a higher percentage of revenue than before, but the focus remains gambling—or gaming, as government officials and corporate execs prefer to call it.

Las Vegas itself is one big casino. The incessant warbling of slot machines greets you upon deplaning at McCarran International Airport. Video poker machines earn 7-Elevens more income than cigarette, coffee, and Slurpee sales combined. You can monkey around with a full electronic deck while grease monkeys pump your gas. In 1998, some 141,485 slot machines were operational in Clark County. Even hair salons are a beehive of gambling activity.

But the epicenter of this bizarre universe is the casino floor. Bugsy Siegel's fabled subterranean tunnels and escape routes at his original Flamingo are nothing compared to the mazes of **Caesars Palace**, the **MGM Grand**, **Circus Circus**, **Riviera** (arguably the most maddening layout), and the other major casinos, and there's a method to the madness: The more disoriented you become, the higher the odds you'll be sucked into the adrenaline high. Oxygen is reputedly pumped into the rooms to reinvigorate gamblers. There are no clocks or windows, lighting remains the same 24 hours a day, and trompe l'oeil skies replete with fleecy clouds are painted on the ceilings to create the illusion of endless daylight, to counteract claustrophobia and cabin fever. Such distractions as cocktail waitress cleavage and rounds of free drinks help keep players woozily rooted in place. All perfectly innocent, of course (and I've got a piece of the Brooklyn Bridge replica at New York-New York to sell you).

Not all casinos are alike. They run the gamut from redneck to blueblood. There are the "high roller" casinos, like **Bellagio**, **Venetian**, **Ceasars Palace**, **Desert Inn**, and **Mirage**. Millions are won and lost in private salons; décor is suitably grand. Then there are the mid-range casinos that offer the same facilities, as well as high-stakes rooms. Grimier and grittier Downtown is the province, mostly, of low rollers and old-time gamblers in ancient, smoky, claustrophobic casinos. One term you'll hear often is locals' hotels/locals' casinos (the "Station" properties—**Boulder Station**, **Texas Station**, **Palace Station**, and **Sunset Station**; **Orleans**; **Santa Fe**; **Fiesta**; **Gold Coast**; **Arizona Charlie's**; and **Sam's Town**). These are generally off-Strip properties patronized by savvy locals for their reasonable restaurants, fun bars, and family-oriented attractions like movie theaters and bowling alleys, as well as friendly casino play. They, too, offer all the action. All major venues feature the usual complement of games: blackjack, baccarat, craps, roulette, keno, and several variations on poker. Most also have some version of the Racing and Sports Book, an area filled with video monitors broadcasting every concievable sporting event; you place your bets at the windows or from your seats. Some even offer Bingo games more competitive than those church functions.

Slots and poker are omnipresent. Believe it or not, slots used to be looked down on as being "for the wives," as they'd say in the '60s; typical pit bosses contemptuously referred to players as "worms." Now every slot area has an impressive SUV or Porsche on display for the winning. **Caesars Palace** now boasts $1,500 slots with $1 million-plus payouts and gold-plated tokens, while the **Las Vegas Hilton** Champagne Slots section is served be a tuxedoed staff.

Look for "progressive slots" (where several machines in the house or connected casinos build up the stakes for higher payouts—like a lottery on speed). And if you play slots or video poker regularly, join the casino's Slot Club for special deals, ranging from cash bonuses to free or discounted meals or tickets.

If you gamble wisely and within your limits, the casinos provide unparalleled people-watching: poker-playing sharks, with the cold-eyed, mind-numbing intensity of serial killers; big-assed, big-haired 25-cent slotniks, robotically feeding the maws of machines; and pinching, leering conventioneers. It's a glorious living theater—at times of the absurd.

The rules, and the odds

The Las Vegas Convention and Visitors Authority and similar organizations put out booklets describing each game and explaining the rules, as well as etiquette (e.g., when to tip dealers, when not to touch your cards). Many casinos offer free helpful "gambling lessons" daily—they do have a vested (or invested) interest, after all. The flip side of this is that pamphlets on addiction are omnipresent, and dealers aren't allowed to seat obviously addicted players (provided they can identify them), and reports suggest that the casinos engender a blase sense of security by relentlessly emphasizing the positive, avoiding words with negative connotations ("lose"), and couching the inherent risks in bland or euphemistic terms.

The best advice is simply to study the rules, watch the good players, don't get swept up in the endorphic excitement,

CASINOS | INTRODUCTION

and gamble sensibly within your means. As Kenny Rogers sang, "You gotta know when to fold 'em." When you're tired, take an invigorating walk...or quit. If you lose your self-imposed $200 limit, consider it money well spent on entertainment. And remember: There's no such thing as a sure system (or lord help us, ESP hunches and lucky silver dollars). Some people swear that there are favorable slot positions (usually by the entrance station, on the theory that they serve as a lure), aka "loose slots." Don't bet on it. Gambling, like life, defies prediction. Only a very few "professionals" earn a living by gaming. Believe me, the odds are stacked in the casino's favor—how else do you think Steve Wynn amassed a $300 million art collection (most of it displayed at **Bellagio**—for $12 a viewing, to boot)?

Casino-favoring odds are built into the rules of each gambling activity (tellingly, they're termed "negative-expectation propositions"). You can beat the slots, the roulette wheel, or the video poker machine short-term, but continue playing, and the house advantage will catch up with—and surpass—you. It's simple mathematics and statistics. Games requiring little skill usually offer the worst odds. Keno leads the pack, followed by roulette, wheel of fortune, slots and video poker, and certain craps situations (die-hard gamblers know that "hard way" bets feature the crappiest odds of all). If you play perfectly (and not even computers do that), the best odds are when the house advantage is 0.5% (blackjack) to 1.4% (craps). Compare that to 5.26% for double-zero roulette and 20% for keno.

Sure, some casinos truthfully advertise higher payouts on

Gambling terms

The casinos have a language of their own, as well. "Virgins" are first-time players, while "voyeurs" watch and wander. A "break in" isn't an attempt to rob the house: It's a novice dealer. "Steamers" are players who quickly increase their bets while winning, "chasers" those who raise their bets when losing (which could lead to their becoming "degenerates"— people who gamble to their detriment). "The grind" refers to low-end betting. "Niece" is self-evident: the young woman accompanying an older man. A tip is a "toke" (probably short for token). A "George" is a generous tipper (clearly old slang, since it refers to the president on the one dollar bill). A "stiff" (aka "DOA") is someone who doesn't tip. A "whale" is a player with a million-dollar-plus credit line, as are Adnan Khashoggi, Bruce Willis, and Dennis Rodman. There are perhaps 250 whales worldwide, most of them obscure Saudi princes, Japanese CFOs, South American playboys, and former dictators' right-hand men.

slots. Yes, there is a statistical advantage in the increasingly rare single- and double-deck blackjack game (that is, if you're Dustin Hoffman in *Rain Man*, or experienced enough to count cards surreptitiously). True, roulette odds decrease significantly from 1:38 to 1:37 when the double zero is eliminated (though the payout—this is where the house edge comes in— is $2 less, or 35:1 and 34:1, respectively). On video poker machines, payoffs vary from machine to machine; look for those offering 6:1 for flushes and 9:1 for a full house (the norm is 5:1 and 8:1). Look also for "progressive slots," payoffs connected to various casinos to maximize payouts.

When all else fails, don't cheat. You'd be surprised how many idiots think they can get away with covertly substituting cards or pilfering a few chips from their inattentive neighbor. Dealers, pit bosses, and floor managers are ever vigilant. And see those elegant opaque black mirrors in the ceiling? That's the "eye in the sky," a security camera broadcasting and videotaping all activity upstairs in the casino manager's lair. Big Brother is indeed watching; some paranoid locals insist that cameras are placed everywhere on the Strip. Even if you're caught innocuously adding a few chips to your bet pile, expect judges to be stonily unsympathetic (after all, casinos make generous contributions to their campaign coffers). And there's no word on when they'll install video poker in the Nevada penal system.

Getting comped

Almost any casino bar with video poker serves a free beer or well drink if you give the bartender a ten and ask for a roll of quarters. (You can then wander off, ostensibly to play machines elsewhere in the casino, cashing in the quarters later. If they catch on, go to a different casino.) Or sit down in a Race and Sports Book, peruse a Racing Form, and look serious; waitresses will serve you, rarely checking whether you bet or not. This sometimes works in the keno area; a few casinos comp drinks while you place even $1 keno bets.

To qualify for a free dinner, let alone a room, you generally have to gamble at a $5 table for four to eight hours. Even experienced gamblers are likely to lose several hundred dollars in that amount of time (hey, at least that $6.95 buffet is all-you-can-eat). The minimum and length of time vary according to the casino; the minimum might be $25 or more at the **Mirage**, **Caesars Palace**, and **Bellagio**.

The locals' hotels usually offer better deals. If you planned on gambling large amounts anyway, say chips of $25 or higher, ask the dealer for a rating card. Whenever you sit at a table, you hand over the card, the dealer enters how much you bet, and you accrue points toward fabulous "free" prizes. The magic words when the suits approach are "can I do anything for you?" Bingo! You're comped. If you feel you've wagered a small fortune and casino staffers don't approach you, ask what level of play merits freebies—or find a friendlier casino (with less snob appeal). You needn't look the part of the high roller; long gone are the days (or rather nights) when dinner jacket and evening gown were practically de rigueur. You could probably wear a diaper and slippers as long as you can back up your credit card slips.

Nonetheless, you can probably forget about those legendary V.I.P. suites. To rate those you must be at least a "premium gambler," guaranteed to wager $100,000 to $500,000. They comprise fewer than 5% of gamblers, yet they account for over 40% of the total casino revenue.

The Lowdown

Friendliest pit staff... Local casinos survive on repeat business and high volume; staffers often form relationships with customers, rather like the folks at "Cheers," where everybody knows your name. These include **Palace Station**, **Sunset Station**, **Texas Station**, **The Fiesta**, **Orleans**, the **Gold Coast**, and best of all, **Sam's Town**. Dealers are friendly, but the crowds are very savvy: a wonderful opportunity to watch and learn how to improve your odds. Patrons at Mardi-Gras themed **Harrah's** are practically encouraged to behave like Bourbon Street revelers; the eager-to-please staffers manage to be both refreshing and terrifying. Excellent gaming lesons, megabucks progressive slots, and numerous promotions further enhance festivities. At **Hard Rock**, the ultra-cool dealers (the men sporting goatees and single earrings) have been known to high-five big winners, while the comparatively nondescript **Bally's**—the most relaxed, least pumped-up mega-casino—has unruffled dealers who suit the almost calm atmosphere. They're particularly friendly at the crap tables, where they offer pointers during slow periods. **New York-New York** is a Disney-fied version of the Big Apple, which means that you won't be mugged in the Central Park-themed casino (you'll have to lose your money the old-fashioned way, at the tables), and the dealers are as polite and cheerful as, well, Disney tour guides.

Cheekiest waitress costumes... Cocktail server costumes can make or break Las Vegas casinos and have accordingly been the sticking point in some labor negotiations. Cocktail waitresses at the **Rio** lost the battle against skimpy costumes yet won the wage war: tit for tat. (Rumor has it that the management liberally grants time off for anyone wishing to undergo, um, medical alterations. Some estimate that 25% of cocktail waitresses in town have undergone "body sculpting.") The thong-cut outfits they almost wear, not to mention seemingly unsupported decolletage, are marvels of engineering skill; no wonder Rio often hosts Larry Flynt in his gold wheelchair. **Orleans** adopted similar diamond/harlequin-patterned outfits that hike up into what can appear to be very uncomfortable positions. Red satin get-ups with provocatively plunging fringe neck- and hemlines earn **Texas Station** the "Debbie Does Dallas" prize. Me-Tarzan-you-Jane awards go to **The Reserve**, where the zebra print with black fringe outfits suggest a bordello at the foot of Mt. Kilimanjaro. **Imperial Palace** waitresses are hardly demure geishas, with silk skirts slit practically to the hip that scream Suzie Wong. **Monte Carlo**'s mademoiselles have a touch of class sprinkled with Gallic naughtiness (significant cleavage); their outfits are fetishistic French-maid black lace with jade and scarlet brocade. The **Hard Rock**'s cocktail waitresses sport leopardskin hotpants, black leggings, and leotards—they look like they could strangle a mike and bring a crowd to its feet. **Caesars Palace** waitresses are perfectly coiffed, manicured, and made up, and barely clad in white, gold-embossed togas cinched with Gucci-esque gold belts: Amazonian delights to behold (but not to hold.) And Caesar's is almost equal opportunity in this rather chauvinistic town: Gals have a chance to leer at the armor-bedecked "centurions" and "gladiators" standing guard.

For nickel-and-dimers... Downtown, **Lady Luck** teems with seniors fresh off the tour buses and honeymooners in RVs who feel lucky just being in Las Vegas. After a recent renovation, it's a brightened-up dump; motherly waitresses push drinks carts around, pouring liberally, and lots of freebies and constant promotions draw a knowledgeable local crowd as well as visitors. The **Gold Spike** boasts most of the town's remaining penny slots. Seniors fight over the coveted seats, and it's so smoky you wish those unsubstantiated claims that casinos pump oxygen through the room were true. **Slots A Fun** is a wild and wonderful cross between a sordid downtown bus depot and a honky-tonk arcade. Maybe it's the 99-cent half-pound hot dogs and 75-cent Heinekens. Or the wall of fame displaying Polaroids of big winners. Or the smell of stale beer and sweat. Don't discount it automatically: it's phenomenal for people-watching. The somewhat rundown **Palace Station** delivers 5-cent slots and 50-cent roulette dollar blackjack tables aplenty. Among the heavy hitters, **Excalibur** has supplanted **Circus Circus** as the big cheese in town. This is where the Simpsons might go on vacation (it's certainly animated enough), with plenty of ye olde slot-o-philes with jangling fanny packs.

Casinos Royale... **Caesars Palace** defines swank. For all its occasional excess, it walks the high wire between kitsch and true luxe. Mirrors and marble columns galore; a restrained color scheme of ivory, gold, black, and white; and staffers clad in togas and tuxes define the Las Vegas experience. The **Las Vegas Hilton** is glittery and old-fashioned, with stained glass and seemingly more Austrian crystal chandeliers than Vienna's Schoenbrunn Palace. The **Desert Inn** is a welcome relief from its mega-casino strip neighbors—small enough to make you feel like a member of an exclusive club, it projects quiet elegance with faux palms, gold leafing, plush carpets, marble accents, classic frosted glass chandeliers, tapered columns, and tuxedoed dealers. Of the aggressively "themed" casinos, the **Mirage** is the most successful— straw ceilings, creepers, tropical carpets, a carved jungle overhead, and separate thatched areas provide just the right exotic note. Downtown, **Golden Nugget** is arguably the only casino that merits being called classy, with understated ambience and marble and brass decor reminiscent of a select European resort.

Old-style flavor... On the Strip, the **Desert Inn** epitomizes the retro-glam Vegas of the Rat Pack, the Vegas of lipstick-smeared cigarettes, unthemed martinis, tuxedoes, and gamblers who suavely lose a cool million, then win it back without batting an eye. **Barbary Coast** epitomizes the bordello theme so prevalent in older Las Vegas casinos: a stunning $2-million stained-glass skylight, acres of red velour, and satellite-sized crystal globe chandeliers. The dealers even wear red garters on their arms. Ironically, the place has a rep as a grind joint (low-end betting), with plenty of retirees fresh off the tour buses and Winnebagos hoping to augment their Social Security checks. The classic **Caesars Palace** strikes the ideal balance between glitz and ritz that one expects of Sin City. Its Palace Casino is nominally higher end, the Forum lower. The high-energy sports book, traditionally where all the heavy betters and bookies hang out, particularly epitomizes old-time gambling adrenaline. **Stardust** is loud in more ways than one. It's always packed, thanks to its plentiful low-end gaming; the decor is retro futuristic, like a wacky episode of "The Jetsons," and the colors are certainly cartoonish. But it combines Las Vegas grime with long-gone glitz: Gum-cracking cigarette girls patrol the premises like in a '40s film noir, while liquid crystal balls and mirrored columns scream the Studio 54 of the '70s. Downtown, **Binion's Horseshoe** is for serious gamblers, even at the low-end tables, where everyone looks gruff and dyspeptic. Talking (especially at the poker and blackjack tables) is kept to a minimum. The legendary home of the World Series of Poker, it has a classic rough-and-tumble pre-glitz feel where you expect to run into Runyonesque characters. And dig the $1 million displayed in a cabinet.

Over the top (even by Vegas standards)... Circus **Circus** has tried to tone down its glaring colors and busy decor, but it's still surreal. Since the Big Top area, with arcades and free circus acts, sits above the main casino, trapeze artists actually somersault mere feet above a few tables. Like a trailer-park version of Camelot, **Excalibur** dresses uncomfortable-looking staffers as troubadours, wizards, jesters, and fair damsels. It's so raucous, smoky, and crowded that you may feel like you're trapped in a dungeon. **Luxor** makes many admirable stabs at authenticity—the entrance *is* impressive, a temple gateway bookended by imposing statues of Ramses, and the beautiful chips are classy enough to bury in your own mausoleum. But the clutter inside—Egyptian statues, hieroglyphics etched like graffiti on the walls, replicas of artifacts from the Temple of Karnak—seems incongruous amid the slots and gaming tables. **Paris** inlcudes winding cobblestone pathways, French wrought iron street lamps, a replica of the Pont Alexandre III bridge, and a miniature Siene. The piece de resistance: Three of the Eiffel Tower's legs extend into the casino through the 40-foot ceiling. **Treasure Island** seems a blatant rip-off of Disney's "Pirates of the Caribbean," with its marine-themed bas relief ceilings and black carpets littered with rope chains and fake doubloons. The **Las Vegas Hilton** has a second casino that is "concessioned" out as a themed lead-in to the Star Trek Experience attraction. This Space Quest casino, bathed in a blueish light, looks like it was created from spare parts of the Enterprise. A giant Lucky the Leprechaun greets guests downtown at **Fitzgerald's**, looking more like Mr. Magoo after laser optical surgery. Inside there's a genuine piece of the Blarney Stone (which, naturally, looks fake) to rub for good luck. Alas, it's not as deliriously kitschy as before, but the ceiling is stamped with gold, and shamrocks are stenciled all over the walls.

Don't live up to their billing... On the Strip, the **Monte Carlo**, despite its superficial elegance, is soulless and second-rate. It strives for a continental air, with stained-glass and mirrored ceilings, carved goudrons, crystal chandeliers, even white-and-brass pay phones. But disco blares, and there are $1 minimums during the week—no wonder the big spenders have deserted it. **Bellagio** is supposed to be the last word in posh, but its casino is actually rather crass and brassy, trimmed with orange and yellow or garishly striped awnings with equally glaring fringe. The low-end **Imperial Palace** is grungier than it should be, given its prime Strip location, with only token attempts at Asian splendor, including Chinese dragons roaring from the ceiling and tinkling wind-chime chandeliers. The **Flamingo Hilton** should be a piece of history, as Bugsy Siegel's legendary gamble to glamorize Las Vegas. Unfortunately, so many expansions and renovations have eliminated the original touches, leaving only a migraine-inducing decor that includes blinding neon and mirrors everywhere. There are several discrete gaming areas in the sprawling **MGM Grand**, featuring rainbow-patterned carpets and gaudy metallic stars—the effect is Cecil B. DeMille on Prozac.

The **Tropicana** dazzles with an amazing stained-glass-and-mirror canopy ceiling (including cavorting topless angels as showgirls) and art nouveau lighting fixtures, but they're totally incongruous amid the otherwise Polynesian jungle of bogus palms, thatching, and loud umbrella-drink colors. the **Rio,** just off the Strip and frequently expanded, hasn't kept up its Carnival theme beyond some token masks; if any casino had a right to go full-blown gaudy and bawdy, this is the one. Downtown, the **Showboat** boasts a weird Mardi-Gras-meets-the-Mississippi theme, with Mardi Gras masks, confetti-patterned carpets, and stained-glass panels of meadows and lakes that are hideously garish when lit, all clashing with the gingerbread trim, rose-shaped glass chandeliers, and almost elegant riverboat murals.

Worth leaving the Strip to see... The **Hard Rock** wittily incorporates its signature musical motifs (guitar-handled slots, piano-shaped roulette tables, saxophone chandeliers); its memorabilia change more often than the Billboard Top 100, but you might see a set of the Doors' drums, an Elvis jumpsuit, a Madonna bustier, or a jewel-encrusted Elton piano. **The Reserve**, with its safari theme, is well over the top, yet carries it off with sheer brio. The concrete columns resemble tree branches; there's a veldt replete with antelopes, elephants, and cheetahs; ivory tusks festoon change booths and so on. But the action here is swinging, and the place never feels like a zoo. The best of the outlying "Station" casinos, **Sunset Station** features two distinct interior designs, one in Mediterranean Revival (faux ceramic arcades and tiled ceilings, a "village" with barrel tile roofs, balconies, and flowered shutters), the other favoring gem colors like amethyst and turquoise, with sinuous grotto-like walls studded with colored glass mosaic work.

High-roller havens... Casinos provide semi-private rooms in little nooks for high-stakes gamblers (technically, they can't deny access to other players, but they find a way to make them uncomfortable). Many high-roller rooms are separated from main action only by a velvet rope or marble railing, allowing you to steal covert peeks. **Caesars Palace** has several rooms with $1,000 minimum tables—tricked out in marble, velvet, and silk, they're opulent without seeming decadent (although the fawning staff seem like they'd peel their customers' grapes upon command). The intimate baccarat rooms are almost European in feel; hands of $100,000 and more are not uncommon. These high-roller areas are hardly bacchanalian in action, but don't be deceived—if someone coughed at the wrong moment during tense action, the gladiators might feed him to the lions. Speaking of roaring lions, the action in the semi-private rooms at the **MGM Grand** draws fat cats. The poker rooms at the **Mirage** are fabled for their killer jackpots and attitude. Other *salons privés* here are awash in Empire and Regency splendor. The snob appeal of **Bellagio** draws moneyed young turks to its private areas; even in the carefully segregated slots area, the ka-chings can't quite drown out the beepers and ringing cell phones. The Race and Sports Book features individual monitors and buttery reclining chairs that belong in a decorative arts museum. The poker salon is particularly impressive, from the luxuriantly padded swivel chairs to the murals depicting masked commedia dell'arte characters. The plush room at the smaller **Desert Inn** is often hushed, but the players there are major indeed. There are two private salons for baccarat alone with etched glass doors, 24K gold ceilings, hand-woven carpets, crystal chandeliers, and private dining rooms. At the equally intimate, but hardly hushed **Hard Rock**, Gen Xers and younger boomers can flaunt their money in congenial surroundings—hey, any place that welcomes Dennis Rodman on a regular basis automatically becomes a big gambling spot (or a big gamble—your call). Traditionally the favored spot for high-profile conventions, the **Las Vegas Hilton** offers baccarat and high-roller sections cushioned with silk-swathed walls and velvet upholstery. The enormous sports book is ultra-luxe and high-tech (the video wall alone is second only in size to NASA's). Blackjack aficionados know it offers the most benificient rules in town. You'll see several bimbos as good-luck charms (this is, after all, where Robert Redford asked Demi Moore to blow on his dice in *Indecent Proposal*). Deep-pocketed customers seem to like the **Venetian**, with its lavish recreations of Venice's landmarks and high guest-room prices helping to keep the riff-raff out. The **Rio** lures many high rollers off the Strip thanks to its superb restaurants and the popular disco, Club Rio. Most of the chips are $25 and up, while much of the room seems like a paean to Lad Culture, with players who read *Maxim* while placing stock orders on the john and avidly await the new SI swimwear issue.

Best bets... Several casinos are justly beloved for their liberal rules or giveaway policies. **Fiesta** advertises itself as the "Royal Flush Capital," with the most players earning that 800-1 payoff. **Excalibur** offers Circus Bucks, a progressive slot machine whose jackpot also starts at $500,000 (all for a $3 pull), and the Sword in the Stone, a free pull for $10,000. Accumulated points at the slot club at **Stardust** earn you cold hard cash (as well as comp meals and shows) instead of game-show prizes, even on the nickel slots. **Tropicana**'s user-friendly Island Winners Club racks up points toward free rooms, meals, and shows very quickly. **Harrah's** offers the innovative "Play an Hour on Us" for first-time Gold Slot Club members: After one hour of tracked play on quarter or higher machines, you're compensated for losses up to $100. Allegedly a higher percentage of slots at **Fitzgerald's** offer cars as prizes than anywhere else in town. Even if that's blarney, $1 craps and 50-cent roulette tables are a phenomenal learning experience, from 4pm to midnight there's good penetration into the blackjack deck before going to a new one, and the casino fun books offer 2-for-1 gaming coupons. **Slots A Fun** is one of the last domains of the penny slot, as is **Gold Spike**. **The Flamingo Hilton** gets into the act with the occasional chance to win a Lincoln Town Car or Caddy convertible playing the 50-cent slots. **Monte Carlo** takes the prize with opportunities to win a BMW on the 25 cent slots. It also offers only single-zero roulette tables. At **Orleans**, poker tables offer occasional "bad-beat" jackpots awarded to losers with the biggest hands, while slot promotions include condo giveaways and $25,000 raffles. Locals are keen on the cozy keno lounge at **Gold Coast**, whose gimmick is "Freeno": register your six favorite numbers and hang around the casino in hopes of winning $100 to $500. A mere $2 for the Gold Coast's popular progressive game can net several hundred thousands of dollars when the meter ticks high enough. Peachy keno indeed. It gains additional lustre for its newly minted $250,000 bingo games, Progressive Bonanza Bingo, and double- and triple-pay sessions. The odds of hitting your numbers remain constant no matter where you play keno, but **The Reserve** tames the beastly keno advantage with a Zero-Catch Pays policy on dollar bets—even if none of your numbers hit, you still win.

The Index

CASINOS | THE INDEX

Bally's. A less-is-more casino that doesn't take itself too seriously.... *Tel 702/739-4111. 3645 Las Vegas Blvd. S.*
(see p. 140)

Barbary Coast. Decorated like Jed Clampett's Beverly Hills mansion, it's often packed due to its strategic Strip location, but with many low-stakes players.... *Tel 702/737-7111. 3595 Las Vegas Blvd. S.* **(see p. 143)**

Bellagio. Enormous and bustling, and an odd blend of old and new money (not that the casino cares, as long as the denomination's right).... *Tel 702/693-7111. 3600 Las Vegas Blvd. S.* **(see pp. 144, 146)**

Binion's Horseshoe. THE place to feel like an old-style gambler, from the "classy" if dingy decor to the stern-faced players.... *Tel 702/382-1600. 128 Fremont St.* **(see p. 143)**

Caesars Palace. It's the closest to "old" Vegas glitz and glamour, with everything on a grand scale, from the classical statues to the cocktail waitresses' breasts.... *Tel 702/731-7110. 3750 Las Vegas Blvd. S.* **(see pp. 141, 142, 143, 145)**

Circus Circus. Still the most surreal experience in town, especially while gambling under the Big Top area.... *Tel 702/734-0410. 2880 Las Vegas Blvd. S.* **(see pp. 142, 143)**

Desert Inn. If Bellagio or The Venetian consider themselves black tie, this is pearl choker: the quintessential European-style intimate casino.... *Tel 702/733-4444. 3145 Las Vegas Blvd. S.* **(see pp. 142, 146)**

Excalibur. This low-rent Arthurian casino entertains boisterous, only occasionally boorish crowds.... *Tel 702/597-7777. 3850 Las Vegas Blvd. S.* **(see pp. 142, 143, 147)**

The Fiesta. With possibly the most promotions and give-aways in town, this locals' casino merits its name, though it's relatively undistinguished otherwise.... *Tel 702/631-7000. 2400 N. Rancho Dr.* **(see p. 140)**

Fitzgerald's. The Irish theme is blessedly less aggressive than it used to be, and you won't find many greener fields for learning the games or scoring deals.... *Tel 702/388-2400. 301 E. Fremont St.* **(see pp. 144, 147)**

Flamingo Hilton. It's big, it's brash, and it draws plenty of package tour groups (founder Bugsy Siegel must be spinning in his grave).... *Tel 702/733-3111. 3555 Las Vegas Blvd. S.* **(see p. 144, 147)**

Gold Coast. Locals come here for keno and bingo bargains, as well as an excellent slot club and variety of machines. One unique attribute: look very hard, and you'll see real windows.... *Tel 702/367-7111. 4000 W. Flamingo Rd.* **(see pp. 140, 147)**

Gold Spike. Decor is like an alcoholic uncle's 1960s ranch house, with soiled shag carpets and fake wood paneling.... *Tel 702/384-8444. 400 E. Ogden Ave.***(see pp. 142, 147)**

Golden Nugget. The class act Downtown—a handsome clientele and stylish digs.... *Tel 702/385-7111. 129 E. Fremont Ave.* **(see p. 142)**

Hard Rock. Youthful vibes and undeniable coolness. You almost feel they'd card (and exclude) anyone *over* 35; the decibel level of the rock music can be deafening.... *Tel 702/693-5000. 4455 Paradise Rd.***(see pp. 140, 141, 145, 146)**

Harrah's. By far the nicest middle-level casino, from attentive staffers to pleasantly restrained surroundings.... *Tel 702/369-5000. 3475 Las Vegas Blvd. S.* **(see pp. 140, 147)**

Imperial Palace. One step above a grind joint, but worth it for promotions, and two bonuses: a drive-through betting window and an excellent tiered race and sport book, with individual monitors.... *Tel 702/731-3311. 3535 Las Vegas Blvd. S.* **(see pp. 141. 144)**

Lady Luck. Utterly lacking in any style—even trashy—but the most generous spot downtown.... *Tel 702/477-3000. 206 N. 3rd St.* **(see p. 141)**

Las Vegas Hilton. An exceptional blend of old-style dash-and-flash and contemporary convenience, catering to business types, but less pretentious than you'd think.... *Tel 702/732-5111. 3000 Paradise Rd.* **(see pp. 142, 144, 146)**

Luxor. Despite the distracting ancient Egypt theme (Holy Ramses!), one of the better mid-level casinos in town.... *Tel 702/262-4000. 3900 Las Vegas Blvd. S.* **(see p. 143)**

MGM Grand. The Hollywood-themed casino offers everything under the stars, running the gambling gamut.... *Tel 702/891-1111. 3799 Las Vegas Blvd. S.* **(see pp. 144, 146)**

Mirage. A seductive combination of tropical langor and pulsating action.... *Tel 702/791-7111. 3400 Las Vegas Blvd. S.* **(see pp. 142, 146)**

Monte Carlo. Five-cent slots mar the classy pretensions of this otherwise attractive room.... *Tel 702/730-7777. 3770 Las Vegas Blvd. S.* **(see pp. 141, 144, 147)**

New York-New York. Teeming masses yearning to breathe free appreciate the fresh air (little smoke and a Central Park theme).... *Tel 702/740-6969. 3790 Las Vegas Blvd. S.* **(see p. 140)**

Orleans. Laissez les bons temps rouler at this exemplary locals' casino.... *Tel 702/365-7111. 4500 W. Tropicana Ave.* **(see pp. 140, 141, 147)**

Palace Station. Noisiest, smokiest, and most dilapidated of the locals' casinos, but ba-da-bing Bingo and inviting service keep this railroad-themed casino on track.... *Tel 702/367-2411. 2411 W. Sahara Ave.* **(see pp. 140, 142)**

Paris. Magnifique schlock in this middle-brow roller casino.... *Tel 702/967–4111. 3655 Las Vegas Blvd. S.* **(see p. 144)**

The Reserve. Tongue-in-cheek safari decor. Loincloths and pith helmets purely optional for guests.... *Tel 702/558-7000. 777 W. Lake Mead Dr.* **(see pp. 141, 145, 147)**

Rio All-Suite Casino Resort. Bustling, huge, slightly impersonal, but wildly popular with a range of gamblers.... *Tel 702/252-7777. 3700 W. Flamingo Rd.* **(see pp. 141, 145, 146)**

Sam's Town. With its Old West decor and warm ambience, this locals' casino's theme song could be "I've Got Slots that Jingle Jangle Jingle".... *Tel 702/456-7777. 5111 Boulder Hwy.* **(see p. 140)**

Showboat. One of the most popular casinos in town with both locals and tourists—a fun-loving atmosphere and good pay-outs.... *Tel 702/385-9123. 2800 Fremont St.* **(see p. 145)**

Slots A Fun. A premier low-stakes (and high-amusement) facility, dirt cheap in more ways than one.... *Tel 702/734-0410. 2880 Las Vegas Blvd. S.* **(see pp. 142, 147)**

Stardust. Wildly popular for its many promotions and festive atmosphere.... *Tel 702/732-6111. 3000 Las Vegas Blvd. S.* **(see pp. 143, 147)**

Sunset Station. A Mediterranean theme and the friendly vibe common to locals' casinos.... *Tel 702/547-7777. 1301 W. Sunset Rd.* **(see pp. 140, 145)**

Texas Station. Stetsons, lariats, and miniature oil derricks pumping above the slot carousels. And of course, a Texas-sized welcome.... *Tel 702/631-1000. 2101 Texas Star Lane.* **(see pp. 140, 141)**

Treasure Island. Despite the goofy pirate theme, it's the most unintimidating property with upper-end pretensions.... *Tel 702/894-7111. 3300 Las Vegas Blvd. S.* **(see p. 144)**

Tropicana. A solidly middle-class, middle-American crowd comes here, despite the fancy decor touches.... *Tel 702/739-2222. 3801 Las Vegas Blvd. S.* **(see pp. 145, 147)**

Venetian. High-glamor stakes, with remarkable duplication of Venetian art and architecture.... *Tel 702/733-5000. 3355 Las Vegas Blvd. S.* **(see p. 146)**

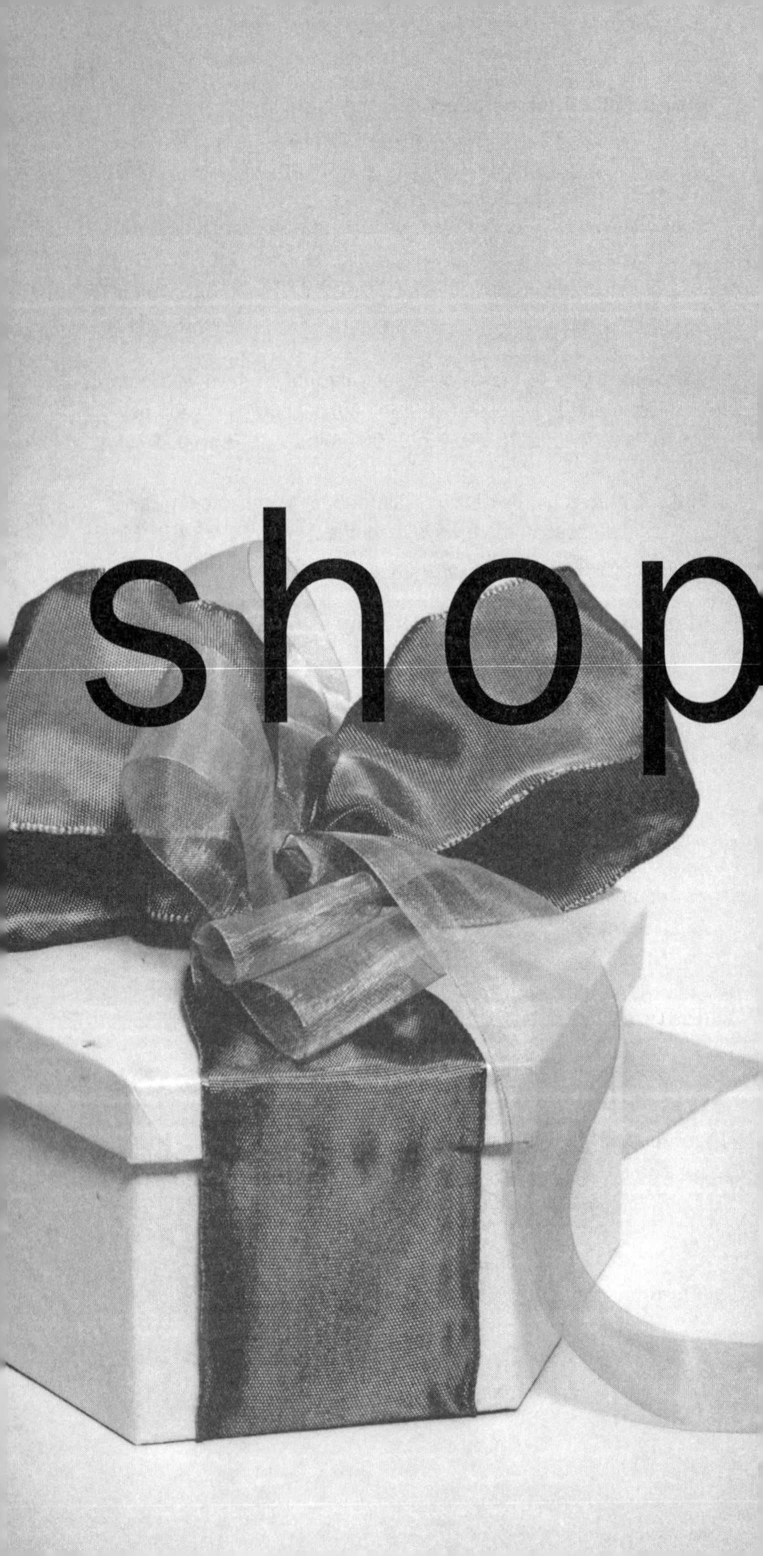
shop

5 ping

Las Vegas no longer peddles only fuzzy dice, Elvis clocks, and rhinestone-studded apparel. From glitzy to ritzy, Las Vegas sells it all.

If you want flash and trash—appliqué, beads, feathers, sequins, bejeweled cowboy boots—you've come to the right place. But today's Las Vegas also offers leading department stores like Saks and Neiman Marcus, as well as hot-shot designer boutiques like Armani and DKNY. You can parade in Prada or get versed in Versace. Lest you think no one comes to Las Vegas to shop, consider this: **Forum Shops at Caesars** enjoys the highest average annual sales per square foot of retail space in the country ($1,200, which is triple the figures elsewhere). As of late 1999, total retail revenue along the four-mile Strip exceeded $18 billion (more than New York's and San Francisco's combined). At this rate, the sounds of cash registers could almost drown out those of slot machines. No wonder that by the end of 2001, four new locations (the 500,000-square-foot Desert Passage in Aladdin; a 280,000-square-foot expansion of Caesars' Forum Shops; a 1 million-square-foot extension of Fashion Show Mall, including Bloomingdale's and Lord & Taylor; and a new 1.3 million-square-foot mall anchored by a triplex 210,000-square-foot Nordstrom between Mandalay Bay and Luxor) will augment retail space by more than three million square feet. Once you get past the glut of glitz, you may find Las Vegas shopping conspicuously deficient in certain areas—like books or cutting-edge club-wear. But the low-brow end of things hasn't disappeared, not by a long shot. For a high price you can buy a $3,500 fur-trimmed Rocky Raccoon slinky or a Coca Cola "Stonehenge" sculpture ($500). Most major productions, theme restaurants, and hotels sell logo merchandise. And don't forget the kitsch souvenirs on tap at such attractions as Liberace Museum, M&M's World, Siegfried & Roy's Secret Garden/Dolphin Habitat, and Star Trek: The Experience (see Diversions). This being Las Vegas, where all the world truly is a stage, window shopping isn't considered sufficiently diverting. Most malls also offer animatronic and laser shows, motion-simulator rides, live pianists—anything to turn you upside down and shake those pockets loose of whatever the casinos didn't.

Target Zones

Shopping areas, by and large, are clustered in mega-malls and hotel arcades, particularly along the Strip (**Las Vegas Boulevard South**). The only streets that offer a variety of stores are **South Maryland Parkway** (anything appealing to college kids and Gen-Xers—retro threads, indie CDs) and **South Rainbow Boulevard** (the interior design drag, with dozens of galleries, furniture stores, and home accessories shops). Representing the "new" (or merely nouveau) upscale Vegas, **Via Bellagio** (Bellagio, tel 702/693-7444, 3600 Las Vegas Blvd. S.) is easily the most affluent and opulent shopping environment. The barrel-vaulted grand hallway contains chandeliers, potted palms, Axminster-style rugs, inlaid marble, an arched skylight of wrought iron and etched glass, and gilded dome. Even the bathrooms have gold-plated fixtures. Prada, Chanel, Armani, Moschino, Hermès, Tiffany, and Gucci all showcase their latest lines. The place has an almost erotic undertow, with mannequins and merchandise lit suggestively, and willowy would-be models behind the counters. Via Bellagio's inspiration was probably **Appian Way** (tel 702/731-7110, 3570 Las Vegas Blvd. S.), the elegant marble-floored arcade in Caesars Palace dominated by its 18-foot replica of Michelangelo's *David;* upscale retailers include Cartier, Ciro, Godiva, and Marshall Rousso. But for the longest time, **Forum Shops at Caesars** (tel 702/893-4800, 3500 Las Vegas Blvd. S.) was THE discriminating destination, and it still houses both upscale (Dior to Dunhill to DKNY, Fendi to Ferragamo, Estée Lauder to Lalique to Polo Ralph Lauren) and populist (NikeTown, Guess?, Warner Brothers, Disney, Banana Republic, Virgin Megastore) among its nearly 100 outlets. The restaurants range accordingly, from Caviarteria and Wolfgang Puck's Chinois and Spago to Planet Hollywood. The Forum Shops at Caesars patented the concept of shopping as entertainment, offering two thundering, smoke-billowing animatronic shows like Lost City of Atlantis, IMAX motion-simulator rides (see Diversions), and a 50,000-gallon saltwater aquarium with hundreds of tropical fish with regular feedings by scuba divers. The design combines the streets of ancient Rome with Milan's La Scala arcades, underneath a "sky" ceiling that passes from sunrise to sunset every hour. The new entrant in the upmarket/extravaganza sweepstakes is the Venetian's **Grand Canal Shoppes** (tel 702/733-5000, 3355 Las Vegas Blvd. S.), a setting of "neighborhoods" lining both sides of the Grand Canal, with gondolas and everything. Designers modeled them from photos of Venice, with genuine marble balconies and cobblestone streets (the brick "exteriors" are cleverly retouched stucco). Street performers (opera singers, magicians, jugglers) and artisans like glass blowers circulate as entertainment. Big-name stores include Ann Taylor, Davidoff, Mikimoto, Donna Karan, Cesare Paciotti, and Lladro; it's a foot fetishist's paradise with

Jimmy Choo (Princess Diana's preferred shoemaker), Ludwig Reiter, Rockport, and Kenneth Cole. The restaurants (see Dining) are the most superlative grouping of any mall in town. Paris's **Rue de la Paix/Le Boulevard** district (tel 702/967-4111, 3655 Las Vegas Blvd. S.) provides a similar "authentic" ambience, albeit on a humbler scale, with street performers, cobblestone walkways, winding alleys, and painted facades from various Parisian *arrondissements*. The gimmick here is that virtually all the shops tend toward the oh-so-Gallic, including a wine-and-cheese emporium (La Cave) and lingerie store (La Vogue). You can even buy Eiffel Tower souvenirs (Tour Eiffel) or Toulouse-Lautrec posters (L'Art de Paris). **Fashion Show Mall** (tel 702/369-8382, 3200 Las Vegas Blvd. S.) plugs along in its own quietly tasteful way. There are plump couches, fake palms, enormous picture windows, marble floors, a high-quality food court, even a pianist on a grand playing classical, jazz, pop, and (ugh) lots of Andrew Lloyd Webber. It features higher-end department stores like Saks Fifth Avenue and Neiman Marcus, and such retailers as Ann Taylor, Bally, Betsey Johnson, Miller Stockman Western Wear, Victoria's Secret, Sharper Image, Louis Vuitton, Polo, Escada, Williams-Sonoma, BCBG, Estée Lauder, The Body Shop, and Sam Goody. There are also four top restaurants and an Elizabeth Arden salon. Needless to say, every major Strip hotel has a shopping arcade where you can pick up apparel, gifts, logo items, T-shirts, electronics, cosmetics, toys, et al. Look for nifty buys at their performers' stores, whether magic or circus sorcery. Among the most notable are **The Tower Shops** (Stratosphere, 2000 Las Vegas Blvd. S), with 40 stores in themed environments (Paris, New York, Hong Kong, etc.); the **Masquerade Village Shops** (Rio All-Suite Casino Resort, 3700 W. Flamingo Rd.), with 26 retailers like Nicole Miller and Speedo; **Street of Dreams** (Monte Carlo, 3770 Las Vegas Blvd. S) where Anne Klein, Bulgari, and Cartier start off the ABCs; and **Star Lane Shops** (MGM Grand, 3799 Las Vegas Blvd. S.), including stellar names such as El Portal (with Coach, Dior, and Fendi leather goods and luggage) and The Knot Shop (ties by Versace, Klein, and Zegna). Circus Circus, Luxor, and Excalibur maintain their kitsch themes throughout the shopping areas and are fun for that reason alone. Away from the Strip down in Henderson, **Galleria at Sunset** (tel 702/434-0202, 1300 W. Sunset Rd.) is the usual lower-middle-class outpost, handsomely designed in Southwestern style with terra-cotta stonework, cascading fountains, sky-lights, and interior landscaping. The duplex mall features 130 outlets like Dillard's, JC Penney, Robinson's, Mervyn's, The Disney Store, The Gap, Eddie Bauer, The Limited, B. Dalton Bookstore, Ann Taylor, and Caché. **Meadows Mall** (tel 702/878-4849, 4300 Meadows Lane), offers 144 stores, anchored by Macy's, Dillard's, Sears, and JC Penney. Families especially enjoy its intricately embellished carousel, indoor oasis pool, live entertainment, and five themed courts, including "Natural History" (with "fossilized" floor replete with desert animal tracks). **Boulevard Mall** (tel 702/732-8949, 3528 S. Maryland Pkwy.), Nevada's largest shopping center, features more than 140 stores and an elaborate food court. Here you'll find comfortably familiar names like Macy's, Sears, Dillard's, Marshalls, The Disney Store, The Limited, The Gap, Radio Shack, Lane Bryant, Bath & Body Works, and Victoria's Secret. There's something for everyone here, from books to home furnishings.

Bargain Hunting

Sorry, folks, this is not the place for endless white sales, though summer predictably offers numerous discounts. But you could scout Maryland Parkway, close to UNLV, for sec-ondhand and cheaper stores. And the further you get from the Strip and Glitter Gulch, the better your chances of finding reasonably priced items (even for the tackiest souvenirs and T-shirts, though of course the selection will be limited). You could also try the locals' casinos: Everything is less expensive at these off-Strip properties. **Belz Factory Outlet World** (tel 702/896-5599, 7400 Las Vegas Blvd. S.) offers a carousel and free laser shows in the courtyards—and no slots! It features more than 140 outlets, such as Saks Off Fifth, Calvin Klein, Fila, Royal Doulton, Esprit, Levi's, Reebok, and Waterford. Further south down the Strip (now just plain old Las Vegas Boulevard), **Factory Stores of America** (tel 702/897-9090, 9155 Las Vegas Blvd. S.) is the country's only outlet center with a casino bar/lounge. The attractive Spanish Mission–style buildings contain over 50 outlets, including Izod, Mikasa, Van Heusen, American Tourister, Geoffrey Beene, and Corning/Revere. For those who don't mind a trek, **Fashion Outlet Las Vegas** (tel 702/874-1400, at Exit 1 off I-15 in Primm, 30 minutes south of the Strip, free shuttle every two hours from New York New York) offers more than 100 designers; shop here for Bally, Banana Republic, Kenneth

Cole, Timberland, Lacoste, Tommy Hilfiger, Benetton, Versace, Gap, J. Crew, Guess?, Jhane Barnes, Burberry, Williams-Sonoma, and Escada. The interior features a fountain with tacky pink flamingos, huge bathing beauties of both sexes supporting one store, horrid murals, and garish marquees (DNKY looks like a sign for a Broadway show).

Hours of Business

Most hotel shopping arcades remain open daily until 10 or 11pm, sometimes later on weekends. The major malls, especially those with dining and entertainment options, are open until at least midnight. Freestanding stores, especially off the Strip, cling to more old-fashioned hours, usually opening at 9 or 10am and closing anywhere from 5 to 7pm.

The Lowdown

Best for kids... At the Forum Shops, **FAO Schwarz** knows how to put on a show. A 48-foot, smoke-spewing Trojan horse guards the entrance; then you dart past animatronic mini-rhinos and Star Wars storm troopers. The toy selection is huge; there's even a private high-roller room where prices run $3,000–$30,000. Also at Forum Shops, **NikeTown**, full of interactive displays, will lift the spirits of any tyke or teen with its selection of Air Jordans and other overpriced sneakers. Across from the Liberace Museum, **Kimberley House of Miniatures** presents Barbie's trip to Las Vegas: Barbie in convertibles, Barbie in showgirl regalia, and many of them vintage collectibles. But it's most remarkable for its darling doll houses, which customers can watch being made, including exquisitely detailed miniatures of Mexican furnishings, musical instruments, and Persian rugs. **Ron Lee's World of Clowns** sells Warners Brothers and Disney characters, as well as its own line of clown figurines; they don't clown around, throwing in a free tour and museum. **Circus Kids** at (natch) Circus Circus offers plenty of razzmatazz with its krazy clown hats and noses, damsels in distress dolls, and glittery tutus and leotards.

Tackiest tchotchkes... **Bonanza Gifts Shop**, which advertises itself as the world's largest souvenir store, is actually a Strip mini-strip mall with such related businesses as Friendly Fergie's Casino Bar. Despite the vast inventory, it isn't as tacky as it should be. Roulette ashtrays, money lollipops (in various denominations), and sparkling dice pencil sharpeners are the best of the bad lot, along with the requisite Elvis memorabilia. The various **Tower of Jewels** shops certainly pile it on with cheap 10K "I Love Vegas" charms, 14K slot charms, panther and crescent moon earrings, and gaudy diamond and pearl items. Or for a remembrance of Sin City, how about **Slightly Sinful**'s T-shirts reading "Peter Gun...Stick 'em up and spread 'em"?

Souvenirs with panache... **Art of Gaming** at Harrah's has a sense of humor about Vegas, selling card games from around the globe, witty statues with torsos modeled after antique one-armed bandits, and mirrored keychains shaped like the "Welcome to Fabulous Las Vegas" sign. **Lost Vegas Gallery** is a priceless source for unique items: pink dice clocks, showgirl Barbies, old postcards from the original hotels (like pink flamingoes from guess where), striking photos from the '50s through the '70s showing the Strip in all its flamboyant glory; there's even an Elvis toilet. Downtown, **Gambler's General Store** sells the truest Vegas souvenirs: gambling books and computer programs, chips, cards, craps tables, even roulette wheels and slot machines (for private use only; every state has different regulations, so ask before buying).

Campier than thou... The Forum Shops has two art galleries that have to be seen to be believed: **Galleria di Sorrento**, which often has outrageous themed art shows, like "Femme Fatales" (artist takes on Naked Maja meets Mata Hari meets Mink) and **Galerie Lassen,** starring marine artist Lassen's oh-so-spiritual images of Hawaiian beaches and playful whales spouting off—Peter Max meets The Sierra Club. There's a 2,700-gallon aquarium at the entrance, life-size sculptures of dolphins and sharks suspended from the ceiling, custom-painted cars, like a 1993 black Lamborgini Diablo, and a video wall projecting soothing sea images. Or, for a Vegas memento, how about a genuine showgirl wig from **Serge's Showgirl Wigs**? It features Raquel Welch's and Dolly Parton's collections, as well as custom designs, all hanging lovingly from beautifully chiseled face dummies mounted on columns. Prices range from $150 to $1,500. (Check the phone listings for cheaper shops advertising "real human hair from $29.95," and hairstyles for the "transvestite/transexual set.") At Excalibur's **Dragon's Lair** you can buy real swords, halberds, shields, even a suit of armor. The kiddies will have to settle for miniature dragons and sorcerers. The **N'Awlins Store** (no, not in the Orleans, instead at the Rio) sells Cajun hot sauce, Mardi Gras masks, and voodoo items like *gris-gris* love potions, Dambala snakes, and dolls bristling with pins. At the Stratosphere, **Cleo's** features hand-crafted foot jewelry (dubbed "shoewels") as well as thumb rings, beaded anklets, toe rings, boot jewels, and waist chains.

For collectors... Get Real Sports sells autographed balls, photos, and clothes (all new—no dirty uniforms or frayed jock straps) from superstars like Michael Jordan, Brett Favre, and Cal Ripken Jr. You can also buy licensed team caps, sweatshirts, helmets, and jackets. **MGM Grand Sports** also traffics in autographed athletic uniforms, baseballs, basketballs, trading cards, and photos. Lots of celeb appearances, too, usually by oldsters such as Stan Musial, Gordie Howe, and Floyd Patterson. **Art Affair** offers animation cells, sports memorabilia, and posters. At Harrah's, **Art of Gaming** features iconic Rat Pack memorabilia from Frank Sinatra and Sammy Davis Jr. The Grand Canal Shoppes' **In Celebration of Golf** includes a re-creation of an old Scottish clubhouse, an art gallery (all golf images), a display of antique golfing memorabilia, and an indoor golf simulator.

Books and record deals... Yes, you can find the biggies: Tower and Virgin Megastore for records, Barnes & Noble and Borders for books. But there are a few idiosyncratic must-sees. Downtown, the **Gamblers Book Shop** offers thousands of titles on gambling history, table game strategies, even volumes about Las Vegas and Nevada history. Clerks even offer their tips on handicapping. **Get Booked** caters to the gay/lesbian population with CDs, jewelry, alternative lifestyle books and posters, and catty/chatty local gossip. **Dead Poet Books** is slightly musty, smells of old hand-tooled leather, and stocks first editions of classics and arcane authors, with everything from metaphysical cookbooks to military memoirs.

Odyssey Records is open 24 hours in a seedy north-of-the-Strip area, but its selection of new alt and indie music may be the best in town. It's a great place to get keyed into the rave scene—if you look the part. The humongous **WOW Superstore** has an immense selection, including many esoteric artists, and serves the best lattes.

Retro-fitting... Whether your fashion passion runs toward "Ralph Kramden" bowling shirts or "Jack Lord" Hawaiian shirts, sequined show costumes or studded rancher's boots, it's at **The Attic** somewhere. This Downtown shops's decor is delectably retro hippie, with zebra carpeting and plush crushed velour seating areas. **Retro Vintage Clothing** displays owner Melina Crisostomo's unerring eye—antique Victorian lace, 1930s Chanel evening wear, Oscar de la Renta tailored business suits, and plenty of accessories, such as gloves, purses, and kooky classic sunglasses. **Pink Gypsy** is big on accessories—Victorian pearl or glass chokers, 1920s flapper rhinestone anklets, bakelite earrings, beaded purses. At **Buffalo Exchange** you can find funky '70s stuff like tan suede leisure shoes and red platform shoes, along with hundreds of jeans, some rather grotty, but some fun, like bell-bottoms with hand-stitched peace symbols.

Haute couture... The **Armani** boutique at Via Bellagio displays clothing fetishistically for maximum impact. Skirts and shirts float in glass cubicles like astronauts in space station compartments. Mannequins sport TVs for heads. Translucent walls are lit from within, imparting an otherworldly glow to the suits, dresses, blouses, and trousers arrayed on single metal rods. Tiny **Ice** almost gets lost amid the old Rome bustle of the Forum Shops, but hunt it down: Owner Dottie Chanin collects one-of-a-kind delights from her various international forays—silver, shawls, sweaters, and hand-painted silk and cut-velvet scarves. Also in the Forum Shops you'll find **Shauna Stein**, which scouts all the fashion shows in New York, Paris, and Milan, and the over-the-top sequined and beaded bags of **Judith Leiber**. New York and Palm Beach socialites seek out the far simpler, stylish exotic skin handbags at **Lana Marks** in the Grand Canal Shoppes. At Appian Way, **Bernini** carries exquisite high-end Italian suits and accessories from Brioni, Moschino, Gianfranco Ferrè, and Zegna.

To beautify your home... If you're looking for fancy with a hint of funk, head to **Unika** for cool post-modern old-fashioned items: distressed armoires, desks, and wine cabinets; marvelous earthenware urns and raku vases; and wrought-iron lamps. **Purr-Deux Designs** offers a precious takeoff on Pierre Deux decorating styles: preserved eucalyptus trees, dried floral wreaths large enough to cover a fan dancer, and burbling wall fountains. Mandalay Bay's **Bali Trading Company** imports the best that Indonesia and the South Pacific have to offer: hand-crafted teak chests, shadow puppets, batiks, hand-woven textiles like Ikat wall hangings, even sarongs. **Amen Wardy Home** at the Forum Shops is like no home on earth: Austrian glassware, ceramic cachepots, exotic wood armoires and screens, and hand-painted dishes. Even the wax fruit looks good. **Showcase Slots and Antiquities** offers antique video poker and slot machines galore, including a 1949 Jennings Sun Chief (the first lighted model), as well as vintage nostalgia items like jukeboxes, neon signs, and barber poles. Amid the rows of booths at **Red Rooster Antique Mall**, you'll find everything from china to clothes to cabinets. You could find something truly special: It's a fine line between antiquarian and junk maven.

Forbidden delights... What trip to Sin City would be complete without a naughty souvenir? **Slightly Sinful** offers boas, G-strings, even schoolgirl uniforms for those who want to play striptease at home; men, too, have a choice of Chippendales-style glitter. Let's not forget lingerie and eveningwear for all fetishes, edible undies, and other sexual accessories from videos to vibrators. Kinky and raunchy don't begin to describe the stock at **Lock Stock and Leather**: handcuffs, whips, cat o' nine tails, latex, clubwear, and other fun holiday gear are featured. Piercings, preferably of remote body parts, are also offered. **Rancho Deluxe Adult Entertainment** is run by maiden-aunt types who don't blink when you request that doubled-headed dildo. Vibrators, S&M gear, vinyl and leather thongs, massage oils: They'll gladly make like Dr. Ruth if you can't decide. **Bare Essentials** carries "fantasy" clothing with strategic holes, as well as more traditional lingerie and men's thongs that leave little to the imagination. **Paradise Electro Stimulations** is serious about stimulating your erogenous zones, with its vibrating accessories in every conceivable shape and size, all connected to a special impulse control unit that reputedly enhances pleasure.

Tattoo you... Owners Bob and Cory show off their creative genius in murals on the walls at **Sin City Tattoo**—a devil with breasts in stilettos sitting on an 8-ball; a female demon in full dominatrix garb with pierced nipples. A flashback to the 1960s, **Tribal Body Piercing** sells jewelry, incense, candles, and hemp products, but its tattoo designs and piercings (including bone and stainless steel) are third-millennium.

The Index

Gambler's General Store. One-stop shopping for gambling paraphernalia.... *Tel 702/382-9903. 800 S. Main St.*
(see p. 159)

Get Booked. Books, CDs, coffee, and light cruising for gays and lesbians.... *Tel 702/737-7780. 4640 Paradise Rd.*
(see p. 160)

Get Real Sports. Signed jock memorabilia.... *Tel 702/248-REAL. 2550 S. Rainbow Blvd., Suite E-19.* **(see p. 160)**

In Celebration of Golf. A virtual golf museum, with memorabilia including trophies and autographed photos.... *Tel 702/733-5000. Grand Canal Shoppes, Venetian, 3355 Las Vegas Blvd. S.* **(see p. 160)**

Judith Leiber. Glitzy handbags.... *Tel. 702/731-7110 Forum Shops at Caesars, 3500 Las Vegas Blvd. S.* **(see p. 161)**

Kimberley House of Miniatures. Watch artisans making unbelievably precise doll houses.... *Tel 702/795-2276. 1775 E. Tropicana Ave.* **(see p. 158)**

Lana Marks. High-end handbags made of exotic animal skins.... *Tel 702/733–5000 Grand Canal Shoppes, Venetian, 3355 Las Vegas Blvd. S.* **(see p. 161)**

Lock Stock and Leather. For all your bondage needs.... *Tel 702/796-9801. 4640 Paradise Rd., #10* **(see p. 162)**

Lost Vegas Gallery. Loving tribute to a vanished era.... *Tel 702/362-0621. Arts Factory, 101 S. Charleston Blvd.*
(see p. 159)

MGM Grand Sports. Memorabilia store.... *Tel 702/891–7777 MGM Grand, 3799 Las Vegas Blvd. S* **(see p. 160)**

N'Awlins Store. Gris-gris dolls and Cajun spices.... *Tel 702/252–7777. Rio All-Suite Casino Resort, 3700 W. Flamingo Rd.* **(see p. 160)**

NikeTown. You know you want to pay too much for that logo sweatshirt. Just do it.... *Tel 702/650-8888. Forum Shops at Caesars, 3500 Las Vegas Blvd. S.* **(see p. 158)**

SHOPPING | THE INDEX

Odyssey Records. Grunge defines the music and the location, but the selection is unbeatable.... *Tel 702/384-4040. 1600 Las Vegas Blvd. S.* **(see p. 161)**

Paradise Electro Stimulations. Everything motorized to stimulate your love muscles. Call for appointments.... *Tel 702/474-2991. 1509 W. Oakey Blvd.* **(see p. 162)**

Pink Gypsy. Costume jewelry, Victorian frou-frou, and modern rip-offs on consignment.... *Tel 702/221-5441. 4001 S. Decatur Blvd. S., #41.* **(see p. 161)**

Purr-Deux Designs. Imaginative if precious home accessories.... *Tel 702/878-2533. 1218 S. Rainbow Blvd.*
(see p. 162)

Rancho Deluxe Adult Entertainment. Sex toys.... *Tel 702/645-6106. 4820 N. Rancho Dr.* **(see p. 162)**

Red Rooster Antique Mall. Endless selection of old stuff, wildly varying in quality.... *Tel 702/382–5253. 307 W. Charleston Blvd.* **(see p. 162)**

Retro Vintage Clothing. Funky and classic vintage clothes and accessories.... *Tel 702/877-8989. 906 S. Valley View Blvd.* **(see p. 161)**

Ron Lee's World of Clowns. Top doll manufacturers, with tour and museum connected to shop.... *Tel 702/434-1700. 330 Carousel Pkwy.* **(see p. 158)**

Serge's Showgirl Wigs. The ultimate in showgirl paraphernalia.... *Tel 702/732-1015. 953 E. Sahara Ave., Suite A-2.*
(see p. 159)

Shauna Stein. Haute couture for truly discriminating women.... *Tel 702/731-7110 Forum Shops at Caesars, 3500 Las Vegas Blvd. S.* **(see p. 161)**

Showcase Slots and Antiquities. Classic pieces of Americana.... *Tel 702/740-5722. 4305 S. Industrial Rd., Suite B-110.* **(see p. 162)**

Sin City Tattoo. Surly atmosphere, but they know their work.... *Tel 702/387-6969. 101 E. Charleston Blvd.* **(see p. 163)**

Slightly Sinful. Leather, lace, and spangles for the sexually playful.... *Tel 702/387-1006. 1232 Las Vegas Blvd. S.*
(see pp. 159,162)

Tower of Jewels. Souvenir jewelry.... *Tel 702/791-0677, Harrah's, 3475 Las Vegas Blvd. S.; Tel 702/736-7355. Bally's, 3645 Las Vegas Blvd. S.; Tel 702/735-4145. Commercial Center, 953 E. Sahara Ave.; Tel 702/382-3387. Fitzgerald's, 301 Fremont St.* **(see p. 159)**

Tribal Body Piercing. For piercings, tattoos, and bongs, catering to both hard-ass bikers and first-timers.... *Tel 702/798-7423. 4800 S. Maryland Pkwy.* **(see p. 163)**

Unika. Tasteful yet fun furnishings and accessories.... *Tel 702/258-0773. 1238 S. Rainbow Blvd.* **(see p. 162)**

WOW Superstore. Mega-store with the best range of CDs.... *Tel 702/364-2500. 4580 Decatur Blvd.* **(see p. 161)**

nigh

6

tlife

"In this town," wrote Hunter S. Thompson, "they love a drunk. Fresh meat." Wine bars, beer bars, martini bars, vodka bars made from ice, cigar bars, oxygen bars, singles bars, bare-all bars: You name it, you'll find a watering hole of your choice. And of course, there are the casino lounges, many offering free shows as a break between gambling and eating.

In Las Vegas, beefy ranchers and red-faced insurance salesmen will always ogle cocktail waitresses and topless dancers. Leather-skinned divorcees still tap long varnished nails while listening to lounge lizards in piano bars. But the possibilities have expanded exponentially; the Strip's new glam image brings in younger, trendier travelers, and dress codes and attitude are making inroads. Corporate sharks of both sexes enact mating rituals in sleek microbreweries and cigar bars. Underage candy ravers clutching dolls, pacifiers, and stuffed animals trance dance in deserted warehouses splashed with graffiti. Pony-tailed neo-hipsters and navel-pierced goth chicks frequent coffeehouses showcasing obscenity-laced poems of existential despair. The club scene here was more sock hop than hip-hop a mere five years ago, but newly trendoid Las Vegas now appropriates the night-crawling frenzy of New York and L.A. Fueled by burgeoning local rave and music scenes, the club craze supports a healthy live music scene outside the casinos, and the casinos compete with discos for customers of every age and musical taste. (There's something for the studious, the studded, and the studly.)

Sources

Most freebie rags (see Sources in Entertainment) offer lounge act listings and the occasional coupon. You'll also find nightlife suggestions in *NEON*, the *Las Vegas Review Journal's* weekend arts section (also accessible online at *www.lvrj.com*), as well as *City Life* and *Las Vegas Weekly*. The catch-all website for conventional conventioneer fare is *www.lvshowbiz.com*. Another option is the gushy but reasonably comprehensive *www.ilovevegas.com*. The edgier *Five/One Magazine* is devoted to the alternative music and culture scene (*www.five-one.com/51mag*); it provides reviews of local bands, a weekly updated *Underground Events Calendar*, and information on raves. Another good source for alternative venues is **Liquid 303 Records** (tel 702/ 383-3285, 320 E. Charleston Blvd., #105. For those who want a sneak peak at the girlie show action, try *www.strip clubreview.com*.

What it Will Cost

Nearly every watering hole offers some kind of entertainment. Covers and minimums vary according to venue and act. Generally, discos and nightclubs charge a $10 cover for men, $5 for women (local women free, according to the "men are boobs, women have boobs" philosophy of marketing). Most local bars have a $3 to $5 cover for their acts. Classier casino lounges levy a one- or two-drink minimum. Name performers, wherever they roost, will up the ante anywhere from $20 to $40. The strip clubs (whether topless or fully bared) usually charge a $10 cover and/or a two-drink minimum (exceptions are "fantasy rooms" and private booths in nude clubs, which may charge $15 or $20). Lap dances invariably run $20, no matter how high-toned or sleazy the venue. They're pretty tame, and no touching or solicitation is allowed. The VIP Rooms are open to any schmo with dough, but often laps are the same price (and no wilder). Note that with one exception, totally nude joints aren't permitted to serve alcohol (which means, ironically, that an 18-year-old can gain entrance to nude but not topless bars).

Liquor laws and drinking hours

The drinking age here is 21, and it's strictly enforced—if you look at all youthful, expect to be carded on and around the Strip approximately every 20 steps. Anything remotely resembling a dance place has a draconic 21-and-over code as well. The city also has remarkably tough drunk-driving laws (given the traffic nightmares and dangerous intersections, that's understandable). Stern local law officers straight from central casting make you feel like you're about to be trapped in a Turkish prison for 20 years. On the plus side, several non-casino bars and clubs offer free cab service back to your hotel if you're sloshed to the gills. Clubs usually don't open, or at least don't start hopping, before 10pm. Lounges and bars usually remain open 24 hours, except for coffeehouses and some non-casino venues. Most bump-and-grind joints open by noon; you can "lap" up the action until 4am, if not all through the night. Liquor flows 24/7. And don't forget that most of the top restaurants (see Dining) have zoo-like bar scenes with an entertaining menagerie of types.

Drugs

Yes, they exist. Yes, they're illegal. But they're plentiful, especially at raves and anywhere the younger set congregates.

Allegedly, it's easy to score vitamins X (MDMA, aka Ecstasy) and K (Ketamine, a feline tranquilizer), and rumors abound that there's plenty of cocaine dealing in the bathrooms of some strip clubs and discos. As one local jokes, that could be why they're all furnished with either stainless steel or black porcelain fixtures.

The Lowdown

Big throbbing dance clubs... Before the club craze finally hit Las Vegas, dance venues were cheesy approximations of big-city-slicker discos. Now fashion fascists increasingly patrol the scene, and the thugs at the door are as self-important as they are in New York and L.A. On the Strip, the three-level **Club Utopia** is as goth as Vegas gets. It not only draws leading DJs from New York and London, it has spawned its own famed spin-meisters like Robert Oleysyck and DJ Speedy. The music is techno, tribal, progressive house, trance, funk, and rave; the lighting system is the city's wildest, running from kaleidoscopic psychedelia to computer-generated disturbing flashes. In numerous dark corners, multiply pierced couples redefine liplock. Hounded by allegations of sex acts performed inside, Utopia brazenly flaunts the rep, throwing such theme nights as *Nymphomaniac's Ball* and *The Black Tie Me Up Ball*. The much more refined **Club Rio**, at the Rio, has brass railings, crystal globes, cushy circular booths, and a stalactite chandelier, but otherwise, it's extremely high-tech, with laser lighting, superior sound, and video banks on either side. A canny mix of canned dance music draws a dressed-up crowd of attractive folks hoping to meet other attractive folks. The Luxor's glitzy **Ra** is an eye-catching blend of barely clad go-go girls, sweeping lasers, and a pretty crowd gyrating to a sensational techno/ska/house mix; scenes of ancient Egypt alternate epileptically with the latest videos on giant screens. Top '80s bands and rappers like Doug E. Fresh and Run DMC occasionally play; *Deca-Dance* '80s nights bring $1,000 cage dancing contests and DJs booming progressive house music. Look for Naked Hollywood (usually the third Thursday of the month) when nudie bar dancers swaddled in latex or lingerie do three quickie peekaboo shows. Trendoid quotient: two cigar lounges, a raw bar, and strong-Armanied dudes in headsets enforce dress codes at the door. Tri-level **Studio 54**, at the MGM Grand, pays homage to its namesake with a big crystal ball, leopard-skin go-go dancers, silver confetti, VIP cocktail waitresses in hot pants and blue spangles, and very pretty bartenders (Steve Rubell would have approved), as well as framed photos of regulars from the old 54, like Andy Warhol, Liza Minnelli, Halston, Liz Taylor, and Truman Capote. But the musical mix is rather uninspired, and, despite the aggressive door staff, half these folk wouldn't have made it in on an off night at 54's New York peak—they look like the clueless thirtysomething brokers and lawyers they are in real life. Just off the Strip, the always-buzzing **Drink and Eat Too** has lost some of its orginal trendiness. GAP poster boys, neo-Reaganites, and anorexic would-be models jostle into its six themed rooms (each with different music and alcoholic specialties) and three dance floors, including a 2,000-foot interior courtyard with frequent live acts. Nearby at **Baby's**, the Hard Rock's ultra-glam underground nightclub, a thousand gorgeous people sweat discreetly to the tunes spun by resident DJ "The Funkler" (aka Mike Fuller) or lounge in intimate rooms on plush leather sofas.

Dancing cheek to chic... Posh and intimate, the Las Vegas Hilton's **The Nightclub** has blue and mauve strobe lights, frosted glass panels, and lasers; the featured act here is energetic Louie Louie, a supremely assured top 40 dance band. The top level of the restaurant/bar/disco **rumjungle** is a sizzling little club; the DJ booth sits right above the *churrascaria* where Brazilian barbecue turns on a spit, and the dance floor adjoins the fire pits. Live entertainment leans toward the exotic, from samba to reggae to jungle trip-hop—the world's two largest conga drums are built right into the floor. **Club Mojo** is the extremely cool after-hours weekend nightclub in House of Blues at Mandalay Bay. Its folk art trappings under sweeping laser beams look almost psychedelic: Alice on acid. The motto is "diversity, unity, love, and energy breed"; the music is whatever's terminally hip at the moment.

Boogie nights... Travolta types prance in white polyester and the occasional Disco Diva drag princess mouths "I Will Survive" wherever '70s retro band Boogie Knights plays—Wednesdays at the Rio's **Club Rio**, Thursdays at

Drink and Eat Too. Resplendent in pimp chic—towering Afro wigs, bell-bottoms, and platform shoes—Boogie Knights rotates among the big clubs. Their equally over-the-top counterpart Jungle Boogie (Chill E. Sauce and J.J. Jive) plays Mondays at the Monte Carlo's **Monte Carlo Brew Pub**, which combines hunkered-down microbrewery coziness with a high-tech dance floor. **Armadillo Lounge**, at the locals' casino Texas Station, crosses *Saturday Night Fever* with Southwestern chic on *Disco Inferno* Thursdays, when the leisure suits and capri pants are favored in desert pastels. There's also swing Sundays and rocking '80s cover band Love Shack on weekends.

Best people-watching... The parking lot of Paradise Road's **Gordon Biersch Brewing Company** tells it all: a sea of beemers and Range Rovers. Local models of both sexes, sleekly handsome as the exposed-brick decor, prowl with their designer Nokias at the ready. When House of Blues' late-night **Club Mojo** holds its *Club Ole* Salsa nights, you can't tell which clings to the ladies more, their dresses or their boyfriends. **Baby's** packs a plethora of Pretty Young Things into its retro-groovy underground space at the Hard Rock, waited upon by a bartending crew in black leather bustiers, hot pants, and studded collars and bracelets. The exhibitionist crowd at **Club Utopia** display enough body piercings to lend new meaning to the term "chain gang"; look for girls in lavender minis and matching mohawks, alongside boys with long lank hair and kohl-rimmed eyes. The beach-party theme of **The Beach** naturally bares lots of smooth tanned flesh—the ogling quotient is high here, with both staff and customers in muscle Ts, halter tops, and cutoffs. Watch for Hot Body contests and Jell-O shot games. **Gipsy** attracts a stand-and-pose ME-lieu: young guppy crowd, a dazzling array of well-stilettoed transvestites, and several curious or unconcerned hets. For maximum eye-popping, keep an eye out for fashion shows of sexy couture, "What would you do for $500?" evenings, and sizzling Monday Latin Nights with the foul-mouthed Miss Cha Cha.

Drinks with a theme... The Sahara may boast the worst major casino lounge in town, the **Casbar Lounge** (get it?), with tacky coffee shop naugahyde seats, hideous keyhole arches, "mujadeens" guarding the entrance, and a suffocating level of smokiness. Like everything else at the Egyptian-themed Luxor, the high-energy **Ra** dance club sports gilt everywhere, while videos of the Pyramids flash on giant screens. It easily out-glitzes Caesars Palace's Egyptian offering, **Cleopatra's Barge**, with its ponderous gold columns, oars, furled sails, and gangplank (so many tipplers have tipped into the drink they installed railings). No mummies, but some guests look embalmed. The **House of Blues Foundation** contains the chain's signature folk art, as well as huge crème de menthe-colored banquettes, but various rooms (with names such as Ganesh, Gothic, and Jacobean) extend the theme, displaying everything from antique Buddhas to oak panels from an English castle to handpainted Shangri-La ceilings. **Gilley's Saloon, Dance Hall & Bar-B-Que** conveys the rustic barn feel of the original Gilley's in Pasadena, Texas, adding cowboy kitsch (and neon): swinging saloon doors, hay bales, wooden posts, barrels, buckets of peanuts (with shells strewn over the floor), and a dance area resembling a corral. Harrah's **La Playa Lounge** relives beach blanket bingo with multicolored palm trees, rocks enmeshed with bright fiber-optic lighting, and a 3-D mural of a day on the sand. Appropriate live music is provided by Latin, surf pop, and Brazilian performers. The Mirage's **Lagoon Saloon** is a more upscale beach, with designer tropical fabrics, rattan chairs, parquet floors, Indonesian thatching, actual sand and shells incorporated into the bar top, and frou-frou frozen drinks. Loincloths are definitely not appropriate attire. Off the Strip near the convention center, **The Beach** diligently recreates a SoCal barn: grass thatching, surfboards, posters of bikinied gals, plastic sharks, even real cars dangling from the ceilings. Dancing is incidental to its keg-party atmosphere and frenzied pickup scene, but the DJs and occasional live bands (including name acts like Mötley Crüe) get the cruisers on their feet.

Class lounge acts... The Bellagio offers a number of cosmopolitan nooks: Choose between the super-sophisticated **Fontana Bar**, whose entertainers range from immaculate pop stylists to high-energy swing bands (Jump Jive and Wail), and the tranquil **Allegro Lounge**, with its smart decor, fine jazz combos, and a vast selection of cognacs, grappas, eaux de vie, single malts, and single batch bourbons. At New York New York, **Hamilton's** oozes sophistication, from the trompe l'oeil mural of the Manhattan skyline at night to the frosted glass windows, marbleized tables, and torch sconces. The jazz acts are first-rate, and moneyed male customers wear their dates (most in slinky black cocktail dresses) like Rolexes. Paris's stage-set Montmartre cafe, **Le Cabaret**, presents veteran chanteuse Denise Clemente and the obviously named house band, Paris Connection, who spice their sets with French-American collaborations, such as Legrand's "Windmills of Your Mind"; they also have fun singing Motown in French.

Tit-illations... Vegas strip clubs don't put as much ease in sleaze as you'd think, but they're an inevitable part of the only-in-Vegas experience. **Club Paradise** strives for class, with opaque glass, cushy sofas and armchairs with remarkably unstained upholstery, and murals of copulating couples and orgies termed "erotic art." Seating is by maître d', name cigars are available, and, if the action doesn't heat up sufficiently, you can go for the flambé dishes: Lobster Bisque (yes, it flames), Steak Diane, and Cherries Jubilee. The tab can run high, but the girls are equally high-rent, several of them "actual centerfolds" from Penthouse and Playboy. **Olympic Gardens** likewise cultivates airs: marble exteriors, arched windows, bronze Rodin lookalikes, and a lingerie shop that, however naughty, emphasizes lace over leather. No surprise it's nicknamed "Disney with tits"; the girls here are clean-cut Barbies without tattoos or piercings. Olympic Gardens crowds up quickly, with a wide range of types from suits to bikers to cyber-geeks; it even offers equal-opportunity ogling, with a ladies' section where buff long-haired men thrust their pelvises. With more than 300 dancers per evening, however, it's a bit mass-produced. *Showgirls* was researched and filmed at **Cheetahs**; don't hold that against it. The place isn't overly campy; many dancers have performed *on* the Strip, and management prides itself on the friendly vibe (how many topless bars urge their bouncers and bartenders to smile and ask how your day's been?). Couples are even encouraged. Most of the gals do gymnastic routines on the poles, tossing their long manes around like whips, playing the G-string like virtuosi. **Girls of Glitter Gulch** is a venerable downtown tourist trap (souvenir baseball caps, mugs, and T-shirts) where assertive gals strip from sequined gowns down to spangly G-strings. The immense **Palomino Club** ain't what it used to be, but it *is* the only 100 percent nude joint in town that serves alcohol. Palomino offers unique old-fashioned burlesque shows (a bride peels off her wedding dress and veil to Mendelsohn's "Wedding March", a cheerleader in red-white-and-blue spangles bumps and grinds to "I'm a Yankee Doodle Dandy"). Uniformly pretty, if slightly hard-bitten, the Palomino girls are also quite persistent; this is one of the more mercenary clubs. The similarly nude **Lil' Darlings** promotes itself as the "Pornocopia of Sex," providing everything from adult boutique (naughty nighties, flourescent condoms, even dildo candles) to private booths (dancers must remain, as one says, at least "Kinsey average length away"). The girls, who look unnervingly young, are drop-dead gorgeous; many sport tattoos and unusual piercings. But the selling point is the Fantasy Rooms, in which ladies cavort singly or in numbers, stroking, teasing, mounting, and punishing various toys. The Shower Room is just gals soaping themselves and giggling with adolescent smirkiness; it wouldn't steam up a shower stall.

Where the Rat Pack might hang out... If they were around today, Sinatra and his cronies would still be able to find suitable watering holes in today's Vegas. Everything about **Bix's**, the only true supper club around, suggests retro-chic: all dinner jackets, classic martinis, swing bands, and lipstick-smeared cigarettes, like you're strolling into a black-and-white 1940s flick about cafe society. Then there's **Hamilton's**, the luxe New York New York lounge owned by perennial pretty boy George Hamilton—Dino, Sammy, Joey, and the Chairman of the Board probably snickered at him when he was a male ingenue, but they'd have to admire his business savvy and self-irony these days. (He's not above selling T-shirts mocking his own rep as patron saint of the tanning parlor.) The MGM Grand's **Brown Derby** would be a natural for the boys, a vast club-by space (lounge plus restaurant) with mahogany paneling, recessed lighting, display cases of crystal, caricatures of the famous (many original), and photos of everyone from George Burns to John Wayne. The lounge menu includes the original restaurant's signature crab cakes, Cobb Salad, and grapefruit cake. In real life, of course, Sinatra performed his first and last shows at the Desert

Inn's quietly elegant **Starlight Lounge**, now home to David Cassidy and Don Reo's "fictional homage," *The Rat Pack is Back*.

See-and-be-scenes... House of Blues Foundation nightly hosts a glamorous international moneyed stampede to Mandalay Bay. Typical sightings include residents (Andre Agassi, Wolfgang Puck) and transients (Oscar de la Hoya, Alanis Morissette, Bruno Kirby, Naomi Campbell, Bruce Willis). Reigning over the idealized Central Park–themed New York New York casino, **Hamilton's** is a haven for well-heeled men and their mannequins. Windowside seats at the opulent **Fontana Bar**, overlooking Lake Bellagio, are coveted even by local power brokers showing off. **Drai's**, the suave Vegas outpost of Angeleno producer/restaurateur Victor Drai (who perpetrated the un-suave *Weekend at Bernie's* and *Woman in Red*), draws its share of Hollywood types, from celebrities to agents with statuesque blondes draped like accessories on their arms. Its candle-lit lounge looks as if Tarzan had redecorated the digs of his rich uncle, Lord Greystoke: overstuffed leopard skin couches and armchairs, leather-tooled books, fireplace, and enormous canvases of palm trees. The retro-Hollywood **Brown Derby** is the in spot for power martinis, buzzing with agents making deals. As for ho-hum star sightings, the faux-Egyptian dance club **Ra** chimes in with the likes of Dennis Rodman and Leo DiCaprio; just off the Strip, the always-packed **Drink and Eat Too** (co-founded by Michael Morton, younger brother of Hard Rock's Peter Morton) has hosted Matthew Perry, Jay Leno, and Charles Barkley.

Vintage Vegas... Like a time warp into the 1970s, **Champagne Café** is slightly seamy: Populated by a few old letches and chain-smoking skanks, it's straight from an indie flick without knowing it. The joint's so redolent of "old" Vegas (that red decor) that if you don't sight Elvis after one drink, there's something wrong with you. Wayne Newton, Anne Murray, and Frankie are the top choices on the juke. Entered through a blue-plate-special coffee shop on the Strip, **Fireside Lounge** is a blast from the past, with its mirrored walls and neon lights. Order the outrageous Scorpion, a flaming bowl of at least 16 spirits. Pink bubble lamps, brass swans, and black lighting make the downtown topless bar **Girls of Glitter Gulch** true retro Sin City. Just off the Strip, **Carluccio's** was owned and decorated by Liberace—need we say more? It features floor-to-ceiling mirrors, a bar shaped like a grand piano, one of his white grands, and part of a hand-carved turn-of-the-century English pub that he admired, had disassembled, and sent to Vegas.

Love shacks... Near the convention center, the premier post-college singles spot, **The Beach**, is like a living, breathing beer commercial—only the Budweiser lizards are missing. If you can't get lucky here after a long drunken horned-up evening, consult the Yellow Pages for escort services. Have a business card ready to exchange at the corporate **Gordon Biersch Brewing Company** down on Paradise Road, where live bands and decent brews draw a yupscale crowd ready to make friends. Flamingo-colored **Pink E's Fun Food and Spirits** looks like prom night on peyote, but hog riders (including yuppies) challenge gals in tight spandex at this pool emporium west of downtown. The astonishing 50-50 male-female ratio (and its chi-chi ambience, fostered by a strictly enforced dress code) makes Rio's **Club Rio** the best meet market dance club, followed by **Ra**, the Luxor's Egyptian temple of excess, where the combination of hot go-go dancers and sexy promotions virtually thrusts singles into one another's arms. Much more subdued than its New Orleans namesake, the **Bourbon Street Cabaret** at Orleans draws handsome young singles who obviously think the Big Easy refers to a one-night stand. At Caesars Palace, slightly older dancers rub against one another in the close confines of **Cleopatra's Barge** (and rub the notably bare-breasted sea nymph figurehead adorning its prow for luck). Go when sultry Singapore singer Anita Sarawale slinks through her set. On the Boulder Highway, **Rockabilly's** is the pickup joint for the Chevy pickup crowd; those with fancy footwork and well-filled Wranglers should lasso an admirer or two. The cruisiest place for gay guys and gals alike is on Paradise Road at **Angles/Lace**, with a mixed crowd, primarily clean-cut and youngish. Both sexes boast stylish buzz cuts and more bicep than is absolutely necessary.

Where to get intimate... Incongruously set in the back of a Strip coffee shop, the lush **Fireside Lounge** has the

NIGHTLIFE | THE LOWDOWN

air of a swingin' '70s bachelor pad—all that's missing are lava lamps and Teddy Pendergrass crooning on the stereo. Blue flames flicker in a pool of water, reflected in mirrored walls; deep-toned neon, brass accents, and candle chandeliers complete the picture. Sneak up to the quiet balcony of **The Nightclub** at the Las Vegas Hilton, where many amorous transactions occur amidst the streamlined Deco-ish decor. At Mandalay Bay, the warren of extravagantly decorated rooms in **House of Blues Foundation** abounds in dark corners, with sumptuous sofas where the violently beautiful and merely wealthy make out. The multiple-environment **Drink and Eat Too** likewise offers plenty of private areas, especially the duplex VIP Room, its Deco-inspired sleek velvet furnishings ideal for lounging and necking. The exotically tropical **Lagoon Saloon** at the Mirage is perfect for those me-Tarzan-you-Jane outings. Its slinky jungle-esque surroundings and sensuous singers (samba, conga, reggae, and jazz) would bring out anyone's inner tiger.

Rainbow nights... Ah, the land of pink sequins, Liberace, and lion tamers—you'd think Las Vegas would be a gay mecca. But it's actually a fairly conservative place, despite the Sin City rep—not homophobic exactly, but rather gay-indifferent. As a result, the gay/lesbian scene is lackluster; there isn't even a truly good gay-owned restaurant where you can eat, drink, and be Mary. **Gipsy** (over on Paradise Road) comes closest to feeling like a classic big-city gay bar, although the decor looks like assorted castoffs from Luxor's and Caesars'—etched glass, hanging vines, broken columns, and Greco-Roman statues. Nearby **Angles/Lace** is the classiest, most comfortable bar by far for both sexes (which isn't saying much), with a tiny mermaid fountain on the patio, highback "thrones" and ottomans, crayon caricatures of regulars, and a fireplace. The occasional midnight drag shows are fun, as is *Sanctuary*, a gothic/industrial/techno dance night usually held on Wednesdays. In the same neighborhood, the leather-and-Levis set stampedes **The Buffalo**, home to the Satyricons Motorcycle Club and Beary Hairy contests. It's really just a neigborhood hangout with bartenders, pool tables, dirty lino floors, and a trophy case with bowling and pool awards—despite the occasional biker-ish posturing, the guys are softies, talking earnestly of tattoo art. No 'tude at the Western-themed

Backstreet, beloved by cowguys and gals for its Sunday beer busts. Thursday nights are the most popular, with free line dancing lessons (best time and place for single dykes to find a partner for dosey-doing). Despite the leather trappings, black walls, and dim lighting, **Eagle** (out near the Boulder Highway), is only a little raunchy. Its Annex is ruby red (like Dorothy's slippers), with ropes, antlers, and harnesses hanging on the walls suggestively.

Wildest decor... The entrance to the **Holy Cow Brewing Company** proudly displays the Holy Cow Hooves of Fame for famous cows' prints (Bessie, Clarabell, Buttercup). Inside are cowhide columns, signs exhorting you to "Moo for a Brew," and slot machines called "Moolah." **Double Down Saloon**'s guests have included Tim Burton and Dr. Timothy Leary, who might as well have consulted on the decor—a riot of psychedelic colors, models of skeletons holding cards, murals of skulls with cherry-red lipstick, and graffiti everywhere, even on the hand-painted tables and shredded chairs. Out at Sunset Station, **Gaudi Bar** is patterned (loosely) after the famed Modernista architect's sinuous designs, with nary a straight line. Add mosaics of broken colored glass, cracked ceramics, stalactites, a fountain sprouting improbably, and a bas relief of Don Quixote—after two martinis if you stare too hard at the walls, you'd be tilting at windmills, too. In its quest to be all things to all people, **Drink and Eat Too** has not one, but five themed environments. There's a grotto-esque enclosed sunken courtyard where live acts (some names) play; the main area and dining room are all exposed pipes and hellish red lighting; the Psychedelic Room sports vivid splashes of purple, orange, yellow, and green; the Tribal Room is a "swinging" cave slung with hammocks and tribal masks; and the two-story VIP Room suggests a streamlined Deco lounge. At Mandalay Bay, **rumjungle** features a 27-foot wall of fire suspended over a moat and waterwalls lit in ever-changing colors. The lounge section has curved acrylic tables in rainbow colors, tortoise-shell maps, and huge glass orb lamps; faux furs cover S-shaped furniture carved from one enormous fallen oak.

Rooms with a view... The big daddy is the glossy **Top of the World**, which commands a 360-degree panoramic view as it slowly rotates atop the Stratosphere, 104 floors above the Strip. Champagne, cognac, and cigarette posters, hardwood tables inlaid with polished black granite, and brass lamps compete the "perfect first date" picture. The town's other high-rise view bar, **Voodoo Lounge** at the Rio, is only on the 51st floor, but in spread-out Vegas that's good enough; many singles come here to share a romantic cocktail while staring at the glittering panorama below. If the view doesn't hypnotize you, the specialty cocktails and voodoo-symbol decor will. **House of Blues Foundation** claims fab views from its terrace, theatrically framed by the giant neon Mandalay Bay and emerald green MGM signs. With enormous picture windows gazing out over the Lower Strip, **Kiefer's** doubles the romantic effect with frosted glass lamps. The picture windows of the high-profile **Fontana Bar** overlook Bellagio's faux version of Lake Como, ringed by cypress trees with impossibly romantic sparkling lights, while the fountains' water show provides a spectacle rivaling anything inside.

True brew... With its loft-like exposed pipes and track lighting, **Gordon Biersch Brewing Co.** is as much nightclub/yuppieteria as microbrewery, but it ferments some mean lager, pilsner, and Marzen. On the Strip, the **Monte Carlo Brew Pub** also sports the techno-industrial warehouse look with brick walls and huge copper vats of fermenting brew (six varieties; standouts include Jackpot Ale, High Roller Red, and Winner's Wheat). Twentysomethings enjoy prowling the overhead catwalk and the patio overlooking a grotto-esque pool. **Holy Cow Brewing Company** crafts surprisingly powerful brews, if you can overlook the bovine kitsch decor; try the Amber Gambler and Hefeweizer (shouldn't that have been "Heifer Weizer"???). The younger professional set hangs out downtown at the handsome **Triple 7 Brewpub** at Main Street Station. The look is 1930s warehouse meets Edwardian railway station; guys will dig relieving themselves on the plastic-wreathed section of the Berlin Wall in the men's room. The five microbrews seem incidental. **Sunset Brewing Company**, at Main Street's sister Sunset Station, is a less frenetic alternative, with good brews, a cigar bar, and terrific live acts ranging from Beatles covers to jazz. Boisterous **Barley's Casino & Brew Pub**, 15 minutes from the Strip in a shopping mall, serves tasty house specialties like the zesty Red Rock and Black Mountain lagers to a regular locals crowd. The draft call at **Crown and Anchor Pub**, near UNLV, is a virtual United Nations of suds, including beers from the Czech Republic, Scotland, Ireland, Germany, Jamaica, Italy, and Mexico. They even do a proper Bondian martini. The British Isles theme is a bit overdone, with nutty nautical touches, darts, Beefeater statues, and heraldic banners. Actual Brit (and Aussie and Kiwi) sightings are more likely at downtown's **Mad Dogs and Englishmen**—expect to be asked for a fag, mate, and your opinion on whose ruggers and footballers rule. Brass plates and mock-Tudor beams can't disguise the neo-punk aura. It's also a big casino dealer hangout, so buy a stickman one of the 45 beers and you might get some tips.

Martini madness... New York New York's upscale cigar bar **Hamilton's** boasts 20 martinis, including many made from flavored vodkas like tangerine and cranberry, and cocktails ranging from the Sour Apple (Midori and Amaretto) to the Lancaster (Martell l'Or cognac with a hint of Marie Brizard anisette and a twist: a mere $135). The martini heresy continues at Sunset Station's **Gaudi Bar**—15 varieties, including chocolate. The decor—a curves-everywhere phantasmagoria—is as outlandish as the designer 'tinis. At least you're on solid ground at **Martini Ranch**, the Texas Station bar where city-slick martinis are served amid longhorns, Texas cowhide, and a fake roaring fireplace. The Rio's **Martini's** is sleeker, with 35 variations. Old movie photos of stars drinking martinis (and, of course, numerous Bonds) and displays of antique shakers, glasses, and tongs make this a martini museum.

Cocktail culture... The lounge at the Italian-flavored **Terrazza Lounge**, at Caesars, provides a full grappa list and a virtual vodka primer. With its dark wood beams, stone columns, Italian tile floors, and cushy chairs, this handsome lounge overlooks Caesars' interior Court of Fountains; jazz trios play Wednesday through Sunday. The Rio's high-rise **Voodoo Lounge** is famed for flair bartenders à la Tom Cruise in *Cocktail* who juggle and throw bottles while mixing more than 40 specialty cocktails in Day-glo colors. Try the Dambala (Absolut Citron, Midori, Chambord, fruit juices). Purple chairs and tables gleam with gold sunbursts, while paintings of Haitian flags and voodoo symbols glow on dark walls. It's a great place to meet airheads of both sexes. The exotically lavish

rumjungle at the Mandalay Bay boasts the world's largest rum bar: more than 160 varieties, each bottle underlit by fiber optics, and drinks to match (or set a match to). But the cutesy **Drink and Eat Too** takes the prize. Drinks like "Sex on the Beach" and "Slippery Nipples" are served in mason jars, baby bottles, and buckets. The main room has a Sake Bar as well as a Beer Bar that sells more than 50 microbrewed and international selections; the Psychedelic Room features a Vodka Bar with various infusions and colors matching the Day-glo decor; the Tribal Room specializes in frozen concoctions; and let's not forget the kamikaze Tequila Bar, with more than 60 brands.

Country roots... Las Vegas was first a dusty Western outpost, then a mob town; today's gun slingers are corporate CEOs quick on the draw with cell phones. Still, C&W rules the airwaves and locals know how to two-step. **Gilley's Saloon, Dance Hall & Bar-B-Que** lassos both the real McCoys and folks in Neiman-Marcus Stetsons and Tony Lama boots. You can ride a mechanical bull ($5 for 10 seconds) but you're projected onto big screens so everyone can see what an idiot you look like. **Rockabilly's** boasts the most energetic two-steppers, most eclectic crowd, and kindest free line-dancing lessons for rookies on its 2,000-square-foot dance floor. Genuine ranchers two-step over to the Sam's Town lounge **Roxy's Saloon** for its fun murals of boom-town dance hall girls, live C&W bands, and exuberant happy hours. Also on the property is the **Western Dance Hall**, a big barn filled with C&W memorabilia where aficionados practice intricate line dancing. There are free nightly line-dancing lessons, but remember, this is the big leagues. **Gold Coast Dance Hall**, in the casino-hotel of the same name, ropes in the older cowpokes, who two-step and swing fluidly around an oval floor nearly as large as a trailer park, often teaching the grandkids on Big Band nights. Down-home **Backstreet** is where gay and lesbian cowpokes strut their stuff. As one bartender chirped merrily, "You can't keep a gay hoedown."

Sports bars... **Final Score Sports Bar**, out at Sam's Town, is a paean to jockdom. Pennants hang everywhere, along with jockeys' racing stripes and autographed photos of boxers, rodeo wranglers, tennis players, and ballplayers. In addition to the expected (pool, darts, air hockey), there's a free-throw cage, a regulation-size basketball court, and even a volleyball pit. **Barley's Casino & Brew Pub** is a preferred hangout for the after-work crowd to egg on their favorite passers and hurlers while downing pitchers of the cheap cold stuff. At throwback Italian restaurant **Piero's**, the UNLV Room is a haven of sports memorabilia (a sign reads Tarkanian Way, after the NCAA-winning ex-Running Rebel basketball coach, one of Tark's sweat-stained towels, and photos autographed by UNLV alumni like Knick Larry Johnson). Topless **Cheetahs,** a favorite with athletes, is so eager to please, there are several TVs so you can check up on your favorite sports teams—and many men do, between, um, innings.

For slackers, Goths, and nihilists... Retro **Café Copioh** caters to the pierced and goateed goth crowd, alongside disaffected philosophy majors and hygienically questionable Euro-wannabes. It features garage-sale chairs with springs popping out and bold rotating artworks, shrouded in a haze of unfiltered Camels. Mocha slushies, fruit smoothies, and pizza bagels fuel poetry readings, open mike ramblings, a Wiccan fortune teller, the occasional live band (including good jazz and blues combos), and satiric comedy skits. Black is de rigueur for **Club Utopia**, along with militia-style club gear, odd dye jobs, piercings in creative places, and Doc Martens. All wear the requisite alienated look, even when they dance. The local dive **Double Down Saloon** is a Paradise Road haven for nonconformists of all types, from sallow cadaverous punks with vermilion hair to spiffy yup-scale types to tattooed burly bikers and their babes. Downtown, the **Enigma Café** clientele crosses slackers with hepcats. Anything (and anyone) goes, wearing anything from thrift-shop chic to multi-hued dashikis. Spoken word and open mike evenings are on tap; several Wednesdays, the garden is given over to obscure movies, which could range from Ed Wood howlers to Italian neo-realist masterpieces. The quintessential hangout **Mermaid Café** is a vividly colored room (mostly in turquoise) filled with hanging plants, paintings, pottery, and lots of comfy couches and throw pillows. There's always something going on, from Monday poetry and palm readings to Friday tarot readings and massages, along with whatever musical act is up.

Frat parties... Like a (slightly) more mature version of MTV Spring Break, **The Beach** greets you at the entrance with stainless steel vats filled with brewskis on ice and neon-bikinied gals offering "a cold one." It's wave upon wave of bodacious babes and pumped-up bros wearing trash-talking T-shirts ("You like that move? So does your girl."). The snarky, smart-ass **Tom & Jerry's** feels like "The Real World" goes out on the town. Rated one of the country's top 100 college bars by *Playboy*, it certainly looks the part, with several dingy if intriguingly decorated rooms—glow-in-the-dark alien paintings, a UNLV sports mural—and an excellent juke, from Alanis to B.B. King to the Clash. As if liberal daily happy hours, drink specials, and ultra-cheap beer weren't enough of a draw, there's also nightly entertainment. The fantasy and shower rooms at **Lil' Darlings** nudie bar draw plenty of local twentysomething bachelors; you could even run into an enthusiastic contingent of gangly college freshmen cheering on the proceedings as if it were a Running Rebels game.

For twentysomethings... Just off the Strip, **The Beach** is an arrested adolescent's wet dream: two vast floors of bars, pool tables, foosball, darts, video games (and poker), pinball, pizza stands, tarot readers, and more than 80 TVs tuned to everything from dirt biking on ESPN to "Loveline" on MTV. At the Monte Carlo, the **Monte Carlo Brew Pub** appeals to every taste: There's a mini-disco with violently strobing lights and live bands; dueling pianos with audience participation; a humidor to satisfy cigar cravings; and 40 TV monitors, some playing videos, others tuned to sporting events. **Baby's** at the Hard Rock has the three requisites for a trendy nightclub: space-age laser shows, frenetically strobing videos, and great dance mix for the party-hearty crowd. Several cozy rooms, each painted in different lipstick colors, are provided for those who wish to get more intimate. Its closest voguish rival, **Club Mojo** at House of Blues in Mandalay Bay, spins righteous house, techno, and funk, offering other late-night lures like go-go dancers, Jäger shots, and the "gyrating decadence of bodies in motion." The soulful, artier crowd hangs out in the UNLV area at **Café Espresso Roma**, which superficially seems unremarkable: huge hand-painted tiles, indifferent student artworks, and equally indifferent biscotti. But the poetry and live music acts are usually enterprising. A camp vision in pink, **Pink E's Fun Food and Spirits**, west of the downtown, draws a local crowd of rocker-wannabes and pool sharks.

For thirtysomethings... The smart set in town hangs out at **Bix's**, enjoying the swing resurgence. This supper club serves admirable nouveau continental food, but draws more people for its sensational swing evenings (Big Band Thursdays), and jazzy dance bands that evoke the Lester Lanin days. Romantically minded trust-fund pretties congregate at the Bellagio's **Fontana Bar** with its brocade booths, plush high-backed shell-patterned chairs, and tiny flickering lamps. At Paris, **Le Cabaret** almost recaptures the feel of a snazzy Left Bank club: the sultry singing sizzles even if the clientele doesn't generate enough smoke. **The Hop**, off the Strip on Tropicana Avenue, is quietly cool, with an intensely danceable R&B mix, occasional Latin and Swing nights, and plenty of plush velvet booths and chairs.

For fortysomethings... Any place catering to sexy twentysomethings attracts a fair share of fortysomethings (guess which gender), and **The Beach** is no exception. Its Spring-Break beer-blast ambiance draws plenty of conventioneers hoping to get lucky: It *is* on Convention Center Drive. A fine-dining spot on the lower Strip, **Kiefer's** does a brisk business with lithe golf-tanned surgeons and portfolio managers displaying their trophy second wives. **Palace Court** at Caesars Palace is a swellegant piano spot whose loyal patrons range from local widderladies to fey dancers between shows. Perfectly mixed cocktails come from an elegant bar with a retractable stained-glass mural, and there's an oak dance floor for touch-dancing. Bellagio's **Allegro Lounge** is a haven where the performers never seem to play anything composed after 1960 and corporate honchos discourse knowledgeably on the peatiness of Islay single malts.

Where locals hang out... If you lived in Vegas, you wouldn't want to party with conventioneers—you'd want to hang in spots the tourists never find. Like the **Double Down Saloon**, a Paradise Road spot where prominent signs read "You puke, you clean" and "Puke Insurance $20"; psychedelic designs and salacious paintings daub the walls; and customers avail themselves of pool tables, condom machines, live bands, and a sublime jukebox that features Tony Bennett to Frank Zappa, Billie Holiday to the Vandals. Videos range from 1940s Buck Rogers serials to midget porn. The house specialty (a jealously guarded secret recipe) is affectionately dubbed "Ass Juice." How could it not be a cherished institution? Arty folk zen out downtown at **Enigma Café**, a no-alcohol haven where you can mellow out—or revivify—on fresh herbal infusions and smoothies. The whole place is regarded as an artwork, from the painted tables to the rotating art exhibits to murals of Bengal tigers and Hindu princesses to the found objects (aka junk) scattered throughout the exquisite garden courtyard. On the west side of town, **Pink E's Fun Food and Spirits** lures a hip "I don't care if I'm hip" crowd, who like the tongue-in-cheek pink decor, plentiful pool tables (more than 50), and rocking bands with names like Sea Monkeys. Locals have nicknamed Cook E. Jar "the head cheese" for his polyester-bedecked lounge singer act at **The Tap House**, off the Strip. He does a wicked parody of Bill Murray's "SNL" lounge lizard parody. **Boston Grill and Bar** in north Vegas is the preeminent place for local bands and draws an enthusiastic, mixed crowd nightly. The **Railhead Saloon** at Boulder Station delivers a sterling selection of almost-has-beens (John Cafferty, Clarence Clemons, Merle Haggard, Jose Feliciano, Gato Barbieri) might-bes, and celebrity vanity acts (Dogstar with Keanu Reeves) for reasonable prices. Cozy is a charitable word for the size of the room. Heading out toward Henderson, **Barley's Casino & Brew Pub** offers something for everyone: great prices for tall cold draft beers; decent pub grub; a fair selection of cigars; low-key low-stakes gambling; pool; and plenty of TVs turned to athletic pursuits. No wonder it's usually crammed with youngish partying patrons.

Cigars, cigarettes... Baby boomers and baby capitalists practice one Upmann-ship at **Hamilton's** in New York New York. In addition to the usual culprits (Dunhill, Macanudo, Davidoff, Romeo y Julietas), smokers can savor owner George Hamilton's own "house blends," created by Upmann. In keeping with its retro-swank rep, **Bix's** offers more than 50 premium brands and a walk-in humidor where you can sniff and twirl to your heart's content. The duplex **Caviarteria,** incongruously snuggled into the Forum Shops at Caesars, offers the big three Cs: caviar, champagne, and cigars. The upstairs martini bar/cigar lounge has track lighting, faux Cubist artworks, slate-blue chairs and banquettes that look more inviting than they are comfortable, and an excellent selection highlighting Upmanns and Montecristos. Among its many themed rooms, the VIP Room at **Drink and Eat Too** caters to corporate climbers with a rotating eight-foot-tall humidor, where you'll find guys comparing the length and thickness of their stogies.

The piano man... The best pianist in town, David Osborne holds forth at **Palace Court**, at Caesars Palace, Thursdays through Mondays; a consummately elegant Bobby Short in the making, he has played for three presidents (Carter, Bush, and Clinton). Phyllis McGuire of the McGuire Sisters (and fabled mobster Sam Giancana's gal pal in the '60s) sometimes holds court here too; she can still curl her vocal cords around a song. The nimble pianists at **Kiefer's** run the gamut of soppy pop ballads from 1920 to the present, upping this lower-Strip restaurant lounge's romantic ante. Another vista venue, the suave **Top of the World** at the Stratosphere, presents the smooth-as-silk Bobby Dickerson at the keyboard. The piano bar at the classic Italian restaurant **Piero's** is bizarre, with zebra carpeting, beige banquettes, bonzai trees, monkey lamps, and paintings of apes reflecting the owner's African obsession. New York New York's **Bar at Times Square** offers NYPD (New York Piano Duo), a majestically silly act that would never fly in the real Times Square. Musical teams on duelling pianos face off with slightly off-color shticks and rousing singalongs to tunes such as "American Pie," "Piano Man," and "Copacabana." They've got the NYC bar look all right—mirrored bar, hardwood floors, ceiling fans, brass accents, black-and-white photos of New York scenes—but the feel is sanitized and Disneyfied. (If only they could have resisted the big red apples dangling everywhere.) Still, it's packed with tourists from crew-cut military cadets to blue-haired retirees.

Jazzin' it up... The Desert Inn's **Starlight Lounge** recalls classier days, with gold or striped booths, picture windows open to the illuminated pool, and Milton Greene photos of Marilyn. The performers, ranging from cabaret greats to the zoot-suited Kid Creole and the Coconuts to the current

NIGHTLIFE | THE LOWDOWN

show, *The Rat Pack is Back*, are a strong draw. The house band at Paris's **Très Jazz**, an Art Deco–style Caribbean restaurant run by the owners of the Black Entertainment Television cable network, is headed by Kendall Lewis (son of famed jazz pianist Ramsey Lewis); Lewis *père* and friends like Nancy Wilson join onstage occasionally. The Rio's atmospheric **Voodoo Lounge** distracts jazz lovers from the high-rise view with the classy funk of Ghalib Ghallab's jazz band, running from "Tiny Bubbles" to "Sittin' on the Dock of the Bay"—as done by Herbie Hancock, Al Jarreau, or Stevie Wonder. **Allegro Lounge** at Bellagio features jazz trios playing everything from Porter to pop; they sooth the clatter and clang of the casino. Out at Sunset Station, the laid-back **Sunset Brewing Company** features the excellent Rocco Barbato with Steven Lee and No Fear Wednesdays through Saturdays. Bobby Barrett does his uncanny Sinatra imitations Mondays at **North Beach Café**, on the west side of town; on weekends, slinky silky local combos play for a few hours, slithering through everything from Astrud Gilberto to Edith Piaf in four languages. Bobby Barrett also performs his Sinatra shtick at the MGM Grand's retro Hollywood **Brown Derby** lounge; the rest of the week there, Larry White croons songs by Porter, Rodgers and Hart, and the other Broadway greats, along with Rat Pack classics. (Pssst...Tom Jones sometimes sings here when he's playing the hotel.) **Bourbon Street Cabaret** at the Orleans offers the Royal Dixie Jazz Band and other top-notch acts in a setting that feels like one of the quieter, more romantic French Quarter night spots. Along with the inevitable Mardi Gras masks, baby and grand pianos hang from the ceilings. Sundays through Tuesdays at New York New York, the plush cigar bar **Hamilton's** showcases the satiny stylings of former Billboard Jazz Artist Award winner James Dixon, whose sound recalls the era when the Duke, the Count, and Lionel were in full swing. Dixon and his trio split the week with the more contemporary Split Decision, led by accomplished guitarist and George Benson–clone Ronnie Rathers.

Singing a blues streak... Off the Strip, the **Sand Dollar Blues Lounge** is smokier than *EFX*, but here at least there's fire: blazing blues (and the occasional Dixieland and Zydeco) sessions by the Ruffnecks (Wednesdays), house band John Earl's 1999 Boogie Man

Band (Thursdays through Saturdays), Faultline (Sundays), Al Ek & All-Star Band (Mondays), and Jimmy Mack Blues Attack (Tuesdays). The knowledgeable crowd ranges from bikers to corporate types. If you can get past the psychedelic-haunted-house decor, locals hangout the **Double Down Saloon** is another hip blues venue, with veteran band Blue Cherry and Friends wailing on Wednesdays.

Where to hear local bands... The local music scene is surprisingly varied, with several up-and-coming bands making the rounds of the leading local venues. As you might expect in cynical Las Vegas, even the melodic pop bands have an edge. Grubby, bare-bones **Boston Grill & Bar** is hardly Cheers, but that's what makes it a prime rock venue. It presents the best mix of acts, from punk to ska to blues; nearly every major local act has paid its dues here. Alas, the sound mix is muddy and the music over-amped. But hardcore music aficionados cheerfully accept its liabilities for the sake of great bookings. Off-the-beaten-path **Legends Lounge** bills itself somewhat ostentatiously as the "premier jam-band club in the west," running the scales from bluegrass to blues. It hosts numerous CD release parties and anything Grateful Dead–related (the owner is a deadhead; Jerry Garcia ties dangle from the walls, and the Dead and Phish play on a loop). The frat-rat hangout **Tom & Jerry's** brings in one-night and regular stands, like Prince cover band Purple Reign, hard rockers Brass Monkey and Mother Ship, and Acoustic Asylum evenings. Where else would there be special tribute nights to the Beastie Boys? Near UNLV, **Café Espresso Roma** remains folk central, with such fine musicians as Steve McCoy and Martin Melancon getting back to their grassroots. The other preeminent folkie hangout is **Enigma Café** downtown, whose weekend performances range from acoustic to zither, with some nationally renowned artists like Danielle Howle dropping by to gig. Texas Station's **Martini Ranch** also books bluesy acts weekends in a space so comfy you can pretend you're home on the range. The **Mermaid Café** roster is heavy on acoustic, blues, and improvisational jazz, but can also run toward sitar and gamelan concerts. In the wee hours, gothic **Club Utopia** often hosts mega-rave bands like Electric Skychurch and the homegrown techno-rave duo Crystal Method (if you don't get the pun, you don't belong at Club Utopia).

NIGHTLIFE | THE LOWDOWN

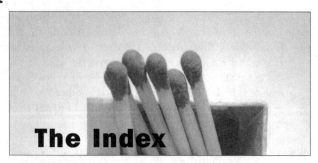

The Index

Bix's. Cool thirtysomethings swing at this sensational supper club throwback.... *Tel 702/889-0800. 4495 S. Buffalo Dr.*
(see pp. 177, 187, 188)

Boston Grill and Bar. Blah decor and lousy acoustics, but it's a top showcase for local bands.... *Tel 702/368-0750. 3411 S. Jones Blvd.* **(see p. 188, 191)**

Bourbon Street Cabaret. Lovingly recreated N'Awlins ambience, with top-notch Jazz.... *Tel 702/365-7111. Orleans, 4500 W. Tropicana Ave.* **(see pp. 179, 190)**

Brown Derby. Vegas goes '50s Hollywood: Forget the tired restaurant and enjoy the lounge's mellow music and energetic buzz.... *Tel 702/891-1111. MGM Grand, 3799 Las Vegas Blvd. S.* **(see pp. 177, 178, 190)**

The Buffalo. There's very little leather posturing in this gay hangout, despite the rough-and-tumble look, just friendly hirsute men shootin' pool and the breeze.... *Tel 702/733-8355. 4640 Paradise Rd.* **(see p. 180)**

Café Copioh. Goth crowd hangout with some pretty intriguing music and poetry nights.... *Tel 702/739-0305. 4550 S. Maryland Pkwy.* **(see p. 185)**

Café Espresso Roma. Youthful crowd, not too edgy, with excellent folk acts.... *Tel 702/369-1540. 4440 S. Maryland Parkway.* **(see pp. 186, 191)**

Carluccio's. This gaudy restaurant, once owned by Liberace, is an over-the-top trip.... *Tel 702/795–3236. Liberace Plaza, 1775 E. Tropicana Ave.* **(see p. 179)**

Casbar Lounge. Old Vegas and deliciously tacky.... *Tel 702/737-2111. The Sahara, 2535 Las Vegas Blvd. S.*
(see p. 174)

Caviarteria. A civilized respite amid the Forum Shops frenzy.... *Tel 702/792-8560. Forum Shops at Caesars, 3500 Las Vegas Blvd. S.* **(see p. 188)**

Champagne Café. Classic 1970s Vegas where folks drink house liquor and scarf down free buffets.... *Tel 702/737-1699. 3557 S. Maryland Parkway.* **(see p. 178)**

Cheetahs. Except for the pole-humping, this genial place feels more like a Gen X keg-party than a topless bar.... *Tel 702/384-0074. 2112 Western Ave.* **(see pp. 175, 186)**

Cleopatra's Barge. This barge replica defines watering hole, since it sits in five feet of water. Great live acts and fun-loving singles.... *Tel 702/731-7110. Caesars Palace, 3570 Las Vegas Blvd. S.* **(see pp. 175, 179)**

Club Mojo. That rare Vegas night spot that would score coolness points anywhere.... *Tel 702/632-7600. House of Blues, Mandalay Bay, 3950 Las Vegas Blvd. S.* **(see pp. 173, 174, 186)**

Club Paradise. The place for Penthouse-petting and pampering; just make sure your wallet bulges more prominently than anything else.... *Tel 702/734-7990. 4416 Paradise Rd.* **(see p. 176)**

Club Rio. A smart set gathers here for its elegant ambience, superb sound system, lookers, theme nights, and middle-of-the-road dance music.... *Tel 702/252-7777. The Rio, 3700 W. Flamingo Rd. Closed Sun–Tue.* **(see pp. 172, 173, 179)**

Club Utopia. Arguably the one truly cutting-edge club in town, a nonstop rave with eclectic music and oh-so-watchable clientele.... *Tel 702/390-4650. 3765 Las Vegas Blvd. S. Closed Sun–Tue.* **(see pp. 172, 174, 185, 191)**

Crown and Anchor Pub. The best variety of on-tap beers, ales, and stouts in town. Occasional live music and easygoing clientele are pluses.... *Tel 702/739-0281. 1350 E. Tropicana Ave.* **(see p. 183)**

Double Down Saloon. Hip and trippy, with lubricious murals and videos, but kickass jukebox and colorful clientele.... *Tel 702/791-5775. 4640 Paradise Rd.* **(see pp. 181, 185, 187, 191)**

Drai's. A sybaritic delight, designed for sipping the perfect martini to jazz accompaniment.... *Tel 702/737-7111. Barbary Coast, 3595 Las Vegas Blvd. S.* **(see p. 178)**

Drink and Eat Too. Model wannabes and rising junior execs

party in a themed rooms, each playing different music.... *Tel 702/796-5519. 200 E. Harmon Ave.*
(see pp. 173, 174, 178, 180, 181, 184, 189)

Eagle. Real leather queens would snicker at this gay bar's harmless attempt; still, it's your best raunchy bet.... *Tel 702/458-8662. 3430 E. Tropicana Ave.* **(see p. 181)**

Enigma Café. The beat days are revived for a bohunk bohemian crowd in art-filled, no-alcohol hangout.... *Tel 702/389-0999. 2 S. 4th St.* **(see pp. 185, 188, 191)**

Final Score Sports Bar. For those who like to watch or play sports.... *Tel 702/456-7777. Sam's Town, 5111 Boulder Hwy.* **(see p. 184)**

Fireside Lounge. Plush '70s decor makes this makeout joint a trip.... *Tel 702/735-7635. Peppermill Inn, 2985 Las Vegas Blvd. S.* **(see pp. 178, 179)**

Fontana Bar. A sophisticated urban-chic cabaret, albeit in ritzy Sin City style.... *Tel 702/693-7111. Bellagio, 3600 Las Vegas Blvd. S.* **(see pp. 175, 178, 182, 187)**

Gaudi Bar. Outrageous decor patterned after the trippy, curvy work of the famed Modernista architect. Good martinis, too.... *Tel 702/547-7777. Sunset Station, 1301 W. Sunset Rd.* **(see pp. 181, 183)**

Gilley's Saloon, Dance Hall & Bar-B-Que. Raucous Texas import for live country music and other cowboy pursuits.... *Tel 702/794-8330. The New Frontier, 3120 Las Vegas Blvd. S. Closed Mon.* **(see pp. 175, 184)**

Gipsy. Jungle ruins decor and snooty gay clientele; dance mixes and special events are torrid.... *Tel 702/731-1919. 4605 Paradise Rd.* **(see pp. 174, 180)**

Girls of Glitter Gulch. A lot of hustling, but the place and drink prices seem unchanged since the 1970s.... *Tel 702/385-4774. 20 E. Fremont St.* **(see pp. 176, 179)**

Gold Coast Dance Hall. Themed music nights, from big band to C&W, lure an older crowd for dancing.... *Tel 702/367-7111. Gold Coast, 4000 W. Flamingo Rd.* **(see p. 184)**

NIGHTLIFE | THE INDEX

Gordon Biersch Brewing Co. This fashionable microbewery is the premier yupster pick-up joint.... *Tel 702/312-5247. 3987 Paradise Rd.* **(see pp. 174, 179, 182)**

Hamilton's. A stunning venue for puffing cigars, sipping single malts, and listening to jazz.... *Tel 702/740-6900. New York New York, 3790 Las Vegas Blvd. S.* **(see pp. 175, 177, 178, 183, 188, 190)**

Holy Cow Brewing Company. The beer (despite several awards) is secondary to singles mingling and video poker addictions.... *Tel 702/732-COWS (2697). 2423 Las Vegas Blvd. S.* **(see pp. 181, 182)**

The Hop. Popular, plush mid-size club catering to white-bread R&B and swing lovers.... *Tel 702/310-5060. 1650 E. Tropicana Ave.* **(see p. 187)**

House of Blues Foundation. You must be gorgeous, famous, or fabulously rich (well-connected will do) to gain admittance to this breathtaking watering hole.... *Tel 702/692-7777. Mandalay Bay, 3950 Las Vegas Blvd. S.* **(see pp. 175, 178, 180, 182)**

Kiefer's. Romantic setting with sensational Strip views and pianists who set the right mood.... *Tel 702/739-8000. Carriage House, 105 E. Harmon Ave.* **(see pp. 182, 187, 189)**

La Playa Lounge. Raucous, riotous beach-themed lounge.... *Tel 702/369-5000. Harrah's, 3475 Las Vegas Blvd. S.* **(see p. 175)**

Lagoon Saloon. An actual slice of rain forest amid the casino's hubbub, with top acts.... *Tel 702/791-7111. Mirage, 3400 Las Vegas Blvd. S.* **(see pp. 175, 180)**

Le Cabaret. Ooh la la: an intimate bar where you expect the chanteuse to wear a feather boa.... *Tel 702/967–4111. Paris, 3655 Las Vegas Blvd. S.* **(see pp. 176, 187)**

Legends Lounge. Out of the way, but showcases the best new local bands; unofficial home to out-of-town Deadheads.... *Tel 702/437-9674. 865 N. Lamb Blvd.* **(see p. 191)**

Lil' Darlings. Lissome girls pick their own music and create interpretive dances at this all-nude club.... *Tel 702/366-1633. 1514 Western Ave.* **(see pp. 177, 186)**

Mad Dogs and Englishmen. Gathering spot for yobbo Brits, along with a motley crew of locals.... *Tel 702/382-5075. 515 Las Vegas Blvd. S.* **(see pp. 183)**

Martini Ranch. Texas Station has several fine bars devoted to specific cocktails (Crazy Mary's for bloodys, Laredo Cantina for margaritas), but this is the best.... *Tel 702/631-1000. Texas Station, 2101 Texas Star Lane.* **(see pp. 183, 191)**

Martini's. Not just a bar, but a virtual shrine to the designer martini.... *Tel 702/252-7777. The Rio, 3700 W. Flamingo Rd.* **(see p. 183)**

Mermaid Café. Wide-ranging crowd, decor, music, at this wonderfully entertaining little spot.... *Tel 702/240-6002. 2910 Lake East Dr.* **(see pp. 185, 191)**

Monte Carlo Brew Pub. Good-looking space with youngish crowd, tasty brews and eats, and fine dance music.... *Tel 702/730-7420. Monte Carlo, 3770 Las Vegas Blvd. S.* **(see pp. 174, 182, 186)**

The Nightclub. Urbane little night spot with superb acts and a nice-looking bunch of traveling business types.... *Tel 702/732-5111. Las Vegas Hilton, 3000 Paradise Rd. Closed Mon–Wed.* **(see pp. 173, 180)**

North Beach Café. Upmarket California-style eatery featuring excellent jazz.... *Tel 702/247-9530. 2605 S. Decatur Blvd.* **(see p. 190)**

Olympic Gardens. The only spot where both men and women get a chance to ogle strippers.... *Tel 702/385-8987. 1531 Las Vegas Blvd. S.* **(see p. 176)**

Palace Court. Celeb pianist David Osborne works this luxe gourmet restaurant lounge.... *Tel 702/731-7110. Caesars Palace, 3570 Las Vegas Blvd. S.* **(see pp. 187, 189)**

Palomino Club. This once high-class outfit has become seedy,

(and dirty).... *Tel 702/891-7254. MGM Grand, 3799 Las Vegas Blvd. S.* **(see p. 173)**

Sunset Brewing Company. Terrific place to kick back, sample some home brew, and listen to live jazz or '60s pop.... *Tel 702/547-7777. Sunset Station, 1301 W. Sunset Road, Henderson.* **(see pp. 182, 190)**

The Tap House. A beloved local dive. Performer Cook E. Jarr can make you laugh so hard you'll cry.... *Tel 702/870–2111. 5589 W. Charleston Blvd.* **(see p. 188)**

Terrazza Lounge. One of the most refined, tranquil spots in town for martinis and music.... *Tel 702/731–7110. Caesars Palace, 3570 Las Vegas Blvd. S.* **(see p. 183)**

Tom & Jerry's. The quintessential college haunt, with cheap eats and beer, ultra-cool jukebox, and rocking live bands.... *Tel 702/736-8550. 4550 S. Maryland Pkwy.* **(see pp. 186, 191)**

Top of the World. This rotating lounge/restaurant, replete with jaw-dropping views, pianist, and single malts, is the classiest pickup joint in Las Vegas.... *Tel 702/380-7711 or 702/383–7711. Stratosphere, 2000 Las Vegas Blvd. S.* **(see pp. 181, 189)**

Très Jazz. This restaurant aims to replicate the Josephine Baker Paris of the 1920s; the house band alone more than lives up to the name.... *Tel 702/967–4111. Paris, 3655 Las Vegas Blvd. S. No music Sun, Mon.* **(see p. 190)**

Triple 7 Brewpub. Downtown hangout with admirable brews and live entertainment.... *Tel 702/387-1896. Main Street Station. 200 N. Main St.* **(see p. 182)**

Voodoo Lounge. Sensational views, marvelous house band, specialty cocktails, funky decor, and playful bartenders equals one hot spot.... *Tel 702/252-7777. The Rio, 3700 W. Flamingo Rd.* **(see pp. 182, 183, 190)**

Western Dance Hall. You'd better know your Mel Tillis from your George Jones if you hope to break your boots in at this country hangout.... *Tel 702/456-7777. 5111 Boulder Hwy.* **(see p. 184)**

enterta

7

inment

High-stepping
gams, jutting
breasts, sequins,
feathers,
rhinestones, and of
course incandescent
stars—

for five decades the statuesque showgirl and the headliner strutted arm-in-arm across the Las Vegas stage. Flashy, fleshy production shows still exist, as well as ever more inventive extravaganzas that often out-"Strip" the name acts. But with competition from so many free attractions—animatronic statues, dancing colored fountains, belching volcanoes, pirate battles—Las Vegas productions have become increasingly high-tech (and high-priced). Sure, Elvis or Sinatra might sell out (pending sightings), but with so many options, audiences are fickle and picky. Las Vegas could never again be Wayne's world, for which we give a hearty "danke schoen, darlin', danke schoen."

The scene runs the gamut: headliners, Broadway musical imports (and knockoffs), comedians, magicians, impression-ists, trash-talking boxers, and acrobats who paint surreal kinetic pictures. You also have your choice of various profes-sional and collegiate sporting events, from baseball to hockey (both ice and roller varieties), as well as actual performing arts like theater, ballet, and even film revivals. Rather than playing front acts in football stadiums, the cutting-edge musicians now sell out smaller venues like **The Joint** at the Hard Rock Hotel and **House of Blues** that appeal to the coveted 21-to-39 demographic. The newer stylish casinos strive for more than just a veneer of class by booking the Luciano Pavarottis, Andrea Bocellis, and Michael Feinsteins. Incidentally, Feinstein (an impeccable show-tune pianist, sort of Harry Connick Jr. without the muscles or voice) fled his Bellagio gig because, rumor has it, people chattered incessantly during his act—proof that Las Vegas isn't necessarily attracting a more cultured crowd, merely a slightly more affluent one.

Locals, however, have become savvier and more sophisti-cated, helping the Las Vegas cultural scene shed its rep as an atomic desert wasteland. The theater and dance companies don't glow in the dark, but they do provide a viable, cheaper, less touristy alternative to the big SRO acts, which lends added credence to that boastful booster moniker, "The Entertainment Capital of the World."

Sources

Front desks, hotel room coffee tables, brochure racks, bars, even taxis practically flaunt free publications, including *Today in Las Vegas*, *Showbiz Weekly*, *24/7*, *Vegas Visitor*, *Enter-tainment Today*, *Las Vegas Today*, *Today in Las Vegas*, and *What's On*. Peddling every act, from hyped headliner to toe-tapping spectacular to stomach-churning lounge lizard, most list venues, prices, and show times, while featuring unreliable "reviews" and gushy celebrity profiles. Many freebie rags include coupons (as do individual casino fun books and even the local Yellow Pages, which also shows seating guides for the large arenas) entitling the bearer to discounts, two-for-one deals, inexpensive dinner tack-ons, even free admittance with a drink purchase.

Local newspapers, such as *Las Vegas Weekly*, *City Life*, and the *Las Vegas Review Journal*, likewise offer complete listings. The first two want to be taken seriously as "alt" publications, but they're simply alternatives to the latter's mainstream Neon section, which is must-reading for its pandering but complete coverage. The **Allied Arts Council** (tel 702/731-5419) is a fine source for cultural activity off the Strip. You can also contact the **Las Vegas Convention and Visitors Authority** (tel 702/892-0711) and request the latest edition of its "Showguide" pamphlet before your trip.

Remember that when productions go on the occasional brief hiatus, the showroom hosts big acts. When magician Lance Burton vanishes for a week from the Monte Carlo, Paul Rodriguez appears in his place; Liza Minnelli, Andrew Dice Clay, or Hall and Oates flesh out the schedule when **Bally's'** flesh-tacular *Jubilee* needs its sequins buffed; Jay Leno spells *EFX* at the **MGM Grand**; and so on.

Getting Tickets

Order tickets to the hot shows as soon as you know your dates; weekends and holiday seats are the hardest to obtain. Many acts sell out months in advance, especially during major convention and event periods. You're best off buying tickets in person at the casinos and other performing arts/sports venues, eliminating the phone surcharge and enabling you to check seat location. **TicketMaster** (tel 702/474-4000) and **AllState Ticketing** (tel 702/597-5970) also sell seats to many productions in advance.

If you haven't planned ahead, know that several major productions do release seats—usually cancellations—in the morning on the day of performance: perfect timing for most bleary-eyed night crawlers. Or you can brave the lines for seats belonging to no-show ticketholders; these often snake for a city block, moving more slowly than rush hour traffic on the Strip. For premier shows like "*O*." get there at least three hours prior to the performance.

Showrooms vary in size and layout. The newest are state-of-the-art and comfortable, with fine sight lines and acoustics. Most major showrooms have several tiers, including regular theater-style seating (occasionally raked) and VIP banquettes or tables. For assigned-seating shows, try to finagle center-stage second- or third-level perches. For general admission shows, line up at least half an hour to an hour before the performance to get better seats.

Although reserved ticketing has become the norm, the greased palm remains a cherished institution; $20 is the going rate for an upgrade in top showrooms. There's an art to bribing: Fold the bill into quarters and quickly shake the maître d's hand. He'll palm the "tip" like a card while surreptitiously checking the denomination. Casino chips are equally acceptable (but use just one—the sound of chips clicking against each other is too blatant).

Ticket prices range from $10 to $100, depending on the act; a dozen or so splashy shows go over the $50 mark, but most are in the $25 to $40 range (which sometimes includes dinner). Prices remain the same for all show times (though some fleshier spectacles may only go topless during the later performance). Most tickets include one or two drinks, but always double check. Be aware that there are several decent, low-priced daytime shows that cater primarily to families and senior groups. Nearly all non-casino arts companies (theater, music, dance) run $10-40 and have irregular schedules and venues. Some casino showrooms (and performing arts centers) book entertainers for limited runs. Other showroom headliners (or revues) run indefinitely, though performers may bop between venues as they become more famous—just like social or corporate ladder-climbing.

But in 1999, three long running shows closed: Luxor's Imagine (replaced indefinitely by Blue Man Group), Harrah's Spellbound (now an open run by Clint Holmes), and Stardust's Enter the Night (welcoming back Mr. Las Vegas, Wayne Newton, who signed a 10-year contract at $25 million per—"Danke Schoen," indeed!—for 40 weeks annually).

The Lowdown

What money does for the imagination... Some shows are so sumptuous, you don't mind that their budgets probably exceeded the GNP of an emerging nation.

The aquatic extravaganza called *"O"* occupies a specially designed $70 million theater at the Bellagio (the production itself cost another $20 million). The pool is 25 feet at its deepest, 150 feet at its longest, and 100 feet at its widest, holding 1.5 million gallons, with seven underwater lifts and numerous contraptions to adjust the pool's size. The skeleton of a ship becomes a giant trapeze; walls form tangled mangrove swamps; the pool turns into fire; lunar modules crawl like crustaceans. Imagine an Esther Williams flick crossed with *Blade Runner*. At the MGM Grand, *EFX* offers flying saucers, animatronic aliens, fire-breathing dragons, and rumbling earthquakes (Sensurround Plus!!!). An incredible 3-D movie of time travel enlivens the H.G. Wells sequence: Music notes explode, planes zoom through clouds, and a sea monster devours the room. The lavish sets and costumes recall *The Wizard of Oz*, *Lord of the Rings*, and "The X-Files" all at the same time. The barrage of mystical, supernatural, and religious elements in *Mystère*, the acrobatic stage spectacle at Treasure Island, creates an effect more sensuous than any flesh show. It starts with a "Big Bang," symbolizing early man embarking on a never-ending journey; primitives banging on Japanese Taiko drums coexist with Renaissance archangels, alien masks, and spinning flying saucers. Acrobats balance on cubes, pyramids, and trapezoids, while colors and shapes shift subtly throughout. Besides feathers, rhinestones, and showgirls' breasts, eye-popping *Jubilee*, which fills the stage at Bally's, includes epic set pieces with remarkable special effects: Samson toppling the temple, a World War I aerial dogfight, and the sinking of the Titanic, complete with exploding blast furnaces and cascading flumes as the boat strikes the berg. The Sanctum Secorum of dinner extravaganza, *Caesars Magical Empire* replicates the Roman Forum, adding a realistically starry sky, grottoes, fountains, a bottomless pit, and stalactites and stalagmites. Even the bars contain animatronic skeletons and holographic wizards. The Magical Empire's Secret Pagoda theater features Chinese dragons and delicate Oriental murals, while the Sultan's Palace has arabesques and mosaics and—only in Las Vegas—black-sequined genies as ushers. Excalibur's *Tournament of Kings* is surprisingly elaborate for a dinner show, with 3-D sets and ornate, reasonably authentic costumes courtesy of Parisian designer Pierre Fresnay. The swordplay is worthy of Errol Flynn, the pyrotechnics awesome (evil wizard Mordred shoots 20-foot flames from his chest and palm), and there's even hand-to-hand combat with mace and battle axe ("No, not your wife," cracks Merlin to a husband in the audience).

And the Liberace award goes to... Those famous animal-act magicians *Siegfried and Roy*, at The Mirage, open with lots of smoke, laser, holograms, and pseudo-mystic incantations. Male and female dancers float about in Darth Vader-ish black masks and long feline leonine manes; bathysphere-like contraptions crush dragons; and finally Siegfried and Roy appear out of fog-shrouded pods in spacesuits with ample codpieces. Think *Cats* meets *Star Wars* as costumed by Jean-Paul Gaultier. The venue where *Splash* is performed at the Riviera is a weird conflation of traditional showroom and grotty grotto. Add fountains, topless mermaids, and a 20,000-gallon aquarium bombarded with multi-hued laser lighting— okay, okay, we've got the idea, already. *Tournament of Kings* ends up more middlebrow than Middle Ages, as audiences root boisterously for whatever country they're assigned. Knights in shining armor and dragon warriors made up like American Gladiators exhort them to shout medieval encouragements like "Huzzah." At the Imperial Palace, the splashy lookalike show *Legends in Concert* utilizes so much sparkle, glitter, and psychedelic lasering, it resembles a cross between a Merv Griffin talk show set, a college production of *Grease*, and a Midwest disco circa 1972. Sumptuous *Jubilee*, at Bally's, is tastefully produced on the whole, but its multi-mirrored opening number makes it look as if thousands of ostrich feathers, dyed in shamelessly artificial hues, fill the stage. The Stratosphere's *Viva Las Vegas* dresses its lovely ladies in costumes so deliriously tacky Bob Mackie would have thrown them in the bin. One outfit resembles a disastrous experiment combining human and bird DNA, given the feathered headdresses and tails; other rhinestoned scarlet getups look like they came from a cathouse in adjacent Nye County.

The bare necessities... A few surviving shows provide a "legit" alternative to nudie bars. Their audience is by no means male-only. A true spectacle of beads, feathers, sequins, rhinestones, and towering headdresses, *Jubilee* is a fitting tribute to its late creator, Donn Arden, nick-named "the Cecil B. DeMille of the showroom." Its 16-minute, $3 million opening, based on Jerry Herman's "Hundreds of Girls" number, features 74 performers (out of a cast of 100) wearing glittering costumes, while huge mirrors create the illusion that thousands of luscious ladies are descending the staircase. These are the real thing: showgirls who combine Ziegfeld Follies panache with Minsky's pizzazz. At *Crazy Girls*, they go from black sequins to biker leather chic. The show is legendary for the ladies' sculptural work—so what if the numbers are obviously lip-synched? It's a cheeky show in the best sense of the word (and word has it that a former lead dancer was actually a remarkably stunning transsexual). Indeed, the Riviera's life-size bronze monument of eight showgirls' backsides (the only ones in town you can fondle) were taken from molds of Crazy Girl cloners. Truly buns of steel, er bronze, it's the ultimate Vegas sculpture so crass it's poetic. The aquatic themed *Splash* has numerous sea nymphs and mermaids slithering around topless, albeit in unflattering costumes (sorry, shells and kelp just don't enhance feminine pulchritude). Maybe that's why the show returns to dry land at intervals, like in the motorcycle racing segment or the *A Chorus Line* ripoff numbers with top hats, beads, feathers, and mirrors. Alas, the showgirls of *Les Folies Bergere*, at the Tropicana, are more erratic than erotic, ranging from apathetic to overly perky. At least the assorted dances, from obligatory cancan to hoedown to jitterbug, as well as a French fashion parade, are mildly diverting.

What a drag... The ribald *An Evening at La Cage*, at the **Riviera**, is more or less played straight. Special honors go to Jimmy Emerson as Roseanne Barr ("Men are like parking spaces: All the good ones are gone and the rest are handicapped.") and the Reba McEntire clone (who actually toured as Reba's concert double during illusionary routines). *Boylesque with Kenny Kerr*, downtown at Jackie Gaughan's Plaza, is slightly darker. The one-liners are trashier; performers even joke (gasp!) about the foibles of gay icons, talking about their drinking, drug abuse, and suicide (e.g. Judy and Marilyn).

Presto!... *Siegfried and Roy* are the *Cats* of Las Vegas; they keep going and going like the Energizer bunny. Their

ENTERTAINMENT | THE LOWDOWN

white tigers are still miraculous, but the real miracle is how Siegfried and Roy stuff themselves into tight leather and sequin outfits. They're clearly bored with the show and each other, so it's rather amusing when Siegfried saws Roy in half—at crotch level—or they rotate on daggers. But these guys are by no means the only magic act in town. At the Monte Carlo, *Lance Burton*'s slight-of-hand tricks are captivating; grander illusions include a Houdini-esque stunt where he escapes the hangman's noose and reappears in the middle of the audience, as well as "The Flying Car" (a levitating and vanishing white Corvette). His studly if smirky good looks help, and he's not above wearing hip- and crotch-hugging pants; one escape routine has him in a studded leather straitjacket. *Steve Wyrick, World Class Magician* sounds like hyperbole, but it isn't. This smaller production at the Sahara's Congo Room is low-key and low-priced but high-quality, with such wow-inducers as a disappearing twin-engine Beechcraft with a 40-foot wingspan (the largest illusion in Las Vegas). Dirk Arthur's accomplished magic act in *Jubilee* might seem incongruous in a show glorifying the American breast obsession. The magical equivalent of a 38D cup, Arthur makes helicopters and sports cars disappear. At *Caesars Magical Empire*, magic takes a back seat to the scintillating settings. During dinner (very unspectacular food), you get simple tricks along the lines of bending spoons and transforming candles into goblets; then the crowd adjourns to the fabulous Sanctum Secorum, which offers two theaters—the intimate Secret Pagoda presents prestidigitation and card tricks, the larger Sultan's Palace hosts bigger-scale illusions like levitations, rope tricks, and turning cockatoos into showgirls. Energetic, friendly strolling prophets and wizards do shtick and simple sleight of hand tricks, agreeably filling the lagtime between shows by sharing "industry secrets" and "union jokes." The good-natured, dreadful humor throughout proves that vaudvile was dead 2,000 years ago.

The impressionists... One of the biggest tickets in town, *Danny Gans* effortlessly fits more than 100 voices into his act, including Homer Simpson, Bill Clinton, Sammy Davis, Jr., Garth Brooks, and Ella Fitzgerald. While he does some unparalleled straight comic bits (a riotous Hepburn/Fonda scene from *On Golden Pond*), his greatest talent lies in bravura singing renditions. Jimmy Stewart and Kermit the Frog endearingly harmonize on "The Rainbow Connection," and Joe Cocker imitates Sinatra swinging on "Hakuna Matata." His tour de force is a "12 Days of Christmas" parody starring Paul Lynde, Andy Rooney, Clint Eastwood, Woody Allen, Mia Farrow, et al. At the Luxor, **Bill Acosta** is snidely referred to as "the Danny Gans impersonator," since his act is remarkably similar, right down to the "12 Days of Christmas" and "On Golden Pond" bits. That said, his impressions are decent, sometimes funny. His roster of impressions is definitely geared toward an older audience—Jack Benny, Ed Sullivan, James Mason, Gomer Pyle, Howard Cosell, even Gabby Hayes—but at least the price is right. **Legends in Concert** rotates its impersonators: you might see versions of Prince, the Four Tops, Garth Brooks, Diana Ross, Dolly Parton, Liberace, Marilyn Monroe, Elton John, Rod Stewart, and Elvis (back after an unaccountable hiatus), singing live with back-up by a scantily clad dance troupe. Once renowned for the physical similarities (reportedly due to enhancements), now most of the shows' performers seem to have blurry features, like third-generation photo reprints. The Stratosphere's musical impersonation show **American Superstars** salutes the likes of Madonna, Michael Jackson, and Gloria Estefan. Refreshingly, you don't get that lip-synching feeling; the performers sing everything rather creditably. They also attempt to remain reasonably au courant, having added Will Smith and the Spice Girls (who are technically British, but why quibble?). If only they'd do Marilyn Manson. **An Evening at La Cage** stars Frank Marino as an NC-17 Joan Rivers. Out of drag, he looks like an ex-*Teen Beat* cover boy, with pouty lips, a long flowing mane of black hair, and sensuous deep blue eyes. But in drag, honey, he looks born to wear fishnets and stilettos. The other "gals" impersonate divas such as Tina Turner, Whoopi Goldberg (eerily authentic), psychic friend Dionne Warwick, Cher, Bette Midler, and Michael Jackson (he may have fathered kids, but he still qualifies for diva status). Kenny Kerr, the drag maestro behind **Boylesque with Kenny Kerr**, now appears at Jackie Gaughan's Plaza, his umpteenth venue since he started camping and vamping three decades ago. But he still looks svelte, sings like Barbra (really), and dishes dirt on local politicians and their pecadilloes, surrounded by top-notch talent.

ENTERTAINMENT | THE LOWDOWN

Broadway babies... Musical theater in Las Vegas once consisted solely of tired third-string road tours or gimmicky shows like *Starlight Express*. While road companies may still be booked for short engagements, today Vegas brings in Broadway cast members to reprise their roles, starring in theaters built to house real musicals. Mirage Resorts has contracted with Jerry Herman (*Mame, Hello Dolly*) to write the score for a 1,500-seat theater at The Mirage yet to be constructed; only the title—*Miss Spectacular*—and director, Frank Galati, are set. Paris premiered the international hit **Notre Dame de Paris** in January 2000: Las Vegas's first US debut of a major musical. David Cassidy (yes, the Partridge Family teen idol) wrote and produced "**At the Copa**," in which he costars with Sheena Easton. It's a fast-paced revue that takes the two (plus dance troupe and orchestra) from the Swing era through the 1970s, and from zoot suits to polyester. The first home-grown product, **EFX**, at the MGM Grand, originally starred Michael Crawford, then David Cassidy, then Tommy Tune, but even they were upstaged by the lavish $45-million production. The plot is feeble (a man hoping to recapture his youthful dreams of being a magician time-travels to the worlds of Merlin, P.T. Barnum, Houdini, and H.G. Wells); the real heart of the show is its overwhelming special effects.

Mandalay Bay got into the act next, snaring the red-hot Broadway revival of **Chicago**, with Chita Rivera (who starred in the original production) and Ben Vereen heading the cast. Subsequent replacements include stage pros like Marilu Henner (veteran of the '90s Broadway version), Jasmine Guy, Hal Linden, and the lissome Charlotte d'Amboise. While it may depart in 2000, the venue will house another recent Broadway hit. **Michael Flatley's Lord of the Dance** no longer stars the self-promoting Flatley himself and is infinitely more palatable for the change. It's ostensibly a tale of ancient warring clans and epic battles between the forces of light and dark (represented—duh—by the Lord of the Dance and the Dark Lord), but plot and ersatz Stonehenge set take a backseat to the scintillating footwork of the 40 dancers. The off-Broadway hit **Forever Plaid** has found a steady Vegas audience in an intimate 200-seat showroom at the Flamingo Hilton. The premise is deliberately absurd: A '60s college glee club, the impossibly squeaky clean Plaids, dies after a collision with a busload of Catholic school virgins en route to the Beatles' first American TV appearance on "The Ed Sullivan Show." They return to earth 30 years later to perform the big gig they missed. It's doo-wop heaven, with a cuddly, feel-good ambience refreshing to find on the Strip.

Headlining showrooms... Las Vegas showrooms still present an eye- and flashbulb-popping lineup of artists. Elvis's former home, the **Las Vegas Hilton**, keeps several class acts like Reba McIntyre and Johnny Mathis under exclusive contract and remains the top venue for touring Broadway shows. It's top-heavy with country performers, one reason why the Academy of Country Music named it "Casino of the Year" in 1998. The **Caesars Palace Circus Maximus** takes no chances and no prisoners with big-name performers like Wynonna, Natalie Cole, or recycled golden oldies like Tony Bennett, Steve Lawrence, and Eydie Gormé, and Legends of Motown (combining acts like the Temptations and Martha Reeves and the Vandellas). The shows are invariably professional; everyone who works this room knows how to give good value (and at these prices, they'd better). **The Venetian Ballroom**, laden with palazzo-like gilt and ceiling frescoes, opened with Vanessa Williams and Michael Bolton. The Desert Inn's historic **Crystal Room**—the first and last venue Sinatra played in town—has superb sight lines and only 636 seats, so audiences are easily drawn into the show, whether the performer is Don Rickles or Al Jarreau. The **MGM Grand Hollywood Theater**, which duplicates the decor of the grand old movie palaces, presents has-beens teetering on the edge of self-parody, like Wayne Newton, Tom Jones, and Rodney Dangerfield. Among local casinos, the **Orleans Showroom** books mostly aging faves who know how to put on a show, from Ray Charles to the Righteous Brothers, Air Supply to Anne Murray.

Music rooms for the hip... Hip smaller spots for music like **House of Blues** at Mandalay Bay and **The Joint** at the Hard Rock Hotel bring in the spectrum from legends to legends-in-the-making, like Sheryl Crow, Chris Isaak, Ringo Starr, Billy Joel, Alanis Morrisette, Bob Dylan, and Neil Young. Both sport signature decor (folk art for **House of Blues**, wonderful posters and signed celebrity guitars at **The Joint**). And both attract the sexiest crowds in town. The **Huntridge Performing Arts Center** and its adjacent, smaller Sanctuary venue book cutting-edge acts, as well as indie and alt icons like Beck and Courtney Love, all of which look wildly incongruous amid the 1940s theater's stunning Art Deco trimmings. The "orchestra pit" (read mosh pit) unleashes as much hormonal posturing as a WWF grudge match.

Yukking it up... Las Vegas has far too many comedy rooms (and even more comedy acts when you factor in lounges, coffeehouses, specialty production acts, and headliners—the ones with TV sitcoms or development deals). Alas, the fabled raunch these days is rarely cutting edge, merely smirky tit-illating jokes from schlock jocks. The **Riviera Comedy Club** consistently offers the best laugh-to-gag ratio, with a roster of stand-up standouts. Its racy, adult-themed late-nite shows, *XXXtreme Comedy*, would have made Redd Foxx blush; it also earns plaudits for innovations like all-gay comedy revues and NC-17 hypnotists. **The Improv**, at Harrah's, is more consistent in quality than the other N.Y./L.A. "institution," **Catch a Rising Star**, with many acts fresh from appearances on Leno, Letterman, and O'Brien. It also presents four comics nightly, whereas most clubs book only three.

Every major production incorporates some comedy routine, from juggling to stand-up. The emcee of *Crazy Girls*, Carol Montgomery, is a brassy Brett Butler looka-like whose jokes marry old-fashioned burlesque to cable TV raunch: call it bawd-ville. Carol gets in your face, asking one hubby if his underpants are "home of the Whopper...offering a happy meal." The women, well, eat it up. *Splash* includes the multi-lingual comic confusion of Dos Latin Cowboys, which is just as racially insensitive as it sounds (not to worry, there are "innocent" homophobic and sexist jokes, too). You can request special seats when you want a loved one razzed. Front row patrons are given rain slickers (you've been warned). Impressionist *Danny Gans* specializes in gentle lampoons and parodies: unlikely celeb duets include Michael Bolton and Dr. Ruth on "When a Man Loves a Woman" and Stevie Wonder serenading Shirley MacLaine with "I Just Called to Say I Was You." He follows an amazing Michael Jackson moonwalk with the older Elvis ("Let me introduce myself. I'm Michael Jackson's former father-in-law. You'd come back, too, if he married your daughter."). If only he'd avoid the cloying moment when he asks our permission to "be Danny Gans for a moment" and sings a song composed for his youngest daughter. She missed Daddy while he was touring 200 days a year; he's been in Vegas for years now.

Top-priced tickets... Is it the lavish production values, the performers' talents, or both? (Or neither?) Whatever the justification, a handful of Vegas shows blithely charge more than $75 a ticket—and the audience pays it. *Mystère*, performed by Montreal's delightfully idiosyncratic Cirque du Soleil, defies description. It's part Pilobolus, part Flying Wallendas, part Olympic gymnastics competition, part Charlie Chaplin—as designed by Hieronymus Bosch and filtered through a Dada sensibility. Haunting images abound: a "baby" floating in a glowing carriage, spaceships and giant snails taking over the stage. Imps frolic and acrobats in whimsical costumes tumble and soar, all to an evocative score influenced by Japanese, African, South American, and classical traditions. As a cast member planted in the audience declares, "There's not a damn thing going on, but it's very Europe and very hip." At the Bellagio, *"O"* is a play on *eau*, the French word for water, and Cirque du Soleil's other show is fluid in every sense. It's literally a three-ring circus, with clowns, dancers, and gymnasts in the air, in the water, and on solid ground. Typically, the images are transcendent. Expect hunchbacks, whip-cracking ringmasters, horse-riding skeletons, snowmen roasting on a spit, and acrobats contorting themselves into crabs. The long-running *Siegfried and Roy* showcases stunning animals, over-the-top production values, and two men who only become animated when talking about their beloved white tigers. They even show home videos of the big cats gamboling at their house. If only they'd crack the whip on the out-of-synch dancers. *Danny Gans* has become the darling of Las Vegas, his show so popular that Steve Wynn built him his own theater at The Mirage, having stolen him from The Rio. Gans *is* a genuine quadruple threat: a singer-impressionist-comedian-actor, gushed over by celebs as varied as Bill Cosby, Joan Rivers, and Celine Dion. The price of admission was 99 smackers at The Rio; Lord only knows what Wynn will charge—and get. At *Caesars Magical Empire*, statuesque golden-clad hostesses offer to take your photo in a chariot, while magicians, seers, sorcerers, and wizards in flowing imperial robes brandish gilded staffs. The physical production is a class act, even if the performers themselves tend to be bargain-basement quality.

Best values... At less than half the price (and overblown spectacle) of Siegfried and Roy, *Lance Burton* bewitches with his down-home demeanor and upscale tricks, in a tasteful magic show free of superfluous smoke, lasers, and melodramatic cape-twirling. *Crazy Girls* delivers more bang, so to speak, for the buck than other flesh shows. It isn't just the Playboy pets come to life; it's the occasional winking kinkiness: voyeuristic mirrors and leather-booted, spanking dominatrices. The Stratosphere lures a younger clientele, so both *American Superstars* and the smaller afternoon showroom spectacular, *Viva Las Vegas*, are generously priced. Phone book coupons provide admission to the latter for a the price of a drink (if you can find a phone book anywhere that hasn't had the coupons torn out). A mere $14.95 nets two drinks and the possibility of a surprise set by Bobcat Goldthwait or Brett Butler at the **Riviera Comedy Club**. Look also for reasonably-priced acts at the **Orleans Showroom** (Crystal Gayle, Neil Sedaka, the Smothers Brothers), or you can take in championship boxing there most Friday nights for $25 to $75.

Family outings... In *Tournament of Kings*, King Arthur invites his fellow monarchs to participate in a competition—the usual Ye Olde Renaissance Faire stuff, but given the million-dollar treatment, and kids love eating without utensils. For all his remarkable illusions, *Lance Burton*'s folksy yet elegant show at the Monte Carlo remains one of the few magic extravaganzas a family can afford. *Caesars Magical Empire* delights kids of all ages (well, 12 and over) with the simple magic acts, spooky settings, and friendly strolling seers and sorcerers. *EFX* features the best animatronics on the Strip, including dragons, aliens, elves, imps, sprites, fairies, goblins, and gremlins of both sexes; throw in flying camels, showgirls, and trapeze and tumbling acts rivaling Cirque du Soleil's. Younger children will probably not even notice the mild raunch. The Flamingo Hilton's *Great Radio City Spectacular* never fails to entertain kids and parents alike, with the Rockettes high-stepping their way through a 20th-century terpsichorean history. *Forever Plaid* could bore the kiddies, but Aunt Martha may glow nostalgically as the starring collegiate quartet harmonizes on nearly 30 golden oldies like "Three Coins in the Fountain" and "Rags to Riches." Harmless audience participation includes playing chopsticks and joining in on soft-shoe routines. Away from the Strip, the remarkably innovative Rainbow Company Children's Theater presents occasionally warped variations on classic fairy tales with a tinge of Roald Dahl-ness that keeps parents on the edge of their seats.

Best movers and shakers... The Rockettes of the *Great Radio City Spectacular* are the high-stepping Clydesdales of the dance world, always perfectly synchronized, though the show overall is awfully hokey (juggler Nino Frediani—imagine Roberto Benigni on speed—and a dog act whose "awww" quotient makes you barf, uh, bark). The finale at *Jubilee* defies the laws of anatomy and physics, with elaborate Bob Mackie-designed headdresses that would topple lesser topless acts. *Mystère*'s international acrobats and aerialists possess bodies as elastic as cords. Acrobats twirl precisely on Chinese poles, bungee aerialists seem weightless, and the troupe uses the theater's sides for "rock climbing." The show's aerial fairy ballet is magnificent, at once ethereal and muscular. That's nothing compared to the same troupe's water show *"O,"* at the Bellagio, whose 75 performers were trained for underwater work. Some of the 16 "nageurs," or synchronized swimmers, won Olympic gold for Canada in 1992, but they had to learn more flowing strokes to swim gracefully through colored lights and bubbles. *Michael Flatley's Lord of the Dance* takes traditional Irish step dancing up a notch, incorporating upper body movement, as well as improbable flamenco, ballet, and disco elements. The 40 dancers define nimble. The stylishly slutty *Crazy Girls* are more soft-core porn cheerleaders than dancers, but the witty choreography displays their assets (performing and otherwise) to the best advantage. The gals work up a sweat, providing a nice sheen as if they were oiled up for competition. *Boylesque with Kenny Kerr* is popular with gays, latent middle-aged businessmen, and women alike for the barely clad, buff male dancers in this drag revue downtown. They actually enjoy what they're doing: winking, flexing, and flirting through their well-executed routines.

Stadium seating... The outdoor **Sam Boyd Stadium** sees everything from the UNLV football team to huge music acts. Its arena counterpart, the **Thomas & Mack Center**, is an acoustic vacuum, with poor sightlines and a murky sound system that a smart teenage band could duplicate in a garage. Alas, many top musical acts still book this echo/torture chamber. The **MGM Grand Garden** is where Barbra Streisand returned to the stage after a 25-year absence in 1993 and Cher asked screaming hordes, "Do you believe?" during her 1999 revival. The Rolling Stones, Bette Midler, Billy Joel, Champions on Ice, and Rod Stewart are other high-octane acts booked here. The **Mandalay Bay Events Center** hits some of the highest notes with primo performers like Pavarotti and championship boxing bouts (Johnny Tapia versus Paul Ayala). Hipper acts like the Goo Goo Dolls draw the twentysomething set here. Smaller outdoor amphitheaters bring in folksier, poppier acts at locals' casinos; the renovated 7,000-seat performing arts center will reopen in mid-to-late 2000 at the new Aladdin, reopening in spring 2000.

Classical moments... Las Vegas remains more plucked brow than highbrow. Still, there are several worthy music and dance companies that play at numerous venues throughout town. The **Las Vegas Symphony Orchestra** is attempting a comeback after a labor strike cancelled the 1998–99 season, unintentionally passing the baton to the new 95-piece **Las Vegas Philharmonic**, which runs the scale from a Pops series where guest John Williams conducted his "Theme from Star Wars" to a monumental mounting of Mahler's Resurrection Symphony, featuring two vocal soloists and a 165-voice chorus. **The Nevada Ballet Theater** dances at **Cashman Field Center**, allowing the company to experiment with occasional outdoor stagings like a ravishing *Romeo and Juliet*. It specializes in classics like *Coppelia*, but is notable for inventive adaptations like *Bram Stoker's Dracula*. The **University Dance Theater**, UNLV's burgeoning student troupe, performs (at various venues) both classical and modern pieces with remarkable energy; the season includes internationally renowned guest artists. **Las Vegas Civic Ballet** usually performs at the **Reed Whipple Cultural Center**; many performances double as unofficial auditions for the Strip shows, so dancers and choreographers alike strut their stuff for agents and casting directors with cell phones bulging like revolvers in their pockets. The cream is annually skimmed from the company, rendering the quality by definition unpredictable.

Premier venues for touring artists are UNLV's **Artemus W. Ham Concert Hall** and **Judy Bayley Theater**. The former boasts superlative acoustics and hosts prestigious guests like the Bolshoi Ballet and Chinese National Orchestra. The latter is a more intimate venue for both experimental and conventional work. The Las Vegas-Clark County Library District is also a major player on the music, dance, and theater scenes; its leading lights are the **Summerlin Library & Performing Arts Center Theater** and **Clark County Library Theater**. Along with the **Winchester Community Center**, **Reed Whipple Cultural Center**, and the **Charleston Heights Arts Center**, they present invariably excellent chamber music groups, young artists recitals, string quartets, folkloric performances, and even ballroom dancing.

The theatah... Fringe theaters are popping up all over town, occasionally mounting productions in some unlikely venues; even senior citizens' centers are fertile meeting spots. The same culture culprits listed above (see Classical moments) stage the more provocative, enterprising troupes' work. **Actors Repertory Theater** is the lone Equity venue in town, presenting fare that tends toward the crowd-pleasing: lavishly mounted musicals (*Oliver*) in the small **Summerlin Library & Performing Arts Center Theater**, farces (*Run for Your Wife*), and the occasional prestige play (*Angels in America*). **Rainbow Company Children's Theater**, ensconced at the **Reed Whipple Cultural Center**, produces delectably twisted kiddie material that doesn't condescend to audiences. Productions are imaginative and nonconformist, as such titles as *No One Will Marry a Princess With a Tree Growing Out of Her Head* attest. **Signature Productions** presents family-friendly musicals like *The Secret Garden* and *Guys and Dolls*; quality is that of a top-notch community players ensemble, with surprisingly high production values. The **Huntridge Performing Arts Theater** ropes in

ENTERTAINMENT | THE LOWDOWN

unusual, challenging productions: anything loosely defined as performance art. Don't miss Jim Rose, icon and protector of the bizarre, who holds actual freak shows (mostly transvestite wrestlers who couldn't get booked on "Jenny Jones" and folks desperate to break into the *Guinness Book of World Records* by eating live chickens or broken glass) in his *Side Show Circus*.

A sporting chance... The wide range of spectator sports includes golf championships at the Desert Inn course, a professional roller hockey team at the Santa Fe, and PBA tournaments at Showboat. The UNLV sports program, tarnished by NCAA probations, is coming back. **Sam Boyd Stadium** hosts football, which promises to become interesting now that legendary USC and L.A. Rams gridiron coach John Robinson has signed on. The university's ugly fieldhouse, the **Thomas & Mack Center**, presents UNLV Runnin' Rebels basketball games when musical mega-acts aren't booked. The ladies have cracked the big time and are generally ranked higher than their male counterparts. **Cashman Field Center** hosts the Padres' AAA farm team, the **Las Vegas Stars**, as well as major league exhibition games in April. It's baseball like it oughta be, right atop the action, even from the $4 general admission seats (field seats are just $7; be prepared for foul balls and flying bats), with mascot Elvee the Bear highfiving the knowledgeable fans and frequent special events and promotions. The biggest boxing bouts are held at Caesar's Palace (see Casinos), **MGM Grand Garden Arena**, and the **Mandalay Bay Events Center**. Ringside seats (when you can get them) run $1,500 and up to watch celebrities like Leonardo DiCaprio, Michelle Pfeiffer, Shaquille O'Neal, Drew Carey, and Madonna chew the fat about whether Mike Tyson will chew his latest opponent's ears. Tickets weren't even made public for Mandalay Bay's "Fight of the Millennium" welterweight championship between Oscar de la Hoya and Felix Trinidad, with an undercard female bout featuring *Playboy* (un)cover girl Mia St. John. So non-high-rollers shouldn't overlook the cozier confines of the **Orleans Showroom**, where Friday night matches might include the IBF Featherweight Championship: $75 for ringside seats.

Overrated... Sure, *Siegfried and Roy* can make elephants disappear, but the overwrought production lumbers along, somehow combining the insipid innocence of *Born Free* with undertones of S&M. And the stars are astonishingly inept at patter—their heavy Barvarian accents sound like the Dana Carvey/Kevin Nealon "Ahnald" parody on "SNL." Groaners range from comic bits like "Is diss your vife or are you on a bizzyness drip...vell, dat's your bizzyness" to wisdom like "Look for magic to enlighten your heart und life." If imitation is the sincerest form of flattery, *Bill Acosta*, at the Luxor, oozes plenty of it, ripping off whole routines from Danny Gans' act (he ostentatiously bills himself as "Man of 1,001 Voices," whereas the more famous and talented Gans humbly says "Man of Many Voices"). And please, Bill, a moratorium on dated material and impressions of long-dead celebs like George Burns or has-beens like Neil Diamond and Ross Perot. *EFX* gives its star Tommy Tune little opportunity to dance dance dance—he sashays more than he taps, and ripped off his own choreography to boot. But then the other dancers scurry out of the way of sets half the time. What was the nine-time Tony winner thinking? The show's over-amped coffee-jingle music and asinine lyrics go beyond disappointing. Fog shrouds nearly half the theater, lasers flash, and more flares are set off than a sea rescue on July 4 (be forewarned: Never sit up front).

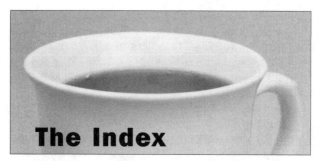

The Index

Actors Repertory Theater. Professional live theater company, playing at different venues off the Strip.... *Tel 702/647-7469.* **(see p. 217)**

American Superstars. Hardly a superstar among productions, but good value: actual live singing, showgirls in rocker-chick black leather, and an enthusiastic young audience.... *Tel 702/380-7711. Broadway Showroom, Stratosphere, 2000*

Las Vegas Blvd. S. Shows at 7 & 10pm (no 10pm show Sun & Tues). Closed Thur. **(see pp. 209, 214)**

An Evening at La Cage. The impressions aren't always sharp, but the humor is: you wouldn't want to cross these cross-dressers, especially Mistress of Ceremonies Frank Marino as Joan Rivers.... Tel 702/796-9433. Mardi Gras Plaza, Riviera, 2901 Las Vegas Blvd. S. Shows 7:30 & 9:30pm Closed Tues. **(see pp. 207, 209)**

Artemus W. Ham Concert Hall. The place to hear national orchestras, as well as the Las Vegas Philharmonic, and view top touring dance troupes.... Tel 702/386-7100. UNLV campus, 4505 S. Maryland Pkwy. **(see p. 217)**

At the Copa. Triple threat David Cassidy time travels with Sheena Easton on this Broadway-style musical revue.... Tel 702/252-7776. Copacabana Showroom, 3700 W. Flamingo Rd. Shows Wed–Fri 8pm; Tues & Sat 7 & 9:30pm. **(see p. 210)**

Bill Acosta. Despite occasional topical humor, this Danny Gans wannabe's impersonations can be somewhat dated.... Tel 702/262-4400. Luxor Live Theater, 3900 Las Vegas Blvd. S. Show at 7pm (also 9:30pm Tues & Sat). Closed Mon. **(see pp. 209, 219)**

Boylesque with Kenny Kerr. Kenny is truly the queen of drag acts, and his equally talented com-madres talk trash, sister.... Tel 702/386-2444. Jackie Gaughan's Plaza, Plaza Showroom, 1 Main St. Shows at 8 & 10pm Closed Sun and Mon. **(see pp. 207, 209, 215)**

Caesars Magical Empire. An elaborately themed, multichambered experience: awful "gourmet" food, but even the hokey comic magicians can't detract from resplendent settings.... Tel 702/731-7333. Caesars Magical Empire, Caesars Palace, 3570 Las Vegas Blvd. S. Dinner/show every 45 minutes 4:30–11:30pm Audience must be 12 years old and over. **(see pp. 205, 208, 213)**

Caesars Palace Circus Maximus. This ellegant showroom plays it safe, with uncontroversial big name acts like Jerry Seinfeld, Julio Iglesias, Clint Black, and Donna Summer....

Tel 702/731-7333. Caesars Palace, 3570 Las Vegas Blvd. S. Show times and prices vary. **(see p. 211)**

Cashman Field Center. Home to the Las Vegas Stars AAA baseball team and Nevada Ballet Theater. The adjoining theater has less character but is comfortable.... *Tel 702/386-7200. 850 Las Vegas Blvd. N.* **(see pp. 216, 218)**

Catch a Rising Star. Spiky acts waiting to get lionized on Leno.... *Tel 702/891-1111. MGM Grand, 3799 Las Vegas Blvd.* **(see p. 212)**

Charleston Heights Arts Center. A snug auditorium that hosts everything from theater to dance, with a penchant for edgy works.... *Tel 702/329-6388. 800 S. Brush St.*
(see p. 217)

Chicago. The sleek, slick mega-hit revival with classic Fosse choreography and a memorably sassy score.... *Tel 702/632-7580. Mandalay Theater, Mandalay Bay, 3950 Las Vegas Blvd. S. Shows Tues–Fri 7:30pm, Sat 7 & 10:30pm, Sun 4 & 7:30pm Closed Mon.* **(see p. 210)**

Clark County Library Theater. This 500-seat thrust theater, the crown jewel of the library system, presents some of the more stimulating cultural fare in town.... *Tel 702/733-7810. 1401 E. Flamingo Rd.* **(see p. 217)**

Crazy Girls. Subtitled "Sensuality and Passion," this is the supreme giggle, wiggle, and jiggle show, with no pretensions to being anything but.... *Tel 702/796-9433. Mardi Gras Plaza, Riviera, 2901 Las Vegas Blvd. S. Shows 8:30 & 10:30pm (also midnight Sat). Closed Mon.*
(see pp. 207, 212, 214, 215)

Crystal Room. A class act: intimate, elegant, with an ineffable sense of tradition sadly lacking in Las Vegas. Performers are eclectic and electric: Gladys Knight is still a pip, Dennis Miller a pop-cultural wiseacre extraordinaire.... *Tel 702/733-4566. Desert Inn, 3145 Las Vegas Blvd. S. Show times and prices vary.* **(see p. 211)**

Danny Gans. Clean-cut and instantly likeable, this red-hot impersonator is the newly anointed King of Vegas.... *Tel*

702/791-7111. The Mirage, 3400 Las Vegas Blvd. S. Shows 8pm. **(see pp. 208, 212, 213)**

EFX. It's blinding and deafening; the book and score are insipid; but the production values boggle the mind, and the price is surprisingly competitive.... *Tel 702/891-7777. MGM Grand, 3799 Las Vegas Blvd. S. Shows 7:30 & 10:30pm Closed Sun & Mon.* **(see pp. 205, 210, 214, 219)**

Forever Plaid. Doo-"whopping" good entertainment for aging baby boomers and the older generation.... *Tel 702/733-3333. Bugsy's Celebrity Theater, Flamingo Hilton, 3555 Las Vegas Blvd. S. Shows 7:30 & 10pm Closed Mon.*
(see pp. 210, 215)

Great Radio City Spectacular. The Radio City Rockettes do their patented synchonized high kicks, while guest stars act as emcees.... *Tel 702/733-3333. Flamingo Hilton, 3555 Las Vegas Blvd. S. Shows 7:45 & 10:30pm Closed Fri.*
(see pp. 214, 215)

House of Blues. This glam venue attracts trendoid twenty and thirtysomethings with eclectic acts like Ruben Blades, Dwight Yoakam, Etta James, and Crash Test Dummies.... *Tel 702/632-7580. Mandalay Bay, 3950 Las Vegas Blvd. S. Show times and prices vary.* **(see p. 211)**

Huntridge Performing Arts Theater. Huge following among college students and slackers; acts here are the height of indie cool. Also a major venue for adventuresome theater and film screenings.... *Tel 702/477-0242. 1208 E. Charleston Blvd. (The Sanctuary is behind the Huntridge, at 1125 S. Morse Pkwy.)* **(see pp. 211, 217)**

The Improv. Consistently books the kind of comics seen on HBO Comedy Showcase and the late-night talk fests.... *Tel 702/369-5111. Harrah's, 3475 Las Vegas Blvd. S. Shows 8 & 10:30pm Closed Mon.* **(see p. 212)**

The Joint. Intimate, yet prestigious enough to attract everyone from Billy Joel to B.B. King to Marilyn Manson. Drawbacks include stratospheric prices and near-fire-hazard crowding (avoid the balcony, which has the worst sight lines).... *Tel 702/226-4650. Hard Rock Hotel, 4455 Paradise Rd. Show times and prices vary.* **(see p. 211)**

Jubilee. Ziegfeld himself would have been proud of this show's lavish production, incredible set pieces, top-notch specialty acts, all "glorifying the American girl" from top to bottom.... *Tel 702/739-4567. Jubilee Theatre, Bally's, 3645 Las Vegas Blvd. S. Shows 7:30 & 10:30pm Closed Tues. Audience must be 18 or older.*
(see pp. 205, 206, 208, 215)

Judy Bayley Theater. This comfortable but ugly 550-seat UNLV campus theater hosts many scintillating touring artists, smaller dance companies, larger student theater productions, and musical recitals.... *Tel 702/895-3900. Boulder Hwy. & Russell Rd.* **(see p. 217)**

Lance Burton: Master Magician. The new breed of magician, with matinee idol looks, hypnotic sleight of hand routines, and a minimum of crude theatrics.... *Tel 702/730-7160. Monte Carlo, 3770 Las Vegas Blvd. S. Shows 7 & 10pm Closed Sun & Mon.* **(see pp. 208, 214)**

Las Vegas Civic Ballet. Uneven range of modern dance, and the occasional classic, at the Reed Whipple Theater.... *Tel 702/229-2415. 821 Las Vegas Blvd. N.* **(see p. 217)**

Las Vegas Hilton. Chic, simple black theater seats 1,700, with excellent sight lines (the furthest seats are just 81 feet from the stage). Styx, LeAnn Rimes, Sinbad, Alan Jackson, and Pat Benatar are typical headliners.... *Tel 702/732-5111. Hilton Theater, 3000 Paradise Rd. Show times and prices vary.* **(see p. 211)**

Las Vegas Philharmonic. The younger of the city's two classical orchestras usually performs at the Artemus Ham hall on the UNLV campus.... *Tel 702/386-7100. 4505 S. Maryland Pkwy.* **(see p. 216)**

Las Vegas Stars. AAA baseball, played at Cashman Field.... *Tel 702/386-7200. 850 Las Vegas Blvd. N. April–Sept.*
(see p. 218

Las Vegas Symphony Orchestra.... *Tel 702/792-4337.*
(see p. 216)

Legends in Concert. Running since 1983, it's the splashiest of the impersonation shows.... *Tel 702/794-3261. Imperial*

ENTERTAINMENT | THE INDEX

Theatre, Imperial Palace, 3535 Las Vegas Blvd. S. Shows 7:30 & 10:30pm Closed Sun. **(see pp. 206, 209)**

Les Folies Bergere. The longest-running production show in the history of Las Vegas entertainment (more than 25,000 performances). Given the tepid production and dinner, all one can ask is *pourquoi?.... Tel 702/739-2411. Tiffany Theatre, Tropicana, 3801 Las Vegas Blvd. S. Shows 8 & 10:30pm Closed Thur.* **(see p. 207)**

Mandalay Bay Events Center. Where to view the big boys like Luciano Pavarotti, the sex symbols like Ricky Martin, the hot gals like Alanis Morissette and Tori Amos, and telegenic world champion pugilists like Oscar de La Hoya. Throw in the odd (sometimes very odd) extravaganza, like a StarSkates Tribute to Barry Manilow starring Kristi Yamaguchi.... *Tel 702/632-7580. Mandalay Bay, 3950 Las Vegas Blvd. S. Show times and prices vary.* **(see pp. 216, 218)**

MGM Grand Garden. This 15,122-seat arena patterned after Madison Square Garden hosts it all: major sporting events (boxing, NHL games), Olympian-crammed ice shows, ballroom and Latin dance championships, and mega-watt musical acts like the Backstreet Boys, 'N Sync, and Barbra.... *Tel 702/891-7777. MGM Grand, 3799 Las Vegas Blvd. S. Show times and prices vary.* **(see pp. 216, 218)**

MGM Grand Hollywood Theater. This intimate space (630 seats) lets audiences feel close to the headliner act(ion); you might be eye level with Tom Jones' thrusting pelvis.... *Tel 702/891-7777. MGM Grand, 3799 Las Vegas Blvd. S. Show times and prices vary.* **(see p. 211)**

Michael Flatley's Lord of the Dance. Extraordinary hoofers render the plot line's Gaelic folk whimsy bearable.... *Tel 702/740-6815. Broadway Theater, New York New York, 3790 Las Vegas Blvd. S. Shows Tues–Wed, Sat 7:30 & 10:30pm; Thurs–Fri 9pm Closed Sun & Mon.* **(see pp. 210, 215)**

Mystère. Mystifying, even maddening, yet hypnotic, this Cirque du Soleil acrobatic tour de force may be the most radiant show you'll ever see.... *Tel 702/894-7722. Treasure Island, 3300 Las Vegas Blvd. S. Shows Wed–Sun 7:30 & 10:30 pm. Closed Mon & Tues.* **(see pp. 205, 213, 215)**

The Nevada Ballet Theater. Classical ballet troupe performs at Cashman Field Center.... *Tel 702/732-3838. 850 Las Vegas Blvd. N.* **(see p. 216)**

Notre Dame de Paris. Vegas does Victor Hugo, at the Paris.... *Tel 877/374-7469. Paris, 3655 Las Vegas Blvd. S. Shows 7:30pm Tues–Sat, & 10:30pm Tues & Sat.* **(see p. 210)**

"O." The peerless Cirque du Soleil's version of an aquacade, with synchronized swimmers, acrobats, gymnasts, and clowns.... *Tel 702/693-7722. Bellagio Theater, 3650 Las Vegas Blvd. S. Shows Fri–Tues* **(see pp. 205, 213, 215)**

Orleans Showroom. Smaller showroom, bigger acts: a high-quality, low-price venue booking intriguing performers like Willie Nelson and the Everly Brothers.... *Tel 702/365-7075. Orleans, 4500 W. Tropicana Ave. Show times and prices vary.* **(see pp. 211, 214, 218)**

Rainbow Company Children's Theater. Superb children's theater with a sophisticated edge.... *Tel 702/229-6553. Reed Whipple Cultural Center, 821 Las Vegas Blvd. N. Showtimes and prices vary.* **(see p. 217)**

Reed Whipple Cultural Center. Ground Zero for Las Vegas culture vultures, it's home to the Las Vegas Civic Ballet, the superlative Rainbow Company Children's Theater, and touring acts in all media, from Irish storytelling to brass quintets to Anthony Zerbe's acclaimed one-man show about e.e. cummings.... *Tel 702/229-6211. 821 Las Vegas Blvd. N.* **(see p. 217)**

Riviera Comedy Club. Dark, smoky, and lined with photos of comic legends. Expect spiky up-and-comers and the occasional national headliner. The XXXtreme Comedy shows are raunchy gross-out fests.... *Tel 702/796-9433. Riviera, 2901 Las Vegas Blvd. S. Shows 8 & 10pm (also Fri & Sat 11:45pm).* **(see pp. 212, 214)**

Sam Boyd Stadium. The UNLV football stadium is well-designed, with levels placed atop one another; it hosts sports events and mammoth outdoor acts like U2, Paul McCartney, Metallica, and George Strait.... *Tel 702/895-3900. UNLV campus, Boulder Highway & Russell Rd.* **(see pp. 216, 218)**

ENTERTAINMENT | THE INDEX

Siegfried and Roy. Yes, the lions, tigers, horses, and elephants are magnificent. Several tricks remain magical, but the leather-clad duo exude contempt for the audience.... *Tel 702/792-7777. Theater Mirage, The Mirage, 3400 Las Vegas Blvd. S. Shows Fri–Tues 7:30 & 11pm*
(see pp. 206, 207, 213, 218)

Signature Productions. Local theater company performs at numerous library theaters and cultural centers.... *Tel 702/878-7529. 3255 Mustang St.* **(see p. 217)**

Splash. Topless girls, ice skaters, motorcycle tricks, and a 20,000-gallon aquarium.... *Tel 702/794-9433. 2901 Las Vegas blvd. S. Shows 7:30 & 10:30 nightly.* **(see pp. 206, 207, 212)**

Steve Wyrick, World Class Magician. The best inexpensive magic show, with some sensational tricks moved from downtown's Lady Luck to The Sahara Congo Room in May 2000.... *Tel 702/737-2515. 2535 Las Vegas Blvd. S. Shows tba at press time.* **(see p. 208)**

Summerlin Library & Performing Arts Center Theater. A charming, state-of-the-art 288-seat proscenium theater staging varied events, including several Actors Repertory Theater and Signature Theater offerings.... *Tel 702/256-5111. 1771 Inner Circle.* **(see p. 217)**

Thomas & Mack Center. Ugly blood-orange-and-white exterior houses a generic barn for the Runnin' Rebels basketball teams, the new hockey team (the WCHL's Wranglers), and enormous acts like Celine Dion, Michael Bolton, and the Ringling Brothers Circus. An adjacent arena hosts smaller events. During scheduling conflicts, basketball is played at the smaller Lied Gymnasium.... *Tel 702/895-3900. UNLV campus, 4500 Maryland Pkwy.* **(see pp. 216, 218)**

Tournament of Kings. Good, evil, jousting, dragons, swashbuckling, fireballing wizards, and Cornish game hen eaten with fingers: Camelot ham-a-lot.... *Tel 702/597-7600. King Arthur's Arena, Excalibur, 3850 Las Vegas Blvd. S. Shows 6 & 8:30pm* **(see pp. 205, 206, 214)**

University Dance Theater. Worthy student dance troupe at UNLV performs modern and classical works at various venues and also lures top guest artists.... *Tel 702/895-3827.* **(see p. 216)**

Venetian Ballroom. Resplendent Italian Baroque theater booking acts to compete with Bellagio.... *Tel 702/948-3007. The Venetian, 3355 Las Vegas Blvd. S. Show times and prices vary.* **(see p. 211)**

Viva Las Vegas. A fast-moving capsulized revue, including showgirls, singers, comedians, and magicians.... *Tel 702/380-7711. Broadway Showroom, Stratosphere, 2000 Las Vegas Blvd. S. Shows 2 & 4pm Closed Sun. Children 6 and older only.* **(see pp. 206, 214)**

Winchester Community Center. Eclectic schedule includes home-grown works like the satire *Lost Vegas* and performances by the vibrant folkloric Mexico Vivo Dance Company.... *Tel 702/455-7340. 3130 S. McLeod Dr.* **(see p. 217)**

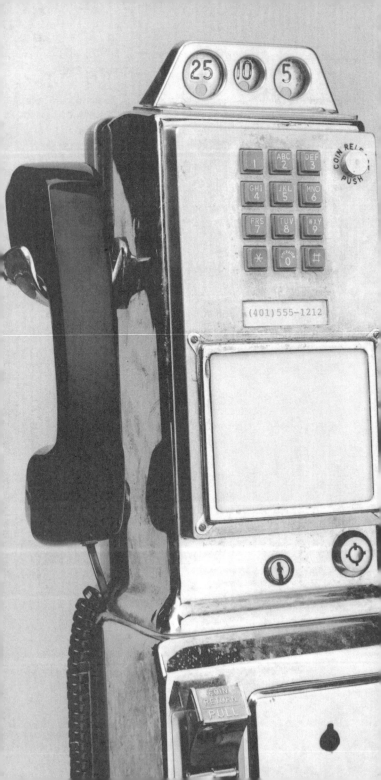

hotlines & other basics

Airports... McCarran International Airport (tel 702/261-5743, 5757 Wayne Newton Blvd.) is conveniently situated, five minutes from the nearest Strip mega-resorts. (It has well over 1,000 slot machines if your fingers are itching; the airport keeps 75 percent of the revenues for maintenance, land acquisition, and construction). Flying in at night you can see the Strip from the runways. It's served by virtually every major domestic airline and several international carriers, from Japan Airlines to Virgin Atlantic.

Airport transportation to the city... Private shuttle buses prowl the arrivals terminal 24 hours daily; flag any of them down. **Bell Trans** (tel 702/739-7990) is the most reliable, with 20-passenger minibuses that patrol all the Strip and downtown hotels. Rates range from $3.50 to $5. Leaving Las Vegas, call at least two hours in advance for departure from your hotel. Several hotels also offer limousine service; check when you make reservations. If you choose to go by taxi, know that there is a $1.20 surcharge for airport drop-off and pickups; taxi fare from the airport to Strip hotels runs $9 to $12, to downtown about $15. There is no bus from the airport.

All-night pharmacies... The vast **Sav-on** (Tel 702/731-

5573, 1360 E. Flamingo Rd. at Maryland Pkwy.) carries all your healthcare and hygienic items.

Buses... Citizens Area Transit (tel 702/CAT-RIDE) operates modern, handicapped-accessible buses over a comprehensive route system between 5:30am and 1:30am. The one-way fare is $1 for adults, 50 cents for children. Route 301 buses, catering primarily to tourists, run up and down the Strip around the clock, starting at the Downtown Transportation Center (Stewart and 4th streets) and ending at the intersection of Sunset and Las Vegas Boulevard (adult fare $1.50). A bus stop can be found on nearly every block. The 302 offers evening strip express service at fewer stops. The hunter-green, oak-paneled **Las Vegas Strip Trolley** (tel 702/382-1404, fare $1.40 in exact change) cars run every 15 minutes daily 9:30am to 2am from Hacienda Avenue north to the Sahara, with a loop to the Las Vegas Hilton.

Car rentals... The usual culprits service the Las Vegas area; most offer inventories including 4WDs, SUVs, Jeeps, minivans, convertibles, and sports cars. **Allstate Car Rental** (tel 702/736-6147/8 or 800/634-6186), Nevada's largest independently owned agency, offers the greatest number of special packages. National brand names include: **Avis** (tel 702/261-5595 or 800/367-2847), **Budget** (tel 702/736-1212 or 800/922-2899), **Dollar** (tel 702/739-8408 or 800/842-2054), **Enterprise** (tel 702/795-8842 or 800/325-8007), **Hertz** (tel 702/736-4900 or 800/654-3131), **National** (tel 702/261-5391 or 800/227-7368), and **Thrifty** (tel 702/896-7600 or 800/367-2277). If you want to tool around in exotic style, **Rent-A-Vette** (tel 702/736-2592) offers a wide array of convertibles, sports cars, and Harley Davidsons.

Child care... Most major Strip properties have baby-sitters either on staff or on call. **Nannies of Las Vegas** (tel 702/395-4009, 2960 W. Sahara Ave., Suite 200) utilizes savvy, mostly long-time residents practiced in taking care of casino employees' kids and high rollers with strollers. For extended stays, they offer live-in and au pair services, with and without accent. **Around the Clock Child Care** (tel 702/365-1040 or 800/798-6768) screens its sitters not only with references but by running checks with the sheriff, health department, and FBI. **Four Seasons Babysitting Service** (tel 702/384-5848) also provides bonded caregivers. Sitters are on call 24/7, but advance notice may be required. There is usually a minimum charge (four hours at $25 to $40 for one or two children), with subsequent hourly rates and surcharges on holidays and for additional children.

Climate... No matter how many times they tell you it's a "dry heat," even at 22% average humidity 110 in the shade will still fry an egg. National Weather Service records for the Las Vegas Valley show average daily highs in the 100s for June, July, and August, which cools off to the low 70s at night. Highs in the 80s are more typical for October and May, with 50s and 60s the normal highs November through March, when lows sometimes drop into the 30s.

Convention center... Las Vegas Convention Center (tel 702/892-7111, 3150 Paradise Rd.) has 1.9 million square feet of meeting space (the world's largest), with nearly 100 meeting rooms, full banquet facilities, and hi-tech audiovisuals. Its rival, Sands Convention Center (tel 702/733-5556, 210 Sands Ave.), by the Venetian, has 1.2 million square feet and comparable facilities.

Coupons... They're everywhere. Check the freebie magazines, available everywhere, such as *Today in Las Vegas*, *Showbiz Weekly*, *24/7*, *Vegas Visitor*, *Entertainment Today*, *Las Vegas Today*, *Today in Las Vegas*, and *What's On*—they may offer coupons worth a few bucks off a show or tour and two-for-one deals on entertainment, even meals. The Yellow Pages has a section devoted to cut-out cut-rate coupons. And ask if your casino provides a "Fun Book" of discounted hotel activities and facilities.

Dentists... If you must grin and bear it while on vacation, ask your concierge or check out local dentists' credentials by contacting the **Clark County Dental Society** (tel 702/733-8700).

Doctors... The **Clark County Medical Society** (tel 702/739-9989, 2590 Russell Rd., 9am–5pm Mon–Fri) makes referrals, with more than 600 recommended physicians, including specialists, in its database. For minor injuries and illnesses as well as referrals, **Family Medical Group** (tel 702/735-3600, 4550 E. Charleston Blvd.) is open daily 8am till 10pm; it offers free shuttle service from your hotel to a medical facility, a pharmacy if necessary, and then back to your hotel.

Driving around... Cars are virtually a necessity of life in Las Vegas. The main highways into town are I-15 and I-515. Visitors can hardly avoid traffic-clogged Las Vegas

Boulevard South, better known as the Strip, which runs more or less north-south parallel to I-15; the main east-west arteries crossing it are Charleston Blvd., Sahara Ave., Flamingo Rd., Tropicana Ave., and Desert Inn Rd. Seat belts are mandatory (traffic cops are vigilant).

Emergencies... Dial **911** for police, fire, and ambulance services. Many locals feel the best emergency room in town is **University Medical Center** (emergency room tel 702/383-2661, 1800 W. Charleston Blvd. at Shadow Lane, open 24 hours). Another good 24-hour bet is **Sunrise Hospital and Medical Center** (tel 702/731-8080, 3186 Maryland Pkwy. between Desert Inn and Sahara roads).

Events hotline... Culture vultures should call the **Las Vegas Cultural Affairs Arts Line** (tel 702/229-5430) for bi-monthly updates on non-Strip performances, including poetry readings, music and dance recitals, and theater, as well as gallery exhibits.

Festivals and special events... The worst times to visit this eternal Mardi Gras are during the major conventions, which occupy not only the convention center but several major hotels. Mid-January brings the vast (100,000-plus conventioners) Consumer Electronics Show, showcasing the latest in—guess what. The Showboat (tel 800/826-2800), with the world's largest bowling alley, hosts the annual PBA Classic, as well as the PBA International, in March. Hoops fans may want to check out the men's and women's WAC Basketball Tournament at the Thomas & Mack Center (see Entertainment). April brings out the beady-eyed sharks and celebrities alike for the 21-day World Series of Poker (Binion's Horseshoe, tel 702/382-1600). April's big convention headache is the National Association of Broadcasters (95,000 attendees), always good for stargazing. The TPC at the Canyons (see Diversions) hosts the TruGreen Chem-Lawn Las Vegas Senior PGA Classic in early-to-mid May. In October, the PGA Tour Las Vegas Invitational (tel 702/382-6616) is plated at three area courses. November brings the biggie: Comdex (nicknamed Comsex by locals for the private shows for horny techno-geeks). With more than 200,000 attendees, it's hard to book a room anywhere. December is a hoot and a hootenanny with the world's top male and female rodeo stars competing in National Finals Rodeo (tel 702/895-

3900), held at the Thomas & Mack. This World Series of ropin', wrestlin', and ridin' every kind of fiesty animal corrals nearly 200,000 rowdy attendees. Pigskin fans can check out Las Vegas Bowl (tel 702/895-3900) at Thomas & Mack Center, where the Big West and Mid-American Conference champions butt heads.

Gay and lesbian resources... The gay/lesbian scene is quiet and the community virtually invisible despite rhinestones and showboys. There are several free publications with resource information, including *Q Tribe*, *Odyssey*, and the biggie, *The Bugle*. The **Gay and Lesbian Center** (tel 702/733-9800, 812 E. Sahara Ave.) sponsors various discussion groups, programs, and the occasional mixer.

Limos... Casinos, wedding chapels, strip joints, and the brothels of nearby Nye County own and operate complimentary limousines. Plus there are fleets of limos for rent by the hour or day. If you want to cruise the Strip in a limo with moon roof, wet bar, hot tub, and a buxom driver, **Bell Trans** (tel 702/739-7990) and **Las Vegas Limo** (tel 702/739-8414) both have sleek fleets. The average price for a town car is $25, a basic limo runs about $33 to $45, and a super stretch averages about $60 to $80 per hour.

Newspapers and magazines... The *Las Vegas Sun* is a bit more maverick than the conservative *Las Vegas Journal* (or RJ), which is best for its Friday Neon section (must-reading for its complete arts coverage; look also for John Smith's columns on Las Vegas wackiness). The weeklies (*City Life* and *Las Vegas Weekly*) are far hipper. *Las Vegas Life* and *Las Vegas Magazine* are the usual glossy city monthlies with insider information, potshots at local bigwigs, the occasional muckracking piece, intriguing columns on local life, and fairly reliable dining, cultural, and shopping listings.

Parking... Most hotel/casinos and malls offer free parking, either as valet parking service (see You Probably Didn't Know) or in huge multi-level self-park garages. Generally, valet parking is the way to go. There's always a free space somewhere—but it may be a hike.

Post offices... Stamps are usually available at hotel front desks or sundry shops. The **Main Post Office** (1001 E. Sunset Rd.) is open till 10pm on weeknights. The **Downtown Station** (301 Stewart Ave.) is a few blocks' walk from the big hotels in that area. **Strip Station** (3100 S. Industrial Blvd.) is one block west of the Strip at

Stardust Way. Call 800/275-7777, even in town, for general information.

Radio and TV stations... The major network affiliates are KVBC Channel 3 (NBC), KVVU Channel 5 (FOX), KLAS Channel 8 (CBS), and KTNV Channel 13 (ABC). Public broadcasting is KLVX Channel 10. UPN (Channel 33) and WB (Channel 21) are usually available. The radio stations follow pretty much the same format as any major American city with a small local music scene—they're often most notable for priceless commercials hyping buffets and "fantabulous" shows. Vital traffic reports are delivered every quarter hour or so during the morning and evening rush hours. C & W dominates the airwaves, with KWNR FM 95.5 and KFMS FM 102 the leaders. Top-40 stations are KMZQ FM 100.5 and KLUC FM 98.5; the former is heavy on female balladeers, the latter plays a bit more dance tracks. The only classic rock station is KKLZ FM 96.3 (supposedly the LZ stands for Led Zep). KEDG FM 103.5 ("The Edge") is virtually the only source for alt sounds. KJUL FM 104 showcases the golden-oldie headliners: Sinatra, Mathis, Streisand. KNPR FM 89.5, the local NPR affiliate, offers the best classical play list. Listen for Nate Tannebaum's "Guess Who's Playing the Classics," where local headliners and politicos share their favorite classical pieces. UNLV's station, KUNV FM 91.5, plays the usual eclectic mix, with the best indie and jazz sounds. And there's plenty of talk radio, including such faves as Rush Limbaugh (KXNT AM 840) and Howard Stern (KXTE FM 107.5), as well as the expected psychobabble drones and chatty entertainment gossips.

Restrooms... Every hotel casino and lobby has facilities, some quite ornate. Favorites: **Via Bellagio** (the hotel's shopping arcade), with gold-plated fixtures; **New York New York**'s Rockefeller Restroom (Murano glass chandeliers and wall sconces, gilded mirrors, silk flowers, custom tile work, and portraits of Mae West over marble and painted fireplaces); and the beaded, translucent glass bathrooms with TV screens outside **Mandalay Bay**'s China Grill.

Taxis... Several taxicab companies serve the Las Vegas Valley. Fares are fairly stratospheric (meters drop at $2.20 to $2.40, 35 cents for every 1/5 mile thereafter or minutes of waiting time). Try **Desert Cab Company** (tel 702/386-

9102); **Yellow/Checker Cab/Star Company** (tel 702/873-2000); and **Whittlesea Taxi** (tel 702/384-6111).

Ticketing... Remember that for top shows, weekend tickets are tighter than a showgirl's spandex. **TicketMaster** (tel 702/474-4000) and **AllState Ticketing** (tel 702/597-5970) sell seats to many productions in advance. (See Entertainment for specific tips).

Tours... **Gray Line** (tel 702/384-1234) is the gray lady of day tours, with air and bus tours to Hoover Dam, Laughlin, Lake Mead, the Grand Canyon, and Red Rock Canyon. **Las Vegas Tour and Travel** (tel 702/739-8975) also offers a complete set of options, including various helicopter tours and a Grand Canyon excursion. There are numerous other companies, specialty and otherwise, in the freebie rags and phone book. Prices are comparable.

Travelers with disabilities... Las Vegas is admirably attentive to the needs of the physically challenged. The bus system is fully outfitted; nearly every hotel has handicapped rooms; pools, spas, casinos, and public restrooms are wheelchair-accessible. Malls have ramps and push-button or electronic entrances. Some hotels even offer special games for hearing or visually impaired players. (This isn't playing good Samaritan—casino resorts must do so to keep their licenses.) But the distance between casino/hotels on the Strip is forbidding, and the casinos themselves are often difficult to negotiate via wheelchairs due to crowds. The **Independent Living Program** (tel 702/870-7050, 6200 W. Oakey Blvd.) is an invaluable resource, providing advice on hotels and restaurants that meet your needs as well as transportation, equipment rental, and help with finding personal attendants.

Visitor information... The best sources for comprehensive information are the **Las Vegas Convention and Visitors Authority** (tel 702/892-0711 or 800/332-5333, 3150 Paradise Rd., open 8am–6pm Mon–Fri, till 5pm Sat, Sun) and the **Las Vegas Chamber of Commerce** (tel 702/735-1616, 711 E. Desert Inn Rd., open 8am–5pm Mon–Fri). Both offer free guides, maps, and brochures, most notably the Chamber's jam-packed Visitors Guide. The LCVA's website, *www.lasvegas24hours.com*, has the most information on every aspect of Las Vegas, including playful videocam highlights of hotels imploding and plentiful related links for discount hotels, show bookings, et al. The *Las Vegas Review Journal* website, *www.lvrj.com* is another

LAS VEGAS | HOTLINES & OTHER BASICS

good info source. The city maintains an excellent site, *www.ci.las-vegas.nv.com*. And there are dozens of other sites dealing with entertainment, gambling, hotels, sightseeing, topless clubs, flying Elvis impersonators, and Area 51. **Clark City Parks and Recreation** (general information tel 702/455-8200, 2601 E. Sunset Rd.) is an invaluable source for recreation (including free tennis) and special events (pops concerts, arts classes) that lure locals.